D0947304

FUTUREPROOF

FUTURE PROOF

HOW TO BUILD RESILIENCE IN AN UNCERTAIN WORLD

JON COAFFEE

YALE UNIVERSITY PRESS
NEW HAVEN AND LONDON

For information about this and other Yale University Press publications, please contact:
U.S. Office: sales.press@yale.edu yalebooks.com
Europe Office: sales@yaleup.co.uk yalebooks.co.uk

Set in Minion Pro by IDSUK (DataConnection) Ltd
Printed in Great Britain by Gomer Press Ltd, Llandysul, Ceredigion, Wales

Library of Congress Control Number: 2019941048

ISBN 978-0-300-22867-0

A catalogue record for this book is available from the British Library.

10 9 8 7 6 5 4 3 2 1

For Maggie

CONTENTS

ACKNOWLEDGEMENTS

The research that underpins this book would not have been possible without financial support from a range of UK research council and European Union awards, whose funding has permitted me the opportunity to engage with many aspects of the futureproofing challenge. I have also received generous support from the University of Warwick.

The range of topics and examples covered in this book has meant that the work supporting it has been a collaborative effort. Special thanks must go to my small team at the Resilient Cities Lab at the University of Warwick; Jonathan Clarke and Rob Rowlands; as well as all numerous research partners whom I have worked with over the last 20 years.

Many people have helped me assemble this book. In particular, my editors at YUP provided superb advice throughout and made valuable suggestions on the manuscript style.

Special thanks are also due to the coffee shops of Moseley in Birmingham, UK, that fuelled the production of the text and provided a convivial working environment that allowed thoughts to flow freely. Coffee houses, as the reader will see, have historically played an important role in the advance of a more resilient world.

INTRODUCTION

There is a tendency in many armies to spend the peace time studying how to fight the last war.

Lieutenant Colonel J. L. Schley, of the US Corps of Engineers, 1929

The Nation's resilience depends upon many decisions and actions that strengthen the ability to respond and adapt.

The Obama Administration, October 2016[1]

At 2.46 p.m. Japan Standard Time on Friday 11 March 2011 an earthquake hit the eastern seaboard of Japan. It was the largest earthquake in recorded history to hit the country and was the fourth most powerful worldwide since modern records began in the early twentieth century. In Tokyo, less than 200 miles from the epicentre, the trembling lasted a full six minutes. Damage resulting from the earthquake itself was just the start. The sudden seismic shock also exposed the underlying vulnerabilities of highly interlinked social and technical systems and, within minutes, the earthquake set off a chain of events that would lead to the so-called triple disaster of 3/11.

The ensuing chaos that unfolded was very much 'Made in Japan'. The essential failings in the response to the events were shaped by the ingrained conventions of a centralised governance culture where 'official' narratives of risk management remained unquestioned.[2] Within minutes, the earthquake triggered tsunamis of almost unprecedented height that flooded large parts of the coastline of northeast Japan. The authorities had not anticipated such a large earthquake hitting the eastern seaboard nor planned for the volume of water and degree of flooding that resulted from the tsunami. The higher than predicted impacts contributed to the confusion that followed as a mixture of poor communication and mishandled evacuation procedures resulted in significant damage and loss of life. More than a million buildings were destroyed with entire villages obliterated. The tsunami alone killed over 15,000 people, and displaced more than 150,000 others. Economic losses have been estimated at anywhere from $250 billion to $500 billion.

Alongside these failures in the response to the earthquake and tsunami, on the coast 140 miles north of Tokyo a parallel set of pre-disaster planning failures were emerging at the Fukushima nuclear power plant. The earthquake had already knocked out electricity at this facility, but emergency backup systems seemed to be functioning properly. Then the tsunami hit. Topping 13.5 metres, it was beyond all predictions. The plant was quickly flooded and its backup generators incapacitated. The complete power loss launched a spiralling catastrophe that captivated the world through global media coverage. Coordinated evacuation did not take place for more than 48 hours and there was a massive failure of the national government to react quickly and communicate ever-increasing radiation levels. This culminated in the largest nuclear disaster since Chernobyl in 1986.

In the years following 3/11, at least 100,000 people who were evacuated from the surrounding area have been unable to return. Many of the displaced are displaying high rates of mental health problems, particularly post-traumatic stress disorder. Six years after the disaster cancer cases have been directly linked to the radiation fallout and genetic mutation of flora and fauna near the Fukushima plant has been observed. The larger legacy of the nuclear disaster, earthquake and tsunami will take decades to be fully realised, and efforts to rebuild the shattered lives of the affected communities are largely yet to begin.

*

Exemplified by the 3/11 disaster in Japan, major disruptive events and their amplification in global and social media have led to an urgent need for the ideas of resilience to be adopted as we attempt to futureproof our world. In a global society mired by uncertainty and crisis, we must learn the lessons which disaster illuminates so that we are better able to survive, thrive and bounce back more effectively from all manner of disruptions. This means engaging in processes that can better anticipate likely risks and develop new ways of reducing the harmful effects of future shocks and stresses.

As a society, we are increasingly compelled to take proactive and preventative action against an array of risks, crises and catastrophe. This is particularly the case for low-probability but high-impact events that have dramatic, far-reaching effects on both localities and global society.[3] The massive impact of these so-called 'black swan' events – exemplified by the 1986 Chernobyl nuclear disaster, 9/11, Hurricanes Katrina in 2005 and Sandy in 2012, and the Tohoku 'triple disaster' in Japan – leads to an immediate effort, whatever the cost, to respond. This inevitably means pulling together, adapting and returning to normal as quickly as possible, all while preparing for the next impending catastrophe. These outlier events are also significant because they often defy the normal laws of insurance coverage that has, for centuries, provided a compensation mechanism against future risk.

Despite such black swan incidents being rare, they have captured the public and political imagination, further fuelling the need for protection against a volatile and unknown future. The growing number of more recent disastrous events and large-scale disruptions that have showcased the vulnerability, connectedness and complexity of contemporary social, economic and political life as we know it has compounded this drive for futureproofing. Such events are no longer exceptional but normal and, we are told, inevitable. Their frequency and impact have grown as we slowly but surely begin to see the real and unanticipated long-term impact of centuries of human progress. The need to respond is pressing and urgent.

Indeed, in early 2018 it was announced that the year 2017 was the costliest on record for the impact of disasters in the United States. Insurance figures set the total economic losses from just hurricanes, earthquakes and wildfires at well over $300 billion. Sixteen separate events within these figures had losses of over $1 billion each and resulted from extreme weather. In California, years of drought were ended with the wettest winter on record. This was not enough to stop the most devastating wildfire season ever taking hold, causing historic levels of death and destruction. Almost 9,000 wildfires ripped through the Golden State, leaving 1.2 million acres of land burnt, 11,000 structures incinerated and leaving nearly 50 people dead.[4] Temperatures peaked at well over 38 degrees Celsius in many parts of the state in what was the third hottest year since records began. San Francisco also reported its highest-ever temperature of 41 degrees Celsius.

The year 2017 also saw a devastating hurricane season in the US with Hurricane Harvey in August unloading a record amount of rain for a tropical storm. This triggered mass flooding that left large parts of Houston underwater and inflicted $125 billion in damage. This tied with Katrina in 2005 as the costliest tropical cyclone ever. The following month Hurricane Irma battered the Florida Keys, the US Virgin Islands and parts of the Caribbean, causing $50 billion worth of damages. Irma was quickly followed by Hurricane Maria, which devastated the US island territory of Puerto Rico, leading to nearly 3,000 deaths and causing the longest grid blackout in US history, with 75 per cent of the island's 3.4 million residents without power for over a month. Requests to Congress for over $100 billion in recovery funds to repair the Puerto Rican electricity grid and other infrastructure were quickly submitted. More generally, requests to the Federal Emergency Management Agency (FEMA) for aid to recover from disaster incidents rose tenfold in 2017 when compared with 2016. Logistically, federal disaster responders were overwhelmed by having to jump from one disaster to another, creating staff shortages that hindered response and recovery efforts.

Although 2017 was an unprecedented year in terms of US and worldwide disasters, we need to stop assuming such disruptive events are rare and unknowable incidents. It is likely that the occurrence and impact of such extreme weather events represent the *new normal*. This is a baseline against which we must act to prepare for a future marked by more frequent and destructive floods, hurricanes and heatwaves as well as the impact of accumulated or 'slow burn' stresses, such as climate change, that reveal themselves over longer time frames.

In addition, if disasters from the weather were not enough, 2017 was an exceptional year for terrorist attacks against the West, particularly across Europe. Over 200 foiled, failed and completed terrorist attacks were reported by EU member states during that year. EUROPOL, the European Union Agency for Law Enforcement Cooperation, argued that such an upsurge in recent attacks represented terrorists' preference for attacking people in crowded areas rather than buildings and infrastructure. Here the aim was indiscriminate killings (London, March and June 2017; Barcelona, August 2017); attacks on symbols of Western lifestyle (Manchester, May 2017) or attacks on symbols of authority (Paris, February, June and August 2017). Similar types of attack also occurred in New York in 2017 when in November a truck was deliberately driven down a bikeway at pedestrians in Lower Manhattan, killing eight people, and in December when a low-tech pipe bomb exploded near the Port Authority buildings, killing four people including the suspect.

As with the occurrence of environmental disasters, the enhanced frequency of terror attacks poses significant questions for authorities of how to be prepared for the unexpected. It is not sufficient for counter-terrorist planning to continue to be undertaken based solely on previous attacks, just as it is foolhardy to assume past weather patterns can predict future extreme events with any degree of accuracy. We are told we must consider the unthinkable and prepare for the worst. In essence, we must learn to be more resilient in the face of an unknown and unpredictable future.

For risks and threats of all kinds, we need to be more forward thinking in our response. It is pointless closing the stable door after the horse has bolted. We should not be like army generals who, it is said, are always fighting the last war. We must arm ourselves for new ones. A singular focus on preparing for past challenges is futile. What we should be doing is paying more attention to enhancing our ability to cope with a wide array of disruptive challenges that may present themselves in the future. These are the challenges that pose significant threats to our current way of living and to our very existence.

LIVING WITH EXISTENTIAL THREAT

The unprecedented ruptures in 'normal' life that we are increasingly experiencing through disruption and disaster did not come out of nowhere. A long backstory shows how ideas of risk and insurance emerged and have evolved over many centuries as a way of seeking to make the future more controllable. More recently, from the late twentieth century, we could also observe how conventional ways of viewing risk were put to the sword by the planet-wide threat of climate change, the global impact of large-scale disaster events and the refusal of insurance to provide cover for certain types of risk.

It has also become evident that long-term trends and ineffective past decisions are increasingly coming back to haunt us. There is nothing 'natural' about a disaster. Nor is it pre-ordained from the heavens. Human progress, together with the systems of organisation that we have developed in an attempt to control the future, are largely to blame. Since the mid-twentieth century, the rapid increase in technological change, population growth and consumption has led to the world around us becoming far more complex, uncertain and unpredictable. This now necessitates a critical need to rethink the relationship of humans with the world around them and a growing realisation that new solutions and approaches are required to ensure our future survival.

This apparently perilous new phase in human history is increasingly characterised by what is often termed in media sound bites as 'existential threat'. This refers to a heightened sense of danger from an array of risks and hazards that threaten the survival of human life on the planet in the near future. However, what is increasingly evident is disconnect between the occurrence of disruptive events and the ability of our current systems to cope. As climate change bites, economic shocks abound and political decisions continue to spawn inequalities and violence, we must acknowledge our greater vulnerability to a multitude of risks and threats. We must also accept that our current policies and practices do not adequately protect us in the short term, nor futureproof us in the medium and long term. Conventional ways of coping with disruption through so-called risk management are no longer good enough. However, currently this way of thinking is precisely what is setting the boundaries of what our collective responses to risk and future disruptions will look like in 20, 50 or 100 years' time.

The struggle to manage the increasing frequency and impact of global risk requires further impetus. In recent decades, this state of affairs has been termed variously as a risk society, the Anthropocene or the age of resilience. What connects these epoch-defining terms is the urgent need to rethink how we assess and manage risk into the future. Traditional ways of assessing and managing risk are still locked into approaches that seek to control the future through an assessment of probability (of a risk event occurring), impact (consequence of a risk event) and the calculation of insurance premiums (projected losses). Our existing risk management and assessment practices appear obdurate and unwilling, or unable, to undergo fundamental change. Key decision-making around risk of all kinds is too reactive and focused upon the present or the near future and based largely on an analysis of the past. In simple terms, how we gear up for a long-term future that is increasingly unpredictable is currently constrained by existing conventions, customs and practices of risk management.

This reflects an enduring friction between those who judge risk based on the calculation of *past* patterns, and those who believe such decisions on risk should be made based on beliefs about an uncertain *future.* Looking to the past to steer us in the present focuses attention on what is *known* and can be dealt with, rather than the *unknown* and the longer-term approaches that are required for futureproofing. This is the 'tyranny of the present' where the future is currently expressed in conventional risk management that looks backwards rather than forwards in envisioning the future.[5] As a society, we need to reframe our views on what constitutes risk and how we deal with it as we progress into an uncertain future. This is an ongoing but slow process.

Since the late 1970s, the impact of mega-risks on global society has begun to shift thinking away from the rear-view mirror perspective on risk management. This reappraisal, catalysed by accidents at nuclear power plants in the US and Soviet Union as the Cold War was in full flight, shone a light on the myth of absolute safety that surrounded nuclear power generation, and an overall sense that governments could keep us safe. It also forced the world to rethink the *global* impact of *local* disasters. The accident that occurred at Three Mile Island nuclear generating station in Pennsylvania on 28 March 1979 was, at the time, the most significant accident in US commercial nuclear power plant history. Initially caused by mechanical failings, the incident was compounded by the initial failure of plant operators to recognise and act on the dangerous situation that was emerging. The partial reactor meltdown that resulted caused the release of radioactive substances into the environment, costing over $1 billion to clean up. The accident served to crystallise anti-nuclear safety concerns among the public and resulted in new regulations for the nuclear industry. It also gave rise to concerns over the wider significance of manufactured risk that was a product of continuing industrialisation.

Such risks and consequences were further illuminated seven years later when on 25 April 1986 a catastrophic nuclear accident occurred at the Chernobyl nuclear power plant in Northern Ukraine, then part of the Soviet Union. The disaster occurred during a late-night test that led to safety systems being incapacitated and triggering uncontrollable reactor conditions and, ultimately, explosions. The resulting fire spewed radioactive products into the atmosphere for over a week. The prevailing wind conditions meant this material was deposited not only across the USSR, but also over considerable parts of Western Europe, contaminating tens of thousands of acres of land. It led to the permanent evacuation of

300,000 Soviet citizens as an exclusion zone was placed around the site. In the long term there has been a range of serious health effects, most prominent among them thyroid cancer, common among the 500,000 clean-up workers.

Writing in the wake of the Chernobyl catastrophe, and at the height of a 'green' environmental movement in Western Europe, which was just waking up to the potentially devastating impact of climate change, eminent sociologist Ulrich Beck labelled this event an 'anthropological shock'.[6] This essentially human-induced catastrophe, whose immediate effects from radiation were invisible to the naked eye, revealed the dangerous extent to which society was at the mercy of centralised institutions and the mass media for information about dangers and risk. Beck's magnum opus on the subject, *Risikogesellschaft*, was published in German in 1986 and translated as *Risk Society: Towards a New Modernity* in 1992. It considered the social impact of new types of risk produced by industrial society.[7] *Risk Society* starkly illuminated the magnitude and boundless nature of the global risks and how these are transforming the way in which risk is imagined, assessed, managed and governed, but never completely eradicated. Along with other notable contributions on how new types of risk are affecting modern civilisation, Beck's work provided the impetus for much reflection on the impact of a set of increasingly common 'mega-scale' risks on the workings of Western society that often elude the very institutions designed for their control.

Critically, at the time of Chernobyl, the catastrophic impact of such mega-risk also questioned the very notion of insurance, the principles of which break down when confronted with unpredictable events that do not tally with past experiences. Increasingly since then the notion of 'insurability' or 'survivability' against an ever-increasing array of shocks and stresses has emerged where financial protection against risk diminishes as the danger grows. This illuminated how specific risks were being excluded from private insurance coverage or made many premiums prohibitively expensive. Insurance, which operates by putting economic values today on future and unpredictable risk, became unviable in many locations with the removal of an insurance safety net, and has had serious implications for where people live and where businesses locate. Fast forward to today and it is now almost impossible in many Western countries to obtain private insurance against terrorism. Flooding insurance often comes with stipulations requiring the installation of mitigation measures before insurance coverage is granted. In California, less than 20 per cent of residents have earthquake insurance due to its vast cost. In other instances, where insurance is purchased, the irrational stipulation of 'like for like' replacement has led to homes being rebuilt in risk-prone areas without better protection being provided. In short, it is often the private insurance companies and their economic calculations that are drawing a line in the sand and marking the boundaries of a risk society and deciding what risks are deemed acceptable and hence insurable, and which risks are not.

Overall, *Risk Society* and other late twentieth-century thinking on risk set in train a process of evolution in our thinking on how to cope with continuous risk. This has resulted in ideas of resilience taking centre stage as we seek to adapt our conventional approaches to managing risk in order to face down future uncertainty in the twenty-first century. Viewed from the perspective of ever-growing uncertainty the world looks very different to the recent past and is cloaked in a new social reality that requires radically different responses.

SURVIVING AND THRIVING IN AN UNCERTAIN FUTURE

Risk Society was a bleak and pessimistic diagnosis of modern society concerned with preparing for the worst. It exposed risks from industrialisation that were now seen to imperil our very survival and placed significant emphasis on the capability of society to withstand disruption without significant impairment of its normal operations. *Risk Society* also displayed a society living in perpetual fear and in a permanent quest for safety and security.

These late twentieth-century understandings of risk as an essential survival narrative in an age of uncertainty have been echoed in more recent discussions on what many have termed the Anthropocene that is serving as a warning sign of our inability to change how we think and act on risk. It was at the start of the new millennium that bioscientists Paul Crutzen and Eugene Stoermer first suggested that human-generated changes to the planet were creating a new geological epoch, which they termed the Anthropocene.[8] Climate change, rapid urbanisation, the deployment of nuclear weapons, large-scale biodiversity loss and accelerating landscape transformation were seen as particular culprits. More recently, in a seminal paper in *Science*,

Colin Waters and others concluded that 'the Anthropocene is functionally and stratigraphically distinct from the Holocene', and began with the 'Great Acceleration' in human activity from around 1750 and the subsequent changes in the Earth System. This was especially pronounced in the mid-twentieth century.[9]

While talking about the Anthropocene in academic and environmental circles has been a popular pursuit over recent years, most people have never heard of it, or do not have a clear idea of its significance. While largely associated with climate change that can be readily evidenced through an analysis of geological strata, it is much more than that. The Anthropocene defines an epoch which began with the Industrial Revolution around 1750 and accelerated in the mid-twentieth century through a rapid increase in technological change, population growth and consumption. It is a new era increasingly characterised by unpredictability and an imperative to rethink the relationship of humans with nature and technology. It is also a narrative about the apprehension for the future of humankind and the need to change our current ways. As Roy Scranton noted in his critically acclaimed book *Learning to Die in the Anthropocene*, survival requires us 'to learn to live with and through the end of our current civilisation. Change, risk, conflict strife and death are the very processes of life, and we cannot avoid them. We must learn to accept and adapt.'[10]

Such bleak scenarios bring global catastrophic risk, or *existential* threats, to the fore as hypothetical impending events that could damage human well-being on a global scale, even crippling or destroying modern civilisation. They also signify the collapse of the underpinnings of modernity, such as scientific innovation and acting in accordance with rational and efficiency-based models. Today, we require a much wider lens for understanding the intimate interconnections between society and nature, and their political significance, than our current tools and approaches provide. The Anthropocene presents a new role for humanity, as the driving force behind planetary systems, while at the same time presenting a world of 'persistent uncertainty';[11] in effect, an unknown and often hostile future for humanity. Under such conditions, the broader safety concerns of nations have to be increasingly rewritten to secure the conditions necessary for human life and our very survival as a species.

In this new risky world, survival is often seen as the best that can happen, but does the evidence back this up, and should we live in fear of the future? Alternatively, are we actually living in an objectively safer world than ever before? In his best-selling book *Risk: The Science and Politics of Fear* Dan Gardner has refuted the idea that we should be more afraid than we have ever been as a result of rising levels of risk. By analysing over a century's worth of life expectancy and human development statistics, he argued that 'we are the healthiest, wealthiest and longest-lived people in history. And we are increasingly afraid. This is one of the great paradoxes of our time'.[12]

But what is skewing our collective thoughts towards perpetual fear and inevitable dystopian futures? The frequency and 24/7 coverage of disaster events that constantly reinforces the vulnerability and complexity of contemporary life is partly to blame. Collective vulnerability is magnified by constant tales of 'when' not 'if' disruption will strike and has foregrounded the political prioritisation of enhanced security – often badged as resilience – as a key policy priority. In other instances, it is the spectacle of unanticipated catastrophe as often depicted in Hollywood 'end of the world' movies such as *The Day After Tomorrow*, *Days of Destruction*, *Aftershock*, *2012* and *Flu* that has driven the interest in attempting to find remedies for a range of natural and manufactured hazards. Such films paint a picture of unbounded and cataclysmic risk that infests our hopes and dreams. This is a vision of society that is merely managing a post-apocalyptic future of rising seas and flooded cities, devastating earthquakes, perpetual economic volatility and rising social inequity. In such portrayals, control – the guiding light of modernity – is increasingly brought into question.

While for some the coming of the Anthropocene embodies a bleak future of perpetual crisis, for others it symbolises the promise of a new dawn where humankind can shape its own destiny through technological and social innovation. These visions are not mutually exclusive. For example, Yuval Noah Harari in *Homo Deus: A Brief History of Tomorrow* anticipates the rise of a new breed of humanity that can 'play God' by manipulating nature through scientific endeavour but eventually ends up destroying itself and everything around it.[13] Others paint a more optimistic picture of living with future risk where the collapse of the modern ways of coping represents a unique possibility for human progress. In this progressive view, there is often an unwavering faith in the power of technology and calls for more effective global governance to better tame an increasingly volatile future. For example, Steven Pinker's 2018 book *Enlightenment*

Now: The Case for Reason, Science, Humanism and Progress makes a detailed defence of rational scientific approaches of the kind that drove forward progress in Europe in the seventeenth and eighteenth centuries – the Enlightenment. Echoing the proverbial saying that 'necessity is the mother of invention', Pinker argues for a newly 'recharged' Enlightenment for the twenty-first century where the challenges we face today can be solved through forward-looking scientific advancement and technological progress and not by falling back on assumptions from a mythical past. Others have also stressed the likely impact of technological advancement in the so-called 'fourth industrial revolution'.[14] Here advances in biotechnology, geo-engineering, big data analysis, machine learning, artificial intelligence, and the effective connection of the Internet of Things will have a significant impact on social progress and risk reduction.[15] The key message here is that society either adapts to new technology through the advance of a 'new cultural renaissance', or perishes.[16]

This call to adapt and embrace technology in order to survive is classic modernity and implies a sort of social Darwinism, where the fittest – in this case the technology developers, decision-makers and others in power – will decide the fate of humanity. But what are the social, organisational and democratic impacts of such a technologically deterministic account? If scientific triumphalism, high technology and a reinvigoration of rational thought are to save civilisation from impending catastrophe, then surely questions must be asked about who has the power to influence technology and who benefits from our ability to manage risk better? In the twenty-first century, as in previous periods of history, the battle for ideas over progress and the way we interpret and act upon risk will come down to the values we hold. Will we be reliant upon conventional and often short-term scientific and rational approaches? Or are we able to embrace new ways of thinking centred upon value systems that are more collaborative and community-centred, and that focus upon enhancing the ability to adapt in conditions of uncertainty for the long term?

ADAPTING IN THE NEW WORLD OF RESILIENCE

In 2013, *Time* magazine declared 'resilience' the new 'buzzword' of our age. It is a phrase or concept that is becoming increasingly prominent across multiple areas of decision-making and has been adopted as a priority action across an increasing range of think-tanks, philanthropic organisations, government institutions, corporations and community groups. The push for resilience stems from the series of existential crises of the current moment – climate change, geopolitical instability (the coming of Trump's America and Brexit), endless wars over resources, widespread terrorism and more frequent weather abnormalities to name but a few – that are forcing us to confront the very foundations that have underpinned modern life. While throughout history existential threat has commonly been seen as a spur to social and technological progress, the complexity and linkage between a wide range of twenty-first-century crises have created a condition of great introspection. This has led to a huge impetus to plan for a turbulent future in the present. It is at this juncture that many proclaim that individuals, communities, organisations, governments, economies and infrastructures will require greater resilience to enable them to both survive and thrive.

For many, resilience offers an integrated approach – often the policy metaphor of choice – for coping with all manner of disruptive events. It is heralded as a new way of engaging with future uncertainty brought about by human-induced changes to the planet. While not geared towards any single shock or stress, resilience is a part of a process which recognises that the future is going to be considerably different from the past. It implies the ability to rebound, pull together or adapt in the face of shocks, extreme events or other forms disruption to 'normal' life. In this way, resilience can be understood as a positive and proactive quality to acquire in light of future uncertainty.

Resilience stresses that in order to prosper in the new age of uncertainty we need to radically change current approaches to dealing with risk. Existing short-term and reactive responses to risk, crisis and uncertainty are broken and no longer sufficient to protect civilisation as the future unfolds. We need to be better able to adapt in order to cope when everything around us is in flux and find new pathways to navigate our deeply changeable world.

Resilience is not found in any one place or in any one type of arrangement. It can mean different things to different people and be applied differently in diverse areas of work. Initially, in the late twentieth and early twenty-first centuries, resilience was mainly seen as the ability to *bounce back* from disruption and return to normality, or business as usual, as quickly as possible. Such a conservative approach sought to maintain the status quo and retain stability and equilibrium at all costs. As the current century has progressed, such bounce-back approaches have been extended by more recent applications of resilience-thinking that have sought to embrace the increased complexity, interconnection and insecurity in the world. These newer approaches to resilience are all about *bouncing forward* to a 'new normal' and putting in place plans for coping with risks that cannot be accurately predicted in advance.

Today, resilience – whether in bounce-back or bounce-forward form – has become increasingly central to reimagining and redesigning life in the twenty-first century where an array of shocks and stresses are already fundamentally reshaping life as we know it. In this sense, learning to adapt in pursuit of greater resilience provides a purported antidote to the volatility of our future world. This will fundamentally involve enhancing the ability of complex and integrated systems to anticipate, absorb or recover from a disruptive event and to adapt successfully to new conditions.

However, resilience is not a new concept. The idea of individuals, communities and ecological systems being resilient and 'thinking' in resilient ways has been a staple of disciplines such as ecology, psychology and disaster management since the early 1970s. However, the popularity of the idea of resilience, at least in the Western world, followed in the wake of the 9/11 attacks in New York and Washington DC. Notions of resilience became a core idea around which security policy was articulated and which led to a dramatic rethinking of existing systems of defence and emergency management. As a result, many nations embraced resilience as an umbrella term for the required effort and resources that had to be put into preparing for security threats in the age of terror. In the US and UK this led to explicit calls for resilience to become the 'national motto' and for resilience principles to be embedded into all organisations and the collective psyche.[17]

Since the tragic events of 9/11, and further fuelled by heightened concerns over sea level rise and abnormal weather extremes induced by climate change, as well as economic meltdown, fiscal austerity and other disruptive challenges, resilience, for many, has come to represent the spirit of the age. Here the capacity to prepare for, withstand, recover and adapt from crisis and uncertainty is increasingly valued. We now commonly see the language and practices of resilience writ large in a range of announcements related to enhancing security, the economy, infrastructure protection and city development. More recently, it has been applied by the United Nations in forging long-term and unified global responses to the challenges of climate change, disaster management and sustainable development. Such increased usage highlights the importance and usefulness of ideas and practices of resilience, showcasing and reinforcing how we collectively need to adapt to tackle the integrated and complex risks we now face.

NEW PATHWAYS FOR FUTUREPROOFING

Today, ideas of resilience and the need to adapt present different viewpoints which allow us to see the future afresh. In the recent past, ideas of reducing vulnerability through probability-based risk management have dominated discussions about how society could hope to 'control' the future and minimise risk and uncertainty. The world prior to the advent of resilience was one with a greater confidence in the capacity of states and governments to secure and control disruptive events as they played out. In this confident and more predictable world of recent history, it appeared that knowledge and understanding could be developed through scientific innovation. Lessons of progress could then be generalised and applied elsewhere. It was a world of policy blueprints and universal one-size-fits-all responses to problems.

In the contemporary world, rising levels of risk, vulnerability and uncertainty have ruptured this predictable worldview. Our thinking has shifted away from traditional ideas that sought stability, certainty and control, and that maximised what is known and minimised what is not known. Today, future planning is increasingly forced to focus on 'unknowns' that cause us to question the value of existing approaches and the tools used to forecast the future. Fundamentally, acting in a resilient way means acknowledging these limits to predicting the future in a world that seems less certain and more complex.[18]

The new age of resilience increasingly adopts a more fluid and pragmatic approach to the world; one that attempts to rethink and to move away from traditional approaches to problems. This also prompts us to think deeply about the idea of social progress and what it means to be 'modern'. Today, this is not predicated upon the world being seen as uniform, linear and unchanging: merely waiting for human knowledge and technologies to develop adequately to solve problems. Technological silver bullets that will solve complex problems are in short supply. Progress today is not so much about acquiring new knowledge as about being more aware of our own intertwined systems of political, social, cultural and economic organisation that are in constant flux.

Emerging resilience approaches are much more about relations, contexts and the processes of change than fixed principles and linear cause-and-effect chains. They are increasingly about how to engage in interaction and build new capacities.[19] While old approaches to risk management, and initial resilience approaches, helped us prepare and plan for accidents and disruption, newer approaches to resilience promote the need to anticipate future challenges and enhance the ability to adapt and continue to move forward positively. This essential requirement to constantly improve resilience and change existing practices is seen as central to effective future action.

As we will see as the book progresses, in recent years there has been a surfacing of many different ways in which the need to change, adapt and embrace resilience principles has played out in different areas. This ranges from the challenges of climate change, to countering the threat of terrorism, ensuring the stable functioning of the economy and protecting essential 'lifeline' services such as water, power and transportation infrastructures. The shift towards resilience approaches as an overarching futureproofing strategy is not without challenge nor is it necessarily neutral in its impact. It poses some fundamental political and ethical questions about who is driving the resilience agenda forwards, which groups do and do not have a say, and who wins and who loses out by resilience efforts? It also foregrounds how the fear of constant shock and disruption is rewiring the relationship between the state and its citizens, forcing us to think through an important two-part question: resilience for whom and by whom?

There is, however, an uneasy paradox at the heart of these understandings of how we best cope with future unknown risk and embrace resilience. While human progress is increasingly responsible for shaping environmental conditions, the ability to control this is hampered by our inability to tackle the complex interactions involved. Are we, as Isabelle Stengers argues, living in catastrophic and barbaric times where governments are incapable of dealing with crises? Is the horrendous situation that engulfed New Orleans in 2005 after Katrina hit, where the poor were abandoned while the rich sheltered, going to become a familiar symbol of our age?[20] Does the political discourse of inevitable catastrophe demand more and more resilience in everything and everyone in order to survive the unknown future that lies in store?

Current attempts to tackle such existential threats have further illuminated the failures of contemporary decision-making and politics. In many ways, the complexity of the modern world, that is often exposed by disaster events, overwhelms and gridlocks existing political and economic institutions at all scales, from the local to the planetary, and must be rethought. Moreover, the shift towards resilience-thinking has highlighted that 'neither traditional risk management strategies nor conventional economic decision-making can be relied on to govern in the face of increasingly likely extreme events'.[21] In reimagining our relationship with risk of all kinds, we will inevitably need to embrace more holistic and integrated ways of assessing risk and mobilising responses across multiple systems, networks and scales. By following such resilience-thinking, decision-makers can seek to transform their practices in a progressive way and will be better able to futureproof their strategies and investments. This requires new, dynamic approaches to deal with risk that encourage new, agile ways of working that embrace learning and adapt when required. Innovative thinking will be required to imagine alternative ways of getting to a desired end point in the future. Resilience favours more choices and recognises that future approaches need to move beyond a narrow range of options calculated from prior experiences and develop more solutions and pathways than a single and rigid Plan A. We need a Plan B, C, D and so on.

Thinking through such possible pathways to adaptation seeks to hardwire resilience-thinking into future planning and action. This is not an arbitrary adjustment of how society and organisations function in response to vulnerability. It is a fundamental redesign of how society thinks about and responds to contemporary and future risk. In short, we urgently need to advance new ways of constructing and enacting policies that are more flexible, agile and adaptable, take a longer-term viewpoint. This will require a coherent joined-up response to the uncertainty, complexity, insecurity and, ultimately, the need for change and transformation, that are due to dominate the twenty-first century.

In seeking solutions to these challenges, the chapters to come will highlight and chart recent futureproofing approaches that have tried to implement resilience across a range of contexts. While in these cases resilience has been implemented in very different ways, there are common threads that connect them.[22] In all cases, resilience is seen as a new way of thinking in relation to managing risk that takes into account the complexities of large integrated systems and organisations. This reflects a consensus about the necessity of adaptation to the uncertainty of future threats. Now that such a consensus has been reached, orchestrating such a coherently joined-up approach to meet the generational challenges global society now faces from risk, disruption and insecurity has become the most significant challenge we collectively have to confront over the coming decades. It is a challenge we must embrace now.

Futureproofing is all about change. It is about mobilising new approaches, by which we can engage more openly with more people and by which individuals, institutions and governments can transition from one way of operating to another and in so doing significantly reshape or transform existing practices. It is about advancing ways of better anticipating the future. It is about modifying our outdated approaches to assessing risk and evolving methods that can better reduce the impact of shocks and stresses from future events. It is not a short-term fix but a long-term endeavour. The transition towards greater resilience and adaptability will not be smooth and even but will be a voyage of discovery. It will involve many difficult decisions, ethical dilemmas and much politicking, and will incorporate new technologies as they emerge. Here the quest for resilience is not a fixed destination but a never-ending journey in which we either adapt or die as we seek to futureproof our world for generations to come.

1

FATE, CHOICE AND THE BIRTH OF RISK

Thou shalt be visited by the Lord of hosts with thunder, and with earthquake, and great noise, with storm and tempest, and the flames of devouring fire.

Isaiah 29:6 (Jerusalem, the City of David, is warned)

Risk is the . . . schema by which a society mobilizes itself when it is confronted with an openness, uncertainties and obstructions of a self-created future and is no longer defined by religion, tradition or the superior power of nature.

Ulrich Beck, *World at Risk*[1]

On 26 April 1986 a systems test at Reactor 4 of the Chernobyl nuclear power plant near Pripyat in the then Soviet republic of Ukraine experienced a sudden and unexpected power surge. Subsequent power spikes ruptured the reactor and set off fires that burned for the next week. This sent plumes of radioactive fallout into the atmosphere over an extensive area, including large areas of the USSR and Western Europe. The local population was evacuated and a 30km exclusion zone swiftly enacted around the plant. Over 300,000 people were displaced permanently and a costly decontamination process begun that is still ongoing today.

The Chernobyl disaster showed that pollution has no borders. Risk was essentially boundless and not constrained by the locality in which it occurred. The accident also heightened concerns about the safety of such reactors and, in subsequent years, led to a dropping-off of new nuclear power plant construction worldwide. Further, it raised concerns about the culture of safety in the nuclear power industry and the way in which many felt the highly centralised Soviet government tried to cover up the accident. The initial alarm that something was wrong at Chernobyl was sounded not in the USSR but at Forsmark, Sweden's second largest nuclear power plant. This early warning played a crucial role in forcing Soviet authorities to open up about the ongoing disaster.

At the time of the accident, nuclear power plants represented the pinnacle of scientific and industrial innovation – of human control over nature – and the ability to produce cheap, safe, decarbonised energy. This was a worldwide movement that since the 1950s had sought to harness the power of the atom in a controlled way to generate 'clean' electricity. While the technology naturally gave rise to concerns about accidents and their possible impacts, it was felt this could be controlled through conventional risk-management procedures. Proper design and backup systems, high-quality components and a well-developed safety culture in operations was deemed sufficient. Such optimism lay in ruins in April 1986.

Twenty-five years after the Chernobyl disaster Pripyat was a ghost city and the area remained contaminated by radiation, being deemed uninhabitable by Ukrainian authorities. Long-term health risk was evident in a large increase in incidences of thyroid cancer among people who were young children at the time of the accident. Many were still suffering psychological trauma because of sudden evacuation, the long-term effects of being a refugee, and the disruption of established social networks. Milk from villages 150 miles away was still five times more radioactive than the Ukrainian government judged safe. Radiation deposited in rain far away in high-lying areas of Britain also led to restrictions being imposed on the way hundreds of farms used land and reared sheep. This was only deemed to have reduced to 'acceptable' levels in 2012.

The 25th anniversary of Chernobyl in 2011 coincided with the escalating crisis at the tsunami-damaged Fukushima Daiichi nuclear power station in Japan. As this newest nuclear accident played out under the global media spotlight, many commentators wondered if we were going to experience 'another Chernobyl'. This stimulated a renewed awareness of the 1986 accident and provided an opportunity to reflect upon the longer-term social and psychological impact – another kind of 'fallout' – from the disaster. Over time, the processing of the world-altering events at Chernobyl has given rise to a wide array of symbolism that has enabled us to better understand some of the important cultural aspects of the disaster's lingering impacts. In poetry, literature and sculpture many Chernobyl-inspired artworks have been frequently imbued with religious meaning to reflect on the tensions between the scientific and the spiritual.

In *Chernobyl Prayer: A Chronicle of the Future* Nobel laureate Svetlana Alexievich compared the Chernobyl accident with the biblical story of Adam and Eve who, after consuming the forbidden fruit, gained access to confidential and forbidden knowledge. The message conveyed is that scientists similarly 'played God' in experimenting with nuclear fission, with devastating consequences. The forced evacuation of hundreds of thousands of people from the exclusion zone is further equated with Adam and Eve's banishment from the Garden of Eden. For Alexievich, the Chernobyl disaster is represented as a form of divine retribution for promoting science over religion.[2] As one excerpt from this harrowing oral history recounts: 'There was a black cloud, and hard rain. The puddles were yellow and green, like someone had poured paint into them. They said it was dust from the flowers. Grandma made us stay in the cellar. She got down on her knees and prayed. And she taught us, too. "Pray! It's the end of the world. It's God's punishment for our sins."'

*

Tracing the deeper development of changes in the way hazards and disasters have been historically viewed, and vulnerability felt, by human civilisations of the past, is vital to understanding the roots of contemporary dilemmas and the growing influence of ideas of resilience in the twenty-first century. There are long-term historical processes that have defined the contours of society and the slowly evolving structures that collectively symbolise how the need to be able to account for hazards and disasters has reshaped our world. This is a story of religious versus scientific explanations, and of enhancing the ability to control the future through better knowledge about what is in store and the likelihood of certain events occurring.

The story of how ideas of resilience emerged as the go-to futureproofing idea in the early years of the twenty-first century, therefore, has a long history dating back to pre-modern times and extends through the advancement of associated ideas of 'risk'. The story begins in the pre-modern era of human civilisation,[3] from around 1500, when fate, divine retribution and mysticism were seen as the primary cause of disaster. Such catastrophic events were seen as historical ruptures and as turning points between past and present conditions. Pre-modern here largely refers to the period before the dawn of the Enlightenment in the sixteenth century, where God was seen as all-powerful, and where superstition and supernatural explanations were widespread and popularised through religious texts. One illustration comes from depictions of the cities of sin – Sodom and Gomorrah from prehistoric Israel in the neighbourhood of the Dead Sea – that have been mentioned in a wide variety of religious books, notably the Book of Genesis in the Old Testament, as well as in the Quran. The story of Sodom and Gomorrah is a morality tale, and the names have become bywords in our modern society, synonymous with unrepentant sin. In biblical texts, the raining down on the city of fire and brimstone which destroyed them was seen as the result of divine retribution; a warning for all that this same event will happen again one day to the wicked.[4]

Such notions of divine retribution came under scrutiny in the Age of Enlightenment (approximately 1650–1800), when commentators began to realise that people *themselves* could change society and alter their way of life. Instead of civilised society being produced completely by the gods, in an atmosphere of scientific advancement there was increasing room for progressive opinions to be voiced. In particular, there was talk of freedom, of people independently making their own lives using their own judgement, and the idea that people *made their own society.*

This chapter will tell the story of this shift in thinking about the true cause of catastrophes from acts of god to human intervention. In this conversion, the relationship between religion and science became reinterpreted through the response to large-scale disaster and claims about its cause. Particularly through the dialogue between great thinkers in response to the devastating Lisbon earthquake of 1755, we will see how traditional ideas of divine cause were challenged by new ideas about the importance of Mother Nature and the need for authorities to take greater accountability for responding to crisis.

This transition was aided by the emerging idea of risk. Risk, as we shall see, from the eighteenth century onwards, became a dominant way of regulating human activity through changes in the way decisions were made. Risk also drove social and economic progress by providing the mechanisms to assess forward-looking choices. Risk was all about calculating the chance that something may happen *in the future.* The concept of risk thus put the 'future at the service of the present' through the help of numbers and risk management, most notably through practices of insurance.[5] As the story of the evolution of ideas of risk progressed through the twentieth century, concerns over mega-risks that threaten human survival became widespread, best exemplified by the Chernobyl accident, and prompted a reappraisal of the role of risk and risk management in modern life. This reflection in turn set the foundations for the emergence of resilience as a long-term strategy of choice for twenty-first century futureproofing.

VULNERABILITIES, HAZARDS AND ACTS OF GOD

In his illuminating book *Against the Gods: The Remarkable Story of Risk*, Peter Bernstein argued that the mastery of risk – the notion that the future can be foreseen or predicated on more than fate or divine intervention – separates modern times from the long brushstrokes of history.[6] Great civilisations, he argued, essentially lived in the past and 'used the ideas of fate, luck and will of the gods where we now tend to substitute risk'.[7]

In the pre-modern era up until the time of the Renaissance (approximately 1300–1500),[8] predicting the future was seen as little more than chance or at best random variation in natural cycles. Risk, or risk-taking, was not a known concept as scientific forecasting was not embraced, even as civilisation advanced. The future was a mirror of the past, remaining shrouded in mystery, and controlled by a single God (in Christianity), or series of deities. It was prescribed only in and through faith and moral behaviour, and within discussions of the afterlife.

In earlier civilisations, we can see these ideas of fate and divine intervention playing out as societies sought to find ways of coping with and explaining hazards that befell them. Early social responses to vulnerability accepted disaster as part of the natural order of things. These were predominantly seen as acts of god – a term that centuries later still endures – where nothing could have been done to mitigate or alter catastrophic events that were coming your way. Such ideas were still prominent in early modern European societies up until the eighteenth century where divine providence – under God's guidance and control – was seen as a the primary cause of disaster.[9] This is not to say that providence was the only view held about the cause of disastrous events.[10] As science evolved so meteorological or geological explanations also took hold, but these 'alternative' accounts were often dismissed by religious leaders who were quick to rebuke those who believed in new and sacrilegious viewpoints.[11]

If we are concerned with exploring and understanding the development of human civilisation in the pre-modern era and how vulnerabilities from hazards were viewed, we will inevitably turn our attention to the places where civilisation as we know it began to take shape – the city. Moral concern about the city has persisted throughout history in every culture and is often connected to the way disaster is perceived.[12] The story of the destruction of Sodom and Gomorrah in Genesis is merely one famous illustration, where the immorality of cities is held to account for their destruction. Another well-known example comes in the fifth century AD from Augustine's *De civitate Dei* (The City of God). Recounting a time of immense change and insecurity, the purpose of the work was at least partly to serve as a warning against the earthly political ambition that had just seen the greatest city on earth laid to waste.[13] The sacking of Rome in AD 410 left the Roman Empire in deep shock and was interpreted by many as a punishment for abandoning conventional Roman religion for Christianity. *The City of God* depicts human history as a conflict between the Earthly City (often referred to as the City of Man), consisting of people who have immersed themselves in the concerns and desires of the present, and the City of God, marked by people who have forgotten earthly pleasure to dedicate themselves to God. History in this sense was seen as one long universal war between God and the Devil and guided by divine intervention or retribution for human misdeeds.

Folk tales that are almost certainly false have commonly linked urban disaster to divine providence as crisis befell cities and their populations.[14] The story of the biblical plagues and subsequent exodus from Egypt provides another illustration that connects epic catastrophe to godly retribution. It is also now generally believed that the ancient Greek philosopher Plato advanced the story of Atlantis in around 360 BC to convey some of his deep thoughts about divinity, ideal societies and the gradual moral corruption of human civilisation. Atlantis is a tale about how a spiritual and utopian society became corrupted by greed, leading to punishment by the gods through destruction by fire and earthquake, with the city finally submerged under the ocean.

In the real world, such a view of divine providence was readily applied to geological hazards and associated volcanoes, earthquakes, landslides and tsunamis that proved the downfall of many cities. For example, volcanic eruptions account for the burial of the Roman city of Pompeii under the ash and lava of Mount Vesuvius and the deaths of around 20,000 people in AD 79, and for the destruction of the Minoan civilisation on Crete following the eruption of the Santorini volcano and subsequent tsunami (circa 1645 to 1500 BC). Earthquakes have also been devastating and equated to acts of god. In ancient Greece, the massive quake that hit Sparta in 464 BC catalysed its decline. The ancient city of Alexandria in modern-day Egypt was also famously destroyed in AD 365 by a tsunami following a massive earthquake epicentred in Crete.

Water-related disasters are also particularly instructive in illuminating beliefs about how God's will is brought to bear on populations in harm's way. English social historians have noted how the origin of the word 'fear' comes from the Old English word *foer*, meaning both danger and a feeling of dread and reverence for God. This meaning was often spread through populations in the early modern world by pamphlets, woodcarvings and other works of art in an attempt to link disastrous events, such as floods and storm surges, with the Apocalypse and God's displeasure. Similar views were held by Egyptian civilisations of the Nile valley and Delta where flooding was both their lifeblood, bringing the gift of rich soil, and the greatest threat. Likewise, in ancient China, catastrophic flooding of urban settlements was endemic on the crowded floodplains of the major rivers such as the Yangtze. The idea that disasters were caused by heavenly misalignment was strong. Here it was commonly believed that heaven gave virtuous leaders a mandate to rule but also expressed its disapproval of evil or corrupt rule through disaster and catastrophe.[15]

Cities were also crucibles of disease. In Europe, where multiple epidemics took hold during the fourteenth century, up to a third of the entire population died in the Black Death between 1346 and 1350.[16] Many thought the pestilence was a punishment from God and made the plague the most fearsome disaster type in early modern Europe. Artistic depictions of the impact of the plague at this time put the blame solely at the feet of human vice, with angels often taking on a deathly role in such images. This symbolised the 'Angel of Death', recounted a number of times in the Bible, notably as the avenger bringing plague to the Egyptians in Exodus. As historian Louise Marshall underscored in her analysis of accounts of the bubonic plague in Italy in the fourteenth century, 'The customary role of angels as bringers of glad tidings and supernatural assistance has here shifted to a sterner role. The punitive capacity of angels as executants of divine punishments.'[17]

As well as coping with a range of environmental hazards and disease, pre-modern era cities had to endure periods of war. The theological underpinning of warfare is important here; it is seen as one of the most devastating disasters visited on human civilisation by God. As historians Jennifer Spinks and Charles Zika have highlighted, we only need turn to the Book of Revelations and its account of the four horsemen of the Apocalypse representing conquest, famine, death *and war* to see the central place of violent struggle in ideas concerning divine retribution.[18] Such retaliation was notably enacted in cities, which were often treated brutally after sieges, often being razed to the ground and ploughed to signify their reconversion to unusable land. In the famous razing of Carthage by the Roman army in 146 BC, the city was literally and symbolically destroyed and most of its inhabitants sold into slavery.[19] The Roman historian Livy presented the Carthaginians' defeat as 'divine retribution' for their vices, which were contrasted with Roman values.[20] Although through history the nature of warfare changed significantly, the idea of war as divine will persisted into the early modern period. In short, viewing disasters or warfare as godly acts was the natural order of things, and they were almost universally seen as part of a heavenly master plan that could not be fully understood by humans.

Theologians and early Enlightenment philosophers who tried to make sense of the disorder and death that disasters or war wrought tended to take the view, in the absence of other explanations, that they were pre-ordained. Divine intervention provided a solitary framework for attempting to understand the chaos and breakdown in the natural and moral order of civilisation; a visible manifestation of God's providence writ large. Disasters were linked to the End of, or Last Days, the Apocalypse, or Day of Judgment 'with its heavenly, ferocious angels blowing trumpets and opening vials that set off waves of utter disaster; its monstrous beasts and false prophets; and its mercilessly riding four horsemen, who trample all under foot'.[21]

CHALLENGING DIVINE RETRIBUTION

Up until the Enlightenment – the Age of Reason – many aspects of decision-making were left to fate or the visions of oracles, with no system of odds to determine future outcomes. Past history and religious-inspired prophecy provided a powerful sense-making system for understanding the disordered chaos of disaster and crisis in the pre-modern period.

While in pre- and early modern times there were some attempts to look at disasters through a scientific lens, there was an overwhelmingly fatalistic acceptance that disasters 'just happen' and could not be prevented. It was not until around 1650, coinciding with the early influence of the Enlightenment, that natural explanations, grounded in emerging science and empiricism, began to challenge moral explanations of divine intervention as a core cause of disaster.

Such a challenge to the status quo reached its zenith in 1755 in the aftermath of the devastating Lisbon earthquake that proved a critical turning point in the battle between supernatural forces and a combination of natural hazards and human-induced phenomena as the cause of disaster. The earthquake struck on the morning of All Saints' Day, 1 November 1755. It lasted around five minutes and caused 5-metre-wide fissures to open in the city centre. Survivors rushed to the open space of the docks for safety and watched as the water receded apace. Forty minutes later the sea returned as a tsunami and engulfed the harbour and downtown area, rushing up the Tagus River. After the tsunami waters receded, the city burned for days. Seismic shocks from the earthquake were felt throughout Europe and further afield. Although estimates vary, this devastating event killed at least 30,000 people and left widespread damage to at least three-quarters of the city. Eighty-five per cent of Lisbon's buildings were destroyed, including famous palaces, churches and libraries.

Such was the significance and impact of this earthquake that it is often referred to by historians as *the first modern disaster*. It represents a disaster event where some opposed supernatural causes and in which the state took some responsibility for disaster response and rebuilding.[22] The timing and location of this devastating earthquake was also crucial. This was a time when ideas of modernity were beginning to take hold, with significant tension building between traditional and new, progressive ideas. The near obsession with thinkers trying to prove the existence of God was slowly being replaced by a focus on reason and a fervour for science. Politically, this led to new ideas about the appropriate role of the state vis-à-vis religion. Prior to the Enlightenment, it was still widely assumed that God ordained kings and that monarchy was the natural order of things in a divine grand plan where kings were not subject to the same laws as ordinary men.

Geographically, at the time, Lisbon was the fourth largest city in Europe after London, Paris and Naples. It was a wealthy trading port and well known as a major city of the Inquisition and as a centre of superstition.[23] The Lisbon earthquake was the first major earthquake to affect a modern European city during the Enlightenment and, as historian Robert Dynes has noted, coincided with a time when 'the bonds of traditional religious authority were being challenged by a growing enthusiasm for intellectual freedom and for reason'.[24] Such talk laid bare the existing tensions between religion and science as driving forces of social progress and led to a broader debate over the nature of modernity.

Therefore, when the devastating Lisbon earthquake occurred in 1755 its timing and location made it the centre point of philosophical and political discussion. Arguments over the links between the catastrophe and God's providence ensued in the earthquake's wake. Given the strong religious beliefs of the population, in the earthquake's aftermath a narrative of the city being punished for its sins was widespread. Some even suggested that the death toll was God's way of controlling the burgeoning population. That the tragedy occurred on All Saints' Day, and annihilated most of the major churches in Lisbon was used as 'evidence' for divine punishment for corruption and sin.

The earthquake, however, forced Western thinkers to confront a world where destruction and suffering could be viewed as a matter of *chance*, and a result of natural hazards, rather than a sign of godly retribution. In the aftermath of the disaster, two important figures debated the philosophical idea of divine providence and the role of evil in contributing to the earthquake in the Enlightenment: Voltaire and Rousseau.[25] The dialogue between these two Enlightenment heavyweights shone a light on the tensions between religion and science, and arguably kick-started what we now think of today as social science.

Voltaire in his 1755 'Poème sur le désastre de Lisbonne' questioned whether a just and compassionate all-powerful God would (or could) seek to punish sins through such terrible means. He believed that all living things seemed doomed to live in a cruel world and thus rejected providence as the disaster's central cause. The philosopher Jean-Jacques Rousseau, to whom Voltaire had sent a copy of his poem, criticised Voltaire's view. In his response, 'Lettre à Monsieur de Voltaire', Rousseau condemned Voltaire for seeking to apply science to spiritual questions and implied that Voltaire must either renounce the concept of providence or conclude that it is beneficial. In their dialogue, Rousseau also famously commented on the social components of disasters, highlighting that catastrophes are of man's own making given how they choose to build their communities. In essence what we see Rousseau arguing for here is the beginnings of a sociological theory of disasters and, more broadly, of social science.[26] As historian José Marques has argued, this comment implied blame should be associated with the unplanned and crowded urban patterns of modern cities as well as with the moral corruption of man in relation to material goods and property.[27] Disasters are not natural or pre-ordained but occur because of social and political actions that enhance vulnerability.

Within a year of the disaster, views from further afield were also being heard. Germany's foremost philosopher at the time, Immanuel Kant,[28] had collected all the available accounts of the earthquake and its effects, publishing them together with his comments and conclusions in three essays. His work attempted to reassure that the disasters should not be viewed as an act of God and endeavoured to show that earthquakes have purely physical causes. He concluded that impending disaster should therefore not incite fear as their effects could be controlled by, for example, engaging in appropriate urban planning.[29] Like Rousseau, Kant's ideas about the causes of the Lisbon earthquake being natural phenomena significantly affected by human activity are, today, echoed in debates about whether or not the term 'natural disaster' is appropriate to use.[30] Significant, Kant was working in a time that was beginning to make use of statistics in order to predict the future and which helped usher in concepts of risk and probability.

CHOICE, NOT FATE

While pre-modern society, and great civilisations such as ancient Rome or China, can be seen to have lived in the past, the advancement of mathematics – in particular ideas associated with probability and uncertainty – ushered in the concept of risk that defied the gods. This idea was non-existent until breakthroughs in maths allowed the chances of particular outcomes occurring to be calculated. It was an idea that was modern, future-orientated and concerned with trying to predict the likelihood of forthcoming events. From the Enlightenment onwards, a better understanding of risk, and how to measure it, drove change and social progress. The ability to rationalise hazards and vulnerabilities into risk allowed society to colonise the future and changed the nature of decision-making for good.

The application of ideas of risk evolved from early work on the laws of probability during the Enlightenment. This was, however, pre-dated by a long history of gambling, games of chance and quite literally the role of the dice that relied on Lady Luck rather than any sense of odds. In the Renaissance era the mathematical tools to assess, measure and control risk were beginning to be discovered. This period of history was ripe for the introduction of the concept of risk given its focus upon social change and future progress, as it blended into the seventeenth-century Enlightenment period. The Renaissance went hand in hand with the (Protestant) Reformation that not only weakened the power of the Catholic Church but also fundamentally changed civilisation's relationship with God. As Peter Bernstein highlighted in *Against the Gods*, in eliminating the confessional, the Reformation essentially warned people that they would have to make *their own decisions* and 'could no longer remain passive in the face of an unknown future'. This meant that 'with this opening up of choices and decisions, people gradually recognised that the future offered opportunity as well as danger'.[31]

But it took a change in social attitudes about the possibilities of the future for luck, instinct and the acceptance of the randomness of nature to be cast aside, and for forecasting and risk management to become part of everyday life. Modern ways of thinking therefore arose out of a greater focus being placed on the autonomous individual rather than the divine providence of an all-powerful God. Early in the seventeenth century René Descartes, a French philosopher, mathematician and scientist, summed this up through this famous saying *Cogito, ergo sum*, 'I think, therefore I am', where he argued that knowledge is no longer just the preserve of God but something grounded in human existence.[32]

Changing attitudes towards scientific discovery led to a rapid expansion of mathematical knowledge in the sixteenth and seventeenth centuries, particularly around ideas of odds and probability. Early ideas of probability emerged very much as a spirit of progress; one that favoured freedom of thought and harboured a desire for experimentation and an insatiable urge to attempt to control the future. By utilising new techniques of numbering and calculation, practices in forecasting improved. These ultimately became key tools for facilitating geographical exploration and global trade, notably with Columbus setting sail in 1492 and discovering a sea route to America. These were daring times and some have argued that the word 'risk' came into English, through Spanish and Portuguese, to refer to sailing in uncharted waters, while its root comes from the Italian *risicare* – 'to dare' – which sees risk 'as a choice rather than a fate'.[33]

Further advances in probability that subsequently informed the management of risk can be traced to a procession of brilliant Italian and French mathematicians. This story begins thanks to a sixteenth-century Italian, Gerolamo Cardano, author of *Liber de Ludo Aleae* (Book on Games of Chance), which was perhaps the first work to focus on probability calculus. This magnum opus can be viewed as a betting manual with gambling and games of chance being put at the service of risk. In this work, Cardano threw dice to understand the basic concepts of probability and in so doing demonstrated that the probability of an event occurring could be assessed by the ratio of favourable outcomes to the total number of possible outcomes. These early ideas of probability grew in significance once mathematicians discovered theories of the frequency of past events that better allowed future risk to be calculated. Notably, *Sopra le Scoperte dei Dadi* (On Playing Dice), the work on probability by Italian polymath Galileo Galilei, further advanced ideas of the quantification of chance.[34] Galileo's pioneering work anticipated mathematical advances in calculus and algebra stemming from Western Europe, and in particular France, over the coming decades of the seventeenth century.

The French connection came from work by mathematicians Blaise Pascal and Pierre de Fermat who both worked on ideas associated with forecasting and are now seen as the fathers of probability.[35] Through their correspondence in 1654, Pascal and Fermat discovered a very important concept that was all but revolutionary at the time. Their key idea, one that is perhaps intuitive to us today, related to equally probable outcomes pertaining to the number of turns required to ensure obtaining a six in the roll of two dice. Advancing ideas by which odds could be more accurately calculated led society to better understand that chance could be tamed and uncertainty brought under some form of control.[36] Therefore, while fate and providence were not completely banished from future gazing, 'after 1654 mumbo jumbo would no longer be the forecasting method of choice'.[37]

THE BIRTH OF INSURANCE

Because of advances in mathematics, calculating probabilities became more sophisticated in Enlightenment Europe and soon a range of types of private insurance developed. Just over a decade after the work of Pascal and Fermat had advanced the theory of probability, their ideas were put into practice with the birth of insurance markets. These were in essence markets for risk, and were seen as a way to redistribute the financial risk of particular outcomes or events.[38] Through statistics, risks were seen as calculable events in the future that could be bet on, or compensated for. Here insurance operated in similar ways to the gambler at a gaming table – by setting premiums to cover long-term losses, moving the focus away from the individual consequences of loss.

Notably, such principles were put to practical use in the aftermath of the Great Fire of London in 1666. On Sunday 2 September, a fire that started in a bakery in Pudding Lane spread across central London, annihilating 80 per cent of the mainly wooden buildings in the vicinity. The cremated dwellings included 13,200 houses, 87 parish churches and other signature buildings including St Paul's Cathedral built during the Middle Ages.[39] Initially, society fell back on assumptions that the disaster was pre-ordained, and the Parliamentary Report on the Great Fire reported in January 1667 that 'nothing hath yet been found to argue it to have been other than the hand of God upon us, a great wind, and the season so very dry'.[40]

In the year following the Great Fire, a new law came to pass allowing organisations to indemnify – to reimburse or compensate – for losses due to fire. This led to groups of underwriters who had previously dealt exclusively in early forms of marine insurance to form insurance companies that offered fire cover. Therefore, Phoenix Assurance, the world's first insurance company – symbolically named after the Greek mythological firebird that burns itself before rising again from its ashes reborn – was established in 1667. This was followed in 1681 by England's first bespoke fire insurance company, Insurance Office for Houses, that offered fire insurance to approximately 5,000 households in London.[41]

While the Great Fire was instrumental in establishing compensatory mechanisms for homeowners, forms of insurance for seafaring pre-dated it. Therefore, just as the idea of risk began on the high seas in the age of exploration, so modern forms of insurance had nautical beginnings.

Marine insurance was the earliest established type of insurance, dating back to Greek and Roman marine loans that were instrumental in the expansion of the Greek and Roman empires.[42] In Ancient Rome in particular, the importance of shipping made cargo insurance essential to guard against piracy, sinking or delays due to bad weather. Essentially, early ideas of risk redistribution were at play that later came to underpin more advanced insurance markets. This allowed lenders to spread the risk by investing and insuring small amounts in many voyages, and made trade profitable, dependable and importantly, less risky. Separate marine insurance contracts were further developed in a number of Italian cities, notably Genoa, in the fourteenth century, and subsequently spread to northern Europe with premiums charged depending on estimates of the variable risk from the seasons and pirates.[43]

London's growing importance as a global centre for trade was increasing demand for marine insurance but it was in the wake of the Great Fire that what many consider the first insurance markets were established. In 1687, a coffee shop was opened by Edward Lloyd near the River Thames in the centre of London which became a favourite haunt for ship owners and merchants who were moored in the nearby London Docks. Given its clientele, it quickly established itself as the authoritative source for shipping news and a place where those prepared to underwrite such ventures congregated. In London an elaborate system emerged, and was sustained, for funding voyages to the New World. Merchants and companies would first seek funding from venture capitalists and, after the voyage was secured, would go to Lloyd's and hand over a copy of the ship's cargo to be read to the investors and underwriters who gathered there. Those interested in taking on the risk for a set premium were asked to sign at the bottom of the manifest beneath the figure denoting what portion of the cargo they were taking responsibility for (hence, underwriting). This meant that a single voyage usually had multiple underwriters who also spread their own risk by taking stakes in several different voyages.

Thus, the first marine insurance market was born in Lloyd's coffee shop in 1688, as Lloyd's insurance, as informal conversations were formalised into business ventures that dealt with risk. It was through these practices of underwriting that insurance could be used to stimulate trade and exploration as well as reduce risk to funders. The logic underpinning such underwriting was that insurance companies could manage the risk of too many policyholders filing claims at once by distributing risk among a number of investors.[44]

In many ways, Lloyd's approach, and that of others in the insurance game, was driven by the work of Pascal and Fermat who had discovered a way to express probabilities and thereby understand levels of risk. In essence, insurance worked best with large sampling sizes where probability of reward and loss could be more accurately determined by looking at past events.[45] This then led to private insurance being established in the late seventeenth century when the practice of risk assessment became increasingly scientific. Armed with Pascal's Triangle (see note 35) to help them determine probabilities, insurance companies quickly expanded their range of business as the formalised practice of underwriting made insurance more inexpensive.

By the end of the seventeenth century, a new discipline of actuarial science was flourishing with its principles especially utilised to offer life insurance as a result of the development of the first 'mortality tables'. Mortality tables – grids of numbers that show the probability of death for members of a given population within a defined period of time – were first created in the late seventeenth century. From these, insurers, using Pascal's work, quickly came up with the first actuary tables, essentially a spreadsheet showing the probability of a person of a certain age dying before their next birthday.[46] This advancement made it easier for insurance brokers to quantify the risk of taking on a new life insurance policy. John Graunt's pioneering work in London during the 1650s and 1660s that focused on public health statistics was highly influential. His book *Natural and Political Observations Made upon the Bills of Mortality*, published in 1662, created the first statistically based estimation of the life expectancy of the population of London. Graunt's innovative work not only illuminated poverty and disparity in London that could be acted upon but, more conceptually, informed the value of sampling and averages. His findings could not only give a picture of what 'normal' was in any given population but also how decisions could be made in conditions that were uncertain.

By the early part of the eighteenth century, further insurance companies were being established in London. These included the Union Fire Insurance Office (1714), the London Insurance Office (1720) and the Governor and Company of the Royal Exchange Insurance Company (1720) who began to develop a common procedure for 'rating' properties according to the risk of loss to which they could give rise. This at first was a basic categorisation including 'common' insurance, 'hazardous' insurance and 'doubly hazardous' insurance, representing low, medium and high levels of risk.

Across the Atlantic in colonial America, insurance companies were also being formed along similar lines, with the first insurance company to underwrite the risk of fire being established in Charles Town (modern-day Charleston) in 1732. It was, however, one of the founding fathers of America, Benjamin Franklin, who helped drive forward the insurance industry in the US, particularly for fire and property, when he founded the Philadelphia Contributionship for the Insurance of Houses from Loss by Fire in 1752. Franklin's company, which is still in operation today, notably warned against certain fire hazards, as well as refusing to insure certain buildings where the fire risk was deemed too high, such as all wooden houses. The company started life as a fund for compensating for fire damage to the property of fire company members but was quickly extended as an insurance programme to all citizens of Philadelphia.

For the next 200 years, up until the late twentieth century, the assessment of risk advanced incrementally, with insurance becoming more sophisticated as the ideas behind probability advanced by Cardano, Pascal, Fermat and others were applied to raw data. From an industry dominated by small, local, single-line mutual companies, the business of insurance has progressed towards the complex multi-line coverage and the multinational companies we see today. As insurance evolved, it highlighted that risk was not something to be feared but something that gave choice and a range of opportunities for action. For example, Jacob Bernoulli's work at the start of the eighteenth century on what became known as the 'law of large numbers' was an attempt to measure uncertainty by calculating the probability of an event occurring through increased sampling. Here unknown probabilities equal greater uncertainty. This simple 'law' explains why insurers can offer more accurate premiums on frequently occurring events than events that occur less often.[47]

Throughout the seventeenth and eighteenth centuries, the increased quantification of risk gave preference to objective measures of progress. This often synthesised 'truth' from the rational application of science, while preserving a role for God. Notably, Isaac Newton's contribution to physics, and in particular the laws of motion, led to the idea of a 'clockwork universe' that resembles a mechanical clock wound up by God – a perfect machine, with its gears governed by the laws of physics.[48] However, by the Industrial Revolution of the eighteenth and nineteenth centuries social progress was placing a premium on scientific research over religious virtues. 'God is dead' according to German philosopher Friedrich Nietzsche who, in the late nineteenth century, used the phrase to sum up the consequences of the Enlightenment on the centrality of the concept of God within Western civilisation. Scientific endeavour had overtaken religion as society's main futureproofing tool.[49]

However, entering the twentieth century, mathematics had taken statistics down an alley that was largely blind to its social impact and was increasingly detached from everyday life. Sociologist Max Weber in his landmark 1905 book *The Protestant Ethic and the Spirit of Capitalism* depicted a shift from traditional social values and organisation through which magic, supernatural and religious ideas lose cultural importance, to what was termed 'rationality', where ideas based on science and practical calculation became dominant.[50] This, he argued, allowed the modern bureaucratic state to run through efficiency, calculability and instrumentalisation (a means to an end), and advance capitalism for the few, not the many. Accordingly, the idea that human behaviour can be controlled through a melding of science, bureaucracy and capitalism, and that this could be dehumanising, emerged. The 'iron cage' was the term coined by Weber for the increased rationalisation inherent in social life, particularly in Western capitalist societies, which traps and controls individuals in overly bureaucratic systems.[51] In this sense, modern institutions were risk management machines. They sought to best determine possible futures by maximising control over areas where they could calculate probabilities and subsequently minimise areas where control was limited by random events. In other words, as mathematicians of the early twentieth century were finding, events that appeared to be random could be ordered and brought under control.[52]

As the twentieth century advanced, so did the demand for such 'risk management' given that a range of newer risks attributable to industrialisation had united with 'old' risks. The First World War in particular proved a watershed time for faith in classical economics that, until that point, had been seen as a riskless system that produced optimal results. The stability it promised was no longer guaranteed.[53] Concern was especially expressed about the way uncertainty was taken into account in calculating risk. In his work on what became known as 'measurable uncertainty'

Frank Knight made a famous distinction between 'risk' (randomness with knowable probabilities) and 'uncertainty' (randomness with unknowable probabilities).[54] Previously accepted ideas in economics, such as perfect competition and forecasting the future through the simple extrapolation of trends, were seen as inherently flawed. Now, uncertainty moved from the periphery to the centre of risk analysis and risk management. The ability to 'calculate uncertainty' in forecasting made it possible, even rational, to allow unexpected outcomes within certain limits.

As rational styles of risk management, notably insurance, began to infiltrate more and more areas of life during the 1970s and 1980s, major catastrophes and political upheavals brought great uncertainty to bear. The Three Mile Island accident in Pennsylvania in 1979 which galvanised anti-nuclear safety concerns among activists and the general public; the release of toxins from an industrial plant in Bhopal, India in 1984; the Chernobyl nuclear meltdown in Ukraine in 1986 which sent radioactive material raining down all over Europe; emerging concerns over climate change impacts such as acid rain and smog; and the fall of the Soviet Empire in the late 1980s; all starkly illuminated the magnitude and boundless nature of the global risks. These were risks that eluded the control and protective institutions of industrial society, transforming the way in which risk of all sorts were reimagined and managed.

This reimagining of society's relationship to risk – as something that is omnipresent and uncertain – questioned the very basis of conventional forms of risk management where traditionally Risk = Consequence × Likelihood.[55] New thinking on the consequences of risk, and risk decision-making, led to a sharp growth in commentary about an emerging type of society where ideas of risk played an increasingly central part. To coin a famous phrase by Karl Marx, all which is solid – in this case, all society's underlying beliefs about calculating risks – had melted into air.

RISK SOCIETY

In the 1980s and 1990s, a number of accounts suggested that concerns about environmental and technological threats became defining characteristics of contemporary society due to the breakdown in the traditional ways of calculating risk. Such accounts emerged primarily around concerns regarding global environmental hazards and the limits of insurance that for centuries had offered financial security against risk. Such interpretations foretold severe environmental, social, economic and political implications of the inability to control such risks. By the end of the twentieth century, risk had evolved into a concept that went well beyond the idea of financial loss, translated into objective financial terms by insurers.

Risk was now seen as something that was 'socially constructed' and came to be viewed as a cultural expression that included individual and public perceptions of indefinable loss. Risk now appeared to be intertwined into the fabric of contemporary society and 'something of an omnipresent issue, casting its spectre over a wide range of practice and experiences'.[56] Our increased knowledge and awareness of the cause and effect of particular risk events, which were viewed as inherently complex and unpredictable, partly drove this. The idea that risk, as one of the consequences of modernity, was under threat ushered in a sense of foreboding. One social commentator employed the metaphor of an out-of-control juggernaut – 'a runaway engine of enormous power which collectively as human beings, we can drive to some extent but which also threatens to rush out of control' – to describe the impact of individually produced risk upon the contemporary world.[57] This was an attempt to show how traditional approaches to controlling uncertainty often had the opposite effect of increasing anxiety about risk through 'the intensity of their focus and attention'.[58]

TRANSITIONING TO A RISK SOCIETY

As we saw in the Introduction, of the new range of 'risk theories' that emerged in the late twentieth century, sociologist Ulrich Beck's *Risk Society* was the most significant. Published in the same year as the Chernobyl nuclear catastrophe in Ukraine, *Risk Society* considered what society might look like when disputes and conflicts about new types of risk produced by industrial society are fully realised. *Risk Society* emerged as the hazards produced by industrial society were increasingly illuminated, magnified and dramatised in the global mass media.[59] *Risk Society* starkly illustrated the magnitude and limitless nature of global risks, and how this had transformed the way in which risk is managed. The vision of *Risk Society* illuminated how social progress had been tempered by new types of risk, increasingly negative risk perceptions fuelled by mass media coverage and the actions of risk management that appeared interwoven into all aspects of contemporary life.

A key aspect of Beck's thesis concerned the ways in which society was associated with a new attitude towards scientific expertise and could reflect upon and adapt to new risks.[60] The increased institutional demands for knowledge about risks in terms of definition, management and assessment, and the changing involvement of welfare agencies, health authorities, the risk management profession and especially insurance companies, were actively changing the way in which risk was defined and managed. Many institutions lost their historical legitimacy as risk controllers. In particular, the insurance industry's ability to reduce the financial uncertainty from risk and to make the incalculable calculable through statistics was under attack. Increasingly it was not possible to insure against all types of risk as, through our own systematically produced hazards, contemporary society balanced 'beyond the insurance limit',[61] creating a situation where financial protection paradoxically diminished as danger grew.

From the 1990s, it became increasingly evident that high-impact risk events such as terrorism, flooding, earthquakes, climate change and industrial accidents were beginning to worry the insurance industry. In some cases, this forced them to withdraw from the specific markets concerned, citing the high cost of their liability as well as the impossibility of calculating the risk involved. It was not that the frequency of such events increased; rather it was that the insured cost of catastrophic losses rose significantly and led to fears of insolvency within the insurance industry. For example, a report in the early 1990s by the UK Chartered Insurance Institute warned that British insurers were only then beginning to realise the scale of risk they were 'carrying on their shoulders'.[62] At this time, there was also a concerted effort among more progressive elements within the US insurance sector to increase their understanding of the insurance impact of extreme events given their concern over their exposure to unknown catastrophic losses.[63] Kenneth Froot's *The Financing of Catastrophe Risk* further illuminated how, as we entered the new millennium, insurance and reinsurance industries were struggling to cope with magnified losses from single or repeat exposures with the potential to impact significantly on the broader US economy.

As such, the provision of private insurance was seen to mark the boundary between calculable risks and incalculable threats in *Risk Society*.

Notably, the tragic events of 9/11 forced everyone to re-examine the risks faced from modern-day terrorism as well as other global risks. The insurance industry had been in difficulty for some time and was experiencing large underwriting losses. Even prior to 9/11, it was widely estimated that insurers were paying out £1.15 in claims for every £1 received in premiums. The insurance industry was subsequently accused of using 9/11 as a catalyst to restructure and streamline, and in doing so raise premiums across the board to make up for falling profits. This further meant that insurers increasingly began to operate policies of 'adverse selection' in an attempt to limit their liability to certain large-scale risks that broke the fundamental rules of insurance. More and more this has forced national governments to get involved and bear part of the risk. Earthquake cover in Japan, general disaster protection in New Zealand and terrorism and flooding coverage in the UK are recent examples of where the state has had to step in to provide a buffer to the insurance industry and to ensure that insurance policies can still be issued for specified risks.

TOWARDS RESILIENCE

Over the many centuries of human progress, the growing ability to calculate risk through probability, and the translation of this into insurance premiums, has had a significant impact on how institutions function and how society views the future. In the Enlightenment, logic and reason embodied in the idea of rationalism provided a refuge for an insecure world where nature was passive and controllable and where previously divine providence was projected as the main cause of disaster or social upheaval. Insecurities were largely managed through strategies of objective statistical risk assessment. Attempts to predict and colonise the future were built into contemporary institutions determined by the 'known knowns' of established knowledge and ingrained in conventional ways of working. Such a worldview was, however, always partial, unstable and backward-facing.

Today, society is living with an almost endless array of perceived risks. Many of these risks have sprung from technological modernisation and the acknowledgment of the vast and complex interconnectivity of global systems. These risks increasingly evade our control and shatter the illusion of modernity. Change is, however, afoot in terms of how society and its protective institutions are seeking to reimagine and construct strategies to manage risk in a world increasingly shaped by human intervention. Such strategies, like *Risk Society*, also illuminate uncertainties, anxieties and lack of predictability inherent in the contemporary world, posing existential concerns over human survival.

With rising levels of risk and vulnerability, global society is experiencing what has been referred to as a 'rupture of continuity'.[64] We are moving away from the modern dream of equilibrium, stability, predictability and control towards new 'postmodern' forms of social organisation where complexity and volatility dominate discussions of an uncertain future. What began as premonitions in the late 1980s about the likely impact of mega-risks have now become fully fledged concerns that have destabilised conventional ways of dealing with risk. This reimagining of our relationship with risk and uncertainty has subsequently catalysed the rise of resilience as a framework through which we can potentially free ourselves from the contours of conventional risk management and embrace future uncertainty and a permanent state of adaptation.

2

THE RESILIENCE TURN AND THE PERMANENT STATE OF ADAPTATION

We live in a complex world. Anyone with a stake in managing some aspect of that world will benefit from a richer understanding of resilience and its implications.

Brian Walker and David Salt, *Resilience Thinking*[1]

Intelligence is the ability to adapt to change.

Attributed to Stephen Hawking's Oxford University graduation speech

In December 2015, just days after world leaders had signed off a global climate change agreement at the UN climate change conference in Paris, Storm Frank wreaked havoc in many areas of the UK as flooding experts warned that the climate was entering an era of 'unknown extremes'. Communities across many towns and villages in northern areas of the UK faced a demoralising and lengthy clean-up operation as the scale of the damage from water and wind became apparent. In many cases, insurance claims took months to be assessed and repairs took over two years to be completed on many affected properties.

As the storm hit, emergency response plans swung into operation but the sheer scale of the damage was overwhelming. Thousands of homes were left without power for days on end. Many others were evacuated. Five hundred soldiers were mobilised to help with the emergency effort, with a further 1,000 put on standby. In some places, emergency response operations continued apace amidst the sound of RAF Chinook helicopters overhead delivering vital aid to cut-off communities, or dropping massive sandbags into exposed gaps in flood barriers in a bid to shore up defences. Many flood protections had proved ineffective, having been built in the wrong place or to inadequate specifications. Amid dire warnings that climate change would lead to more frequent extreme weather and severe flooding, the perilous state of the large-scale barriers was illuminated after many were overcome by the sheer volume of water. A complete rethink of all UK flood defences was called for.

The UK prime minister, visiting the flood-prone city of York, posed for photographs with army helpers as floodwaters continued to rise alarmingly. Large parts of this city were subsequently submerged. Hours before, in direct response to the devastation wrought, a senior figure in the UK Environment Agency noted that we could no longer prepare for such serious flooding incidents in the traditional way: 'We are moving from known extremes to unknown extremes . . . we will need to have a complete rethink [and] move from not just providing better defences . . . but looking at increasing resilience.' What he meant was that in addition to the major £2.3 billion programme of flood defences, we should make infrastructure, homes and communities more resilient so that lives can be saved and recovery time minimised.[2]

The lessons learnt from Storm Frank increasingly challenged the legitimacy of technically engineered approaches to hazard mitigation and the traditional basis of risk management. Greater resilience was required to make responses proactive, adaptive and focused on everyday applications such as solid floors, waterproof plaster and moving electric sockets up the wall to avoid rising floodwaters. This, it was hoped, would get people back home quickly and promote business as usual. An additional focus on improving flood-warning systems and community resilience-building programmes was called for that would give emergency responders and citizens more time to take action in the event of future flooding.

Improving resilience in this context also meant thinking about the strategic actions required. Ironically, a fortnight before Storm Frank hit, a national government review of flood resilience had been announced that was to see the government update worst-case-scenario planning, consider the future impacts of climate change and carry out a risk assessment of critical infrastructure such as electricity substations. Such work was subsequently fast-tracked as questions continued to be asked about the effectiveness of the government's response to the most recent events. In the unfolding chaos, Storm Frank was labelled a 'preventable disaster'.

Preparation for severe flooding had clearly been too focused on major flood defences in isolation. There was a failure to take a holistic view and look at a range of other factors such as at land management, drainage and insurance incentives. Notably, after severe floods in 2007, which affected 55,000 homes, a government-commissioned independent review had recommended *not* building on floodplains. This had been largely ignored by property developers keen to make a fast buck, with one in ten houses over the last 30 years being built in areas susceptible to flooding.[3]

If this story sounds familiar, it is probably because of the remarkable increase in similar disruptive events that have starkly highlighted the requirement for enhanced resilience, as well as the failings of earlier decision-making. This is especially critical as, by recent estimates, there are one billion people globally living on land vulnerable to flooding – a figure that will rise to two billion by 2050, with the cities of the developing world being particularly vulnerable.[4] We urgently need to better understand that such disruptions often result not just from failures in the design of defences but in the decision-making process. Better understanding these failures and promoting a more comprehensive and integrated engagement with the complexities of cause and effect, together with the uncertainty of future threats, holds the key to enhancing resilience.

FROM RISK TO RESILIENCE

In the early twenty-first century – catalysed by the devastating events of 9/11, the release of the fourth Intergovernmental Panel on Climate Change (IPCC) report in 2007 highlighting unequivocal evidence of a warming climate and the financial crash of 2007/8 – ideas and practices of resilience have risen rapidly to become one of the key terms in international policy and academic discussions regarding how best to cope with an uncertain future. The word resilience comes from the Latin *resilire* – 'to leap back' – and although it is predominantly a Western-centred approach, it is an idea that has travelled far in a short space of time and has been embraced across the globe. It is a term that has quickly become central to a broader turn in local, national and global governance towards specific forms of intervention and coordination. Whatever the subject of concern – whether questions of security or conflict management, the response to economic crisis, the mitigation of climate change, reshaping organisations to be more agile, the challenges of urban poverty or disaster management – questions of resilience will be at the forefront of discussion. Leading international institutions, such as the United Nations, the European Union, the World Bank and the International Monetary Fund, government agencies and departments, international non-governmental organisations and community groups are all busily promoting the importance of resilience. They all express various ideas of what it might be and how it could be achieved, together with differing ways to measure it.

However, with the rapid rise of resilience has come ambiguity as to how it should be built and how different practices and approaches should come together to use it.[5] The ways in which ideas and practices of resilience have emerged within popular discussion have varied from country to country and been focused in distinctive ways linked to the particular risks and threats faced. In the UK and the US, post-9/11 security threats from terrorism drove the popularity of resilience as the go-to term to describe attempts to keep the homeland safe. Conversely, in mainland Europe the use of resilience emerged more slowly and has predominantly been associated with climate change adaptation and the response to devastating flooding. Throughout the Western world, the financial meltdown that started in 2007 also catapulted ideas of resilience to general attention. In all cases though, the view that risk of one kind or another has been advanced and enhanced by human progress or poor decision-making has significantly contributed to the rise of resilience as the policy metaphor of choice for coping with growing complexity and managing future uncertainty.

The twenty-first century is progressively seeing a turn away from conventional approaches to risk and towards resilience. Despite being very different concepts, both risk and resilience are closely associated with a deep engagement with uncertainty and can be put into operation alongside each other. As highlighted in the previous chapter, the management of risk has traditionally focused on ordering, probability and a requirement for optimisation and control. Risk-based approaches have traditionally been technically focused and have paid only limited attention to social and organisational factors. There has also been a tendency for risk management to concentrate on making *specific parts* of a system more robust or efficient. By contrast, resilience approaches should go beyond and extend risk management to address the difficulties of managing the complex and integrated social and technical systems that underpin modern life. They are also about specifically prepping to manage the complexity and uncertainty of future threats. The focus of resilience here is very much on the outcomes for the *whole system* and better understanding the relationships and trade-offs between different parts or elements of the system.

Risk and resilience are therefore very different – yet related – concepts dealing with different aspects of an integrated cycle of action. If we consider the widely accepted definition of resilience from the US National Academy of Sciences – 'the ability to anticipate, prepare for, and adapt to changing conditions and withstand, respond to, and recover rapidly from disruptions' – then, as Igor Linkov from the US Corps of Engineers has persuasively argued, risk is central to resilience. He notes that 'adapt' and 'recover' are resilience concepts; 'withstand' and 'respond to' are risk concepts. Where a risk-based view focuses on gearing up to plan for disruption, resilience goes further by seeking to establish how systems can best recover and adapt from adverse events.[6]

Still, advocates and critics disagree over many aspects of resilience: whether it is a new postmodern approach capable of redirecting international policy discussions or just meaningless jargon;[7] whether it allows greater community empowerment or maintains current structures of power; whether it opens up possibilities for radical transformation or merely conserves or reproduces conventional economic and organisational understandings; whether it is about maintaining stability and the status quo or encouraging risk-taking and change; and so on.

BECOMING RESILIENT

The world before resilience was one with a greater confidence in the capacity of states and governments to secure and control events. In this confident 'modern' world, it appeared that knowledge and understanding could grow and that solutions to problems could be learnt. These lessons could be generalised and applied elsewhere. Best practices could be easily identified and transferred anywhere. Arguably, the world of resilience is one with less confidence in our existing knowledge and the ability to advance one-size-fits-all solutions. It is a world that seems less certain and infinitely more volatile and complex.[8] We live in an era where clarity is less likely, and separations between threats and response, human and nature, problems and solutions, past and future, seem less stable than before.[9]

Resilience is often defined in relation to this new awareness of insecurity, uncertainty or complexity. It is commonly seen as the capacity to prepare for, respond to or recover from problems, perturbations and disturbances which cannot necessarily be predicted or foreseen. If the modern world was about control and minimising future uncertainty, the 'post'-modern period acknowledges and prepares for future risk and uncertainty of outcomes. As Donald Rumsfeld famously noted in a US Defence Department briefing in February 2002, 'There are known knowns. These are things we know that we know. There are known unknowns. That is to say, there are things that we know we don't know. However, there are also unknown unknowns. There are things we don't know we don't know.'[10]

Rumsfeld's statement has become a maxim for the contemporary world. Such ideas are increasingly used in strategic planning and risk management to laminate the unknown onto the assessment of risk in order to improve potential outcomes. For the promoters of resilience, this new dynamic and risk-sensitive approach enables a more open and fluid approach to the world, one that attempts to rethink and to move away from traditional approaches to problems. The characteristics of a more open approach often include a more iterative or process-based approach to problems, working with difficulties, being sensitive to feedback and not assuming that there is an immediate or fail-safe cure or solution. The reason for resilience approaches often involving less certainty and more caution is a greater awareness of unintended consequences or side effects when acting in the world. For these reasons, resilience is seen as a more experimental and more context-dependent approach, less prone to generalisations about what works and what does not. Problems are not always seen as something external to us but often as symptoms or expressions of our lack of understanding of, or failure to be alert to, changes in our own environment. Problems might also be seen as an expression of obduracy; an inability to change how we work and how decisions are made.

Resilience frames the world in a different way from risk management and has proved to be a term or approach that can be applied in a flexible fashion across a range of challenges when trying to make sense of the range of potential disruptions facing global society. The increased volatility that we face in the epoch of the Anthropocene requires a new response that moves us on from ideas of sustainability that have pervaded global agendas since the early 1990s.[11] In essence, where sustainability often seeks stability, resilience is based on ideas of change, which makes it particularly helpful for managing a complex and uncertain future. As Andrew Zolli has succinctly noted, 'Where sustainability aims to put the world back into balance, resilience looks for ways to manage in an imbalanced world.'[12]

Despite the confusion caused by the multiple uses of resilience, the general framework of resilience approaches seems to fairly coherently reflect a number of shifts in awareness and policy-making in the international arena. These have cast doubt on modernist assumptions about the inevitability of social progress as well as in relation to specific questions of security, the environment and development, urban planning and so on, where the external world was seen to be uniform and unchanging. This was a world merely waiting for human knowledge to develop adequately enough to solve problems.

Resilience, by contrast, is underpinned by the belief that complex life is no longer bounded by fixed laws, structures or assumptions, and that rational behaviour and predictive methods cannot be relied upon to help us progress and remain safe. There is no precise set of policies or interventions by which we can protect ourselves. By contrast, if we adopt resilience-thinking then how we respond to crisis, shocks and disruption is enabled by learning, self-reflection and, above all, adaptation. Progress today is not so much about creating knowledge blueprints, but rather about being more aware of the complex integration of our own systems of organisation – politically, culturally, socially and economically. It is also about the interactive effects of these forms of organisation with the external, changing environment and international context. In this sense, resilience approaches seem to be much more about relationships, connections and contexts than about fixed rules and linear cause and effect assumptions.[13] Resilience is more about understanding the cyclical nature of the world around us. This has commonly led to resilience processes being depicted as a cycle of action – most often with preparedness, response, mitigation and recovery/adaptation elements – rather than a set of steps that you climb incrementally as you progress.

Resilience approaches are also often about how to engage in processes of interaction between different aspects of the world and using feedback in more responsive ways to track progress. Resilience can, in many ways, be seen as symptomatic of the world today where more open, inclusive, pragmatic and contextual solutions to problems are sought in coping with an uncertain future. As geographer Kevin Grove has noted, ideas of resilience are an attempt to break through the grid of positivist social science, representing a 'will to design' new approaches that seek to synthesise diverse forms of knowledge and develop collaborative solutions to complex problems.[14]

FRAMING RESILIENCE

While resilience can be framed in myriad ways, we can identify two broad approaches that have been influential. Initially, resilience was about maintaining the status quo and retaining equilibrium at all costs. Gradually such *bounce-back* resilience has given way to more radical approaches, which see the world as much more in flux. These so-called evolutionary approaches focus upon a *bounce-forward* and 'new normal' model of resilience, seeking to construct an approach more applicable to increasingly complex systems that impact on all aspects of human life on earth.

Bounce-back resilience focuses on maintaining stability and balance, and seeks to regulate a return to a pre-existing or 'normal' condition. This type of approach has been associated largely with ecological models of resilience that have dominated resilience discourse since the early 1970s. For all the talk of the multiple areas into which resilience has been jettisoned, the use and application of the term 'resilience' is broadly acknowledged to have emerged from C. S. 'Buzz' Holling's 1970s studies of systems ecology and his subsequent work with the Resilience Alliance.[15] Holling's ideas, best portrayed in the classic 1973 publication *Resilience and Stability of Ecological Systems*, represented a shift in conventional thinking, demonstrating a more dynamic process that he termed the 'adaptive cycle'. This deviated from earlier understandings of ecological systems, which assumed a stable basis. The adaptive cycle, though, was essentially an equilibrium model in which resilience was seen as the ability of a system to either return to a steady state or to absorb shock events and persist under stress.

In Holling's words, ecological resilience is the magnitude of change a system can absorb before it 'flips' and alters structure to another 'stability domain'.[16] Ecological resilience was about change and unpredictability but with a view to return to equilibrium. This resilience approach sought to organise any system internally to enable a smooth and efficient return to functioning after a disruption or setback. Within this broad framing, some bounce-back approaches might focus on internal capacities of the community or society to be resilient to disruption. Others will assess levels of redundancy, slack or spare capacity that can be built into a system to provide a buffer against disturbance. There could also be a focus on questions of variety and diversity, avoiding over-reliance on particular resources, their sources of supply or centres of coordination that if disabled could prove destabilising.

The bounce-back approach sometimes makes a distinction between the *inside*, to be made resilient, and the threat or problem on the *outside*, as something to be resilient against. The threat of cyber-attacks against critical infrastructure may serve as a good example. Here such an attack is often conceived as an external threat, one difficult to prevent and therefore necessitating the preparation of ways of rebounding to normal functioning should major infrastructural facilities or lifelines be damaged. In such a situation, the central focus is on returning to normal functioning as quickly as possible. In this instance, resilience is about restoring an orderly flow of electricity, water or commerce, and limiting the impact of disruption on broader society or the economy.

Such resilience approaches are concerned with bouncing back after an event but nevertheless encourage changes in the present. These changes are geared less towards preventing risks, threats or problems from taking place than towards recognising problems, responding to them and recovering with the minimum of disruption. So rather than working on the external world in a direct way, this type of resilience tends to work indirectly, often starting with the process of working on the properties of the internal ecosystem, system or society to help it rebound. This is an important shift away from traditional approaches to problem-solving, focusing on the complicated and integrated parts of a system. The aim is not to achieve specific outcomes in themselves but to be able to respond to external disturbance, much as a thermostat works on the basis of adapting to feedback from temperature changes in the external environment.

Increasingly, equilibrium or bounce-back approaches to resilience have come under fire as their influence has spread, particularly into the area of climate adaptation. They have been viewed by some as inherently conservative and not able to fully reflect the volatility and complexity of real life. They are seen as enacting pre-programmed responses based on tried and tested procedures. To return to the previous metaphor, a thermostat measures room temperature against a standard setting and turns the heat source up or down accordingly to how it is programmed. It asks a one-dimensional question to elicit a one-dimensional answer. It is a simple cause and effect response.

For many, such an approach is too divorced from the complex reality of modern life to be applied appropriately to a range of social and policy areas.[17] As geographer Katrina Brown has highlighted, such a view of resilience 'promotes a scientific and technical approach akin to "imposed rationality" that is alien to the practice of ordinary people . . . is depoliticized and does not take account of the institutions within which practices and management are embedded'.[18] Therefore, while the term 'resilience' has its roots in the natural sciences, particularly ecology, conventional approaches are not amenable to wholesale transfer into today's complex social and political world.

If equilibrium approaches represented the first generation of resilience-thinking, and are still perhaps the dominant approach in many areas, then second-generation resilience can be seen as more evolutionary. Such approaches have advanced as a reaction to the acknowledged limitations of bounce-back models. In newer, bounce-forward approaches, resilience is intimately connected to ideas of complexity thinking. In thinking through resilience, the dynamic and unpredictable nature of interlinked systems with many feedback loops that move systems away from equilibrium is emphasised. Small changes in one part of the system can have big effects on other parts, and thus systems are forced to evolve, adapt and self-organise in order to engage with future uncertainty. In many ways such approaches represent an 'extension' to established risk management or resilience approaches where the central aim is not 'bouncing back' but rather growth and development. This can be accomplished through an increased awareness of interconnections, and the importance placed on *processes of change* rather than short-term outputs and medium-term outcomes.

Resilience is no longer about returning to the equilibrium, or maintaining the status quo, but is seen to be a process of ongoing transformation, adaptation and the building of capacities that facilitates 'bouncing forward'. It is a way of thinking about problems with emphasis placed on the process of 'self-regulation' or self-organisation.

Resilience as transformation or as evolutionary self-growth presupposes a very different relationship between the society and the outside world than bounce-back approaches. The evolutionary approach in many ways can be seen to follow the earlier equilibrium approach of not working directly on an external world but focusing on internal forms of organisation in relation to the external world. In this case, however, rather than aiming to maintain balance and stability, the aspiration is to generate new and innovative ways of thinking and organising. For example Judith Rodin, the former president of the US-based Rockefeller Foundation, referred to this as the 'resilience dividend', where resilience-thinking enables communities and societies to 'bounce back better' by learning more about themselves and building new forms of relationship and self-awareness.[19] Here, external stimuli and disruptions become important, as they can be catalysts for enabling this process of learning and self-reassessment. Even if there is no disastrous event, these sensitivities to changes can be applied to improve and rethink everyday processes, allowing us to revaluate how we live with risk and vulnerability in the present and how we might alter this in the future. This creates a shift towards organising and governing on the basis of resilience per se, independently of whether there is a disaster, crisis or unexpected disruption.

In this framing of resilience, problems are no longer considered as entirely external threats but also as products of historical, or existing, social and organisational processes. Similarly, resilience practices and policies are not merely about technical development but are also focused on social and political adaptive changes that are required to help us cope in an increasingly complex and volatile world. New forms of governance – the ability to organise and mobilise collective action – based on the awareness of problems and threats that emerge out of interactions between society and the external environment are therefore required.[20] This approach moves well beyond perspectives of prevention and bounce-back framings of resilience. It enables a fundamental re-evaluation of traditional forms of knowledge and organisation that fail to take into account the unintended consequences of narrow and rational problem-solving approaches. The earlier story of Storm Frank provides a classic example of this where the construction of flood defences made water systems more volatile and undermined natural protections. Similarly, the failure of the levee system in New Orleans, when Hurricane Katrina hit in 2005, illuminated how ground subsidence caused by the tapping of underground aquifers and the erosion of freshwater marshes by oil and gas exploration in the

Gulf of Mexico contributed to the devastation. This means that organising our resilient responses should be seen as a circular process of governing the unintended consequences of previous attempts to solve problems, being wary of the possibility that this stores up further problems for the future, and attempting to break out of this destructive loop through new, more imaginative, bounce-forward methods. Such approaches therefore embrace adaptability and seek to work with the uncertainty the future holds, rather than simply attempting to control or defend against it.

Today, the principles of resilience carry tremendous influence in futureproofing our world. Resilience affects how many people, politicians and organisations think about the future and look at the short-, medium- and long-term issues. It changes the way in which we advance the knowledge, objectives and actions involved. Resilience recognises the wide range of interconnected issues and the greater number of stakeholders that should come together as new solutions are sought with anticipation, adaptation and flexibility as core attributes. This breaks conventional approaches to dealing with risk out of their preoccupation with order, certainty and stability, and reacting through short-term fixes. In this transition from equilibrium to more transformative approaches, resilience is as much about a set of learning processes as it is about outputs and outcomes. The potentially positive force of resilience is in destabilising the status quo and shining a light on how future vulnerabilities might be tackled in a proactive, transformative and adaptive way.

THE AGE OF PERMANENT ADAPTATION

Solving what Tim Harford in his book *Adapt* refers to as 'complex, fast moving problems in a complex, fast moving world'[21] not only promotes the idea of resilience but also endorses the need to be able to adapt rapidly to changing and volatile situations in the future. This is an acknowledgement that former 'expert' judgement has failed to fully appreciate the persistent uncertainty of the modern world and is insufficient to forecast the future with any great degree of accuracy. Conventional approaches to forecasting that privileged linear thinking and the simple exploitation of trends are seen as broken. Today's complex problems throw up an array of possible outcomes, some of which are 'unknowable', requiring us to come up with a range of plausible options and scenarios that we can pick from or move between. Put more crudely, and in the language of Charles Darwin's 1859 theory of evolution, to encourage adaptation requires *variation* and *selection*. As Darwin, in *Origin of Species*, noted, 'The species that survives is the one that is able to adapt to and to adjust best to the changing environment in which it finds itself.' Simply put, adapt, or die.[22]

Ideas surrounding adaptability, together with the capacity to respond to risk in agile ways, are at the heart of resilience. Here, resilience practices seek to enhance the adaptability of critical systems and to proactively respond to the occurrence or threat of disruption. Resilience is also about change, doing things differently, and encouraging approaches to problems that are inventive, experimental and 'safe to fail'. Resilience is about diversity and variation leading to innovation. Resilience and the ability to adapt is also about the real-world trial and error testing of these innovations for their contribution to problem-solving, survival and social and economic progress. Thus taking the time to reflect, learn and act on feedback are incredibly important processes, however uncomfortable, in today's fast-paced world.

ADAPTING FROM FAILURE

Seeing resilience as the need to adapt sits in contrast to many conventional approaches to dealing with risk that can be considered fail-safe or 'maladaptive'. Maladaptation can be broadly understood to mean a process that is 'inappropriate', no longer 'fit for purpose' or which increases rather than reduces vulnerability. Sometimes maladaptation can occur because of well-meaning adaptation strategies.[23] Notably, many large-scale engineering features have a low likelihood of failure but catastrophic consequences when tipping points are reached. These are seen as the points at which a series of small changes is significant enough to cause a larger change or effect that can't be stopped. For example, during the nuclear accident in Japan in 2011 the sea walls at Fukushima nuclear power facility were compromised, causing power loss that affected the ability of the station to cool its reactors. In this case, there was no uncompromised backup system or Plan B in operation. This starkly illuminated a lack of adaptability and a fragmented system of governance where different parts of the same overall system undermined each other's objectives, increasing vulnerability and leading to failure.[24] We must recognise, better understand and then remove such maladaptive factors before new adaptations can be implemented and resilience enhanced.

Learning the lessons from previous experiences of disruption has therefore become a key feature of resilience narratives that seek to understand why those tasked with dealing with risk are often seen to make poor decisions that increase, rather than reduce, risk. Often this appears to be the result of a failure to change where adaptation attempts overwhelmingly support the status quo and promote 'business as usual'. In many cases, the resilience discourse itself appears to be focused on short-term fixes and an equilibrium-based approach to recovery efforts rather than approaches that seek to change established modes of action. In other situations, we might see that the ability or capacity to adapt has been exhausted by a lack of slack, or what engineers call redundancy, in any given system. Very complex systems, where there are lots of interconnections between different parts, are a classic example of situations that might be seen as having a good degree of 'robustness' at the level of individual parts or components yet are not very resilient as a whole. For example, an earthquake might produce a cascade effect where a range of interlinked systems falls like a line of dominoes. The quake might knock out an electricity gird and cause fires that in turn stop many other systems from functioning. Such complex systems have been termed robust-yet-fragile systems,[25] meaning that while designed to cope or defend against disruption through ensuring toughness, they are susceptible to unexpected threats due to lack of compensatory systems, slack or redundancy. As Andrew Zolli and Ann Marie Healy noted in their best-selling book *Resilience: Why Things Bounce Back*, the paradox of such robust-yet-fragile systems makes the properties of resilience both an advantage and disadvantage. This highlights how the increasingly complex systems of the modern world that have embraced risk management have often become inherently brittle and unstable because of their interconnectedness. As they note, 'As complexity of that compensatory system grows, it becomes a source of fragility itself – approaching a tipping point where even small disturbances, if they occur in the right place, can bring the system to its knees.'[26]

Understanding such maladaptation also means shining a light on poor decision-making, which has increased vulnerability or led to a reduction in a willingness to adapt. In many ways resilience is the response to maladaptation, delivered through the enhancement of what many refer to as adaptive capacity (or adaptability). This is the capability to adapt to stress and shock as quickly as possible. It might simply be the capacity for humans to accept and cope with change. The systems, organisations or individuals best able to adapt to new circumstances or perceived vulnerabilities will be the most resilient.

In an age of unforeseeable disruption and volatility, increasing adaptive capacity allows for uncertainty, change and new forms of practice to be integrated in governing linked systems and is arguably the key element of new ways of thinking about resilience. Here adaptive capacity denotes 'the ability to adapt to change circumstances while fulfilling one's core purpose'.[27] Adaptive capacity is the product of the resources that a system requires to adapt and learn, and the way in which particular individuals or groups can mobilise these resources effectively to mitigate the impact of known risks or unknown disruptions. Adaptability is therefore a proactive, dynamic and adjustable capacity that allows more flexibility and responsiveness, and highlights the need to engage in collective decision-making efforts that are learning-based. By definition, it will also provide more options, scenarios or pathways that might be followed when disruption occurs rather than following one preferred option that has been calculated, in advance, from past trends.

BEYOND DESTINY BY TRENDS

In 1906, the San Francisco Bay area was hit by a massive earthquake that killed nearly 3,000 people, destroyed 80 per cent of the city, swallowed entire city blocks, ruptured water mains and ignited enormous fires that burned for days. At this time, only rudimentary forecasting based on historical time series data was being used to predict when future quakes might occur. Indeed, in the quake's aftermath some much-needed – but false – assurance was given to the public that the Bay Area was safe for a good number of years from further seismic shock events. As the president of the American Association of Geographers noted in his annual address in 1909, this was a worrying development, and 'reasoning of this general tenor probably underlies the greater number of lay forecasts, and is in particular responsible for the wide-spread popular belief that a place recently devastated is ipso facto immune for several decades, or at least for several years'.[28]

In contrast to this less-than-accurate forecasting, in 2018 predicting when the next 'big one' would hit was underpinned by high-tech forecasting science, but still worked largely with probabilities and predictive methods. By using such methods, the US Geological Survey and other scientists concluded that there was a 72 per cent probability of at least one magnitude 7.2 or greater quake, capable of causing widespread damage, striking somewhere in the San Francisco Bay Area in the next thirty years with the most vulnerable fault line described as a 'tectonic time bomb'.

This is just the latest of a large number of predictive models that have been produced to assess risk and its impact in this seismic zone with a view to enhancing resilience. In response to such forecasts, for many decades the local Geological Survey in California has been developing earthquake scenarios for planning purposes. These have focused on specific faults, and are intended to depict the potential consequences of earthquakes of different magnitudes. Using information from recent earthquakes in New Zealand and Nepal, improved mapping of active faults and a new model for estimating earthquake probabilities, scientists recently worked on earthquake probabilities and updated the 30-year earthquake forecast for California. Computer simulations of scenarios provided detailed pictures of the degree of shaking we should expect in such earthquakes.[29] The scenarios focused on predicted ground motions and associated chances of fault rupture, liquefaction and landslide potential. They also provided estimates of economic losses, damage to infrastructure and social impact associated with the potential high-magnitude seismic activity.

As well as looking at the hazard impacts, mitigation efforts and resilience actions for communities, the possible worst-case devastation scenarios were also set out. Here the scientists' best guess was that a 7.0 magnitude quake centred on the Hayward Fault line would kill around 800 people and injure 18,000.[30] Damage to infrastructure would be devastating with more than 2,500 people having to be pulled from collapsed buildings. Water supply would be severely affected, taking up to 30 days for an acceptable service to be restored. As in the 1906 quake, fire would devastate vast tracts of the city. The main shock of the earthquake would probably ignite more than 400 fires over an area big enough to consume 52,000 homes, killing hundreds. Potential damage costs were estimated at $30 billion. While this scenario is just one of many possibilities for the impact of the rupturing of a major fault line, scientists have also produced computer-simulated scenarios based on multiple fault lines rupturing at the same time. In such a scenario, death and destruction would be many times worse.

ANTICIPATION THROUGH FORECASTING

For the many problems we face, earthquake-prone California being just one, enhancing the ability to adapt in good time will likely be the primary means by which potential damages are avoided. In such endeavours, the way in which the future is predicted or forecast is of paramount importance. The advancement of such sentinel capacities has proven key to the way risk has been assessed and how resilience has developed as the current futureproofing strategy of choice.

Forecasting abounds in the modern 24/7 world. Whether you are concerned with when the next big quake will hit, the state of the economy, who will win the election, which sports teams will make the play-offs or just the weekly weather, conjecture and prediction of future conditions is everywhere we look. Over time, forecasts and scenarios have become a staple of future gazing but they have limits. This affects our ability to put in place and test appropriate resilience plans and processes.

As we highlighted in the last chapter, risk and uncertainty are central to forecasting techniques linked to how we can better predict what the future *will* look like and undertake necessary planning (predicting what the future *should* look like). Forecasting, however, is a conventional way of thinking about the future and makes its predictions by looking backwards using past data, commonly presented as trends. Yet such data is both at the mercy of obtaining accurate historical data and the growing realisation that as civilisation has progressed it has become more complex and interconnected. This means that when the factors that lead to what is being projected are not well known, it is difficult to produce reliable predictors of future destiny.

Even as advances in mathematics allow us to better work with degrees of uncertainty or predict risk, they cannot exclude chaos. It was during the 1960s that major changes took place in the way scientific research was viewed and practised, leading to the questioning of such rational and calculated approaches. These traditional approaches had focused on trend analysis to predict a *probable* future, and arguably did so in a way that was seen as objective and value neutral. They could not, however, account for contextual factors and unpredictable or incalculable events.

In the 1960s and 1970s, this realisation led to chaos theory emerging as a new branch of mathematics concerned with the science of predicting the behaviour of 'inherently unpredictable' systems. What was advanced was a mathematical toolkit that allowed us to extract beautifully ordered structures from a sea of disorder. Chaos theory provided a window into the complex workings of diverse and connected systems. Early studies into natural phenomena, notably the weather, highlighted that such natural systems were not random but had underlying patterns and were in a constant state of flux because of constant feedback loops.[31] The most well-known example that emerged out of chaos theory in action was first presented by Edward Lorenz at the 1972 American Association for the Advancement of Science conference and was entitled 'Predictability: Does the Flap of a Butterfly's Wings in Brazil Set Off a Tornado in Texas?'. This 'butterfly effect' described how a small change in one part of a complex 'non-linear' system could result in large differences in the overall system. In Lorenz's example a butterfly flapping its wings in South America could, hypothetically at least, cause extreme weather in Texas: the flapping wing represents a small change in the initial condition of the system, which causes a chain reaction leading to larger-scale phenomena. Had the butterfly not flapped its wings, the trajectory of the system might have been vastly different. What the ideas behind chaos theory illuminated was that minute differences in initial conditions can yield widely diverging outcomes for such dynamic systems. This key lesson – that everything affects everything else – renders long-term prediction impossible in general. The world is complex, and basic extrapolations of 'trends' into the near future can result in unreliable predictions.[32]

Advances such as chaos theory underlined the fact that conventional forecasting approaches are never going to accurately detect a tipping point or random shift in the trajectory of a system, which is ever more necessary in our unpredictable world. And, ironically, as our ability has evolved to develop ever more sophisticated future modelling and crunch even more data towards that end, so we better understand the limits of prediction. The more we know the more we realise we do not know and this places restrictions on what is foreseeable. It has further required us to think outside the box of straight-line linear forecasting and evolve fresh approaches where the ability to adapt, and view the future as a range of competing alternative visions, should be valued above all.

DIFFERENT PICTURES OF THE FUTURE

The shift from a predictive, or probable, future to embrace a range of alternative, preferred or possible futures has its roots in scenario planning. Scenario planning – a strategic approach used to make long-term future plans – emerged out of a dissatisfaction with past approaches that considered only one likely future. This was usually depicted from a straight line on a graph that extended current trends into the future and which systematically failed to consider how changes in society, the economy, politics or the environment would affect such projections. Scenario planning initially evolved through the work of the RAND Corporation for the US military in the 1950s where a group of analysts would generate simulation games based on known facts and key driving forces that were identified by considering social, technical, economic, environmental and political trends. In essence, this approach described the future in a number of different stories as if written by people in the future.

Having different scenarios allowed strategic planners to navigate between the false certainty of a single-end-point trend forecast and the infinite number of possible futures that could be envisioned.[33] Such scenario planning approaches sought to generate alternative outcomes, each of which is formed by a series of contributory events. The beauty of scenario planning is that it rallies against human habits that conventionally lead us to assume the future will look like the past and that if any change occurs it will happen slowly and steadily. What developing a range of scenarios does is highlight how and why different outcomes might occur, particularly those that happen quickly and with significant impact. The process of producing such scenarios also develops deep insight into the probable drivers of change and helps us prepare us for the variety of possibilities that the future may hold.

In general, scenario planning builds on forecasting methods by recognising that the future is not predictable or linear and that multiple factors combine in intricate ways to produce uncertain future outcomes. These are presented as plausible scenario storylines based on the most powerful drivers of change (such as demographic shifts, economic facts or global temperature rise). Scenarios therefore allow us to challenge conventional wisdom and think innovatively. While in some scientific circles scenario planning might lack legitimacy as a predictive forecasting technique, it can be seen as a really good way of reframing ideas of an uncertain future and ways to progress there that permit change and adaptation to occur as the future unfolds.

MORE THAN A PLAN A

Enhancing the resilience of future systems requires a change both in the way we deploy certain techniques and methods to try to predict the future, and in attitude to the way such a task is approached. For example, since the early 1970s, oil giant Shell have heavily used scenario planning as a way of changing mindsets about how external trends might affect their business in advance of developing detailed strategies.[34]

In his book *Elastic: Flexible Thinking in a Constantly Changing World*, Leonard Mlodinow persuasively argues that changing individual and organisational behaviour to think in new, flexible, ways leads to greater success as the ability to adapt becomes ever more important. Out goes conventional linear thinking, where 'groupthink' often dominates, and in come more adaptive styles of thinking that allow unconventional perspectives to be considered.[35] Anticipating and responding to a deeply uncertain future requires new and flexible ways to allow communities, governments and businesses to evaluate alternative routes forward in planning for, and responding to, complex challenges.

The problem here for decision-makers is that the conventional 'rules' for strategising the future have not progressed sufficiently to accommodate new complex risks that could have unprecedented impact, simultaneously, across many areas. This has meant that decisions about the need to adapt in the medium and long term are seldom recognised, with the focus still on ad hoc adaptation and managing short-term considerations. In many cases, this has resulted in conventional ways of future planning, including many traditional resilience approaches, which are inherently maladaptive. These are often approaches that have relied explicitly on top-down scenarios that are used to induce change but which do not engage with a full range of interested communities or stakeholders. This reopens a social question we posed earlier regarding whose future is being forecast and by which scientific methods: resilience for whom by whom?

To make good decisions you need more than a Plan A to explore a set of possible actions based on alternative developments over time, allowing greater understanding of what decisions need to be made, by whom and over what time scale. One new type of approach that is proving popular is adaptive pathways, that aim to draw together ideas associated with future scenario planning and an assessment of the range and scope of policy decisions that need to be made in response to long-term change.[36]

The adaptive pathway approach is a process that identifies the challenges for which we need to adapt and works through the different outcomes based on what interventions are required and when they might be implemented. After long-term future challenges have been identified, an adaptation plan is developed with a range of identified pathways. This specifies actions to be taken immediately in order to be prepared for the near future, and decisions that need to be made now to keep options open to adapt if needed over a longer time frame. Such an approach utilises a risk-based decision framework to identify potential lock-ins where prior decisions are fixed for the near future, and tipping points that should be avoided. Such thinking allows small or large adjustments to be made in response to new information and changing circumstances which ensures that learning, feedback and experimentation are built into the decision-making process.[37]

The adaptive pathway method also allows a range of stakeholders to consider a wide portfolio of adaptation actions and provides the potential to shift from one policy pathway to another when circumstances dictate. This might be when an action has reached its sell-by date or is no longer seen as effective. Where such an approach differs significantly from traditional approaches is that it is not underpinned by classical economics where optimisation is sought, and which we now recognise as inflexible with little slack or redundancy built into the system or process. By contrast, flexibility is incorporated into such adaptation planning through an adjustable set of plans developed and implemented as knowledge and understanding of changing circumstances proceeds.[38]

Such approaches acknowledge the need to live with some degree of risk. The assumption with the adaptive pathways approach is that flexible types of adaptation, as opposed to limited or inflexible adaptation, will keep risk within acceptable levels. To enable such a flexible approach, 'trigger points' are built into the pathways plan whereby processes are assessed and revisions made if necessary, particularly if tipping points are approached. In other words, given the uncertainty and unpredictability associated with any one risk or collection of risks, constant monitoring is undertaken and options are left open to deal with different scenarios as the future plays out.

Whist some of the ideas underpinning this approach are not novel in resilience studies,[39] current pathways approaches essentially mainstream adaptive and resilience-thinking into future planning. This provides an alternative to relying on short-term, incremental changes that in most cases will fail to shift organisation custom and practice from a linear thinking and a risk-based mindset. Such an approach provides flexibility around when action is required, rather than being forced to take irreversible and reactive decisions about one or a small number of 'best options'. It further encourages decision-makers to consider a wider variety of outcomes, to ask a range of 'what if' questions and to make decisions about future options over a longer period, when more complete information might be available. This kind of approach ultimately seeks to embed adaptability and resilience into decision-making to ensure that the plans adopted are not necessarily fixed or locked in if – and when – the future turns out to be different from what we can assume today.

PRACTISING RESILIENCE

Resilience is everywhere today, rapidly becoming a principal framing device for political discourse to assess and understand the resistance and adaptability to enduring stresses and shock events of people, households and communities. Additionally, it is used to describe the properties and ability of interconnected and complex systems to adapt and change in the midst of failure. In this sense, resilience represents a break from previous eras of history where stability was sought through methods that attempted to model the future from the past and fit social requirements to those predictions. Today, in contrast to equilibrium 'bounce-back' models that seek a recovery to a stable state, resilience in a more contemporary guise should be considered as an ongoing process – a never-ending journey – that seeks to understand and adapt to the complexities of constant change. Resilience provides a bridge between short-term responses and longer-term future planning. The tools and approaches used to assess and monitor such resiliency – its permanent state of flux and its adaptive capacities – have also evolved over many decades. Evolving from modern approaches based on the mathematics of prediction and probability, we now have a toolkit of approaches whereby different interpretations and complex interconnections are brought to bear in envisioning a range of alternative futures that can be implemented and adapted in a flexible fashion.

Resilience can be seen in a number of ways, which can both easily overlap and be seen as contradictory, depending on our angle or level of analysis. Therefore, rather than focusing on fixed definitions of resilience it is perhaps more useful to see resilience as forming the basis of a range of discussions in a number of fields that seek to rethink traditional policy approaches and embrace complexity and adaptability. Resilience begins with the assumption that problems cannot be prevented, ring-fenced, solved or cured in conventional ways. Thus, resilience operates to frame discussions of a quite fundamental nature – of how we might rethink forms of social, political or economic organisation. These ways of reflecting on required changes in structures, habits and forms of understanding range in focus depending on the type of futureproofing action required. Some practices of resilience will be about preparatory policy-making to bounce back and retain stability, while others will consist of more radical calls for high-tech forms of awareness and real-time responsiveness. All of them will involve fundamental questions of long-term policy development, community and stakeholder engagement, feedback effects and interactive relationships.

In thinking through how the call to be resilient is changing our thinking patterns, we need also to consider the broader implication of change which does not necessarily fall evenly. Economically, change induced by resilience is not cost neutral and is often inefficient or costlier, at least in the short term. Resilience is not necessarily an optimised system highly calibrated to yield maximum benefit. It is often about acceptable levels of action for dealing with acceptable levels of risk. Here the potential social and environmental benefits of resilience are often traded off with economic motives that dominate the global neoliberal landscape. Socially too, resilience often yields disparities between who benefits and who loses out from adaptation options. Also worth mentioning as a key feature of emerging resilience approaches is the growing importance of digitisation.

Increasingly, digital connectedness, (big) data availability, artificial intelligence and predictive technologies are reshaping how society responds to risk, crisis and uncertainty. In other instances, utilising digital technologies serves to produce further dangers and social disparities, notably concerning privacy and civil liberties and the concentration of risk in intertwined cyber-enabled systems that might be vulnerable to hacking. Therefore, balancing resilience actions with economics, social concerns and the utility of the digital world cross-cut through how we should think about adapting our current approaches to improving resilience and futureproofing.

As we will see, these new ways of enhancing resilience and embracing the requirement to adapt have many and varied applications and implications in the real world. Different interventions to cope with a range of disruptive challenges and risks are sought, with different ways of organising and fostering adaptation. The following chapters will illuminate a range of different resilience approaches to understand how they are being used and how effective they will be for coping with a range of risks as an uncertain future reveals itself.

3

ANTICIPATING CLIMATE ARMAGEDDON

We know that if we continue on our current path of allowing emissions to rise year after year, climate change will change everything about our world ... And we don't have to do anything to bring about this future. All we have to do is nothing.

Naomi Klein, *This Changes Everything*[1]

It's freezing and snowing in New York – we need global warming!

A tweet by Donald J. Trump, 7 November 2012

It has long been known that Miami is, slowly but surely, sinking into the ocean with sea level rise widely predicted to finish the job off by the end of the century. If urgent action is not taken the city will become a modern-day Atlantis, condemned to the oceans because of an inability, or unwillingness, to act. Such a worst-case doomsday scenario, where Miami is rendered uninhabitable in only a few decades, has received a lot of attention in recent years as the prospect of irreversible climate change comes into plain sight.

Miami has become synonymous with the scenario depicted by Ashley Dawson in *Extreme City* where communities are now facing 'the peril and the promise of urban life in the age of climate change', with the Organisation for Economic Cooperation and Development further viewing Miami as the second most flood-imperilled city in the world.[2] One recent study showed that in the last decade alone, flooding in Miami Beach has increased by 400 per cent despite hundreds of millions of dollars being spent on mitigation measures such as pumps and the raising of roads.[3] In another warning, the Union of Concerned Scientists argued that evidence points to more than 1 million homes in South Florida facing 'chronic flooding' by the end of the current century, accounting for 40 per cent of chronically flooded properties in America.[4] Beyond the damage to homes and infrastructure, flooding also threatens the supply of drinking water together with plant and animal life. Yet more scenarios see the Miami area set to experience over 200 deadly heat days a year by 2100 with 2.5 million Miamians becoming climate refugees in the same time span.[5]

While there are ongoing disputes about the exact science underpinning climate change and sea level rise projections, what is certain is that the city needs to transform how it functions before it is submerged. The flat topography and porous underlying geology, combined with unregulated building regimes, have created a disaster situation waiting to happen as sea levels climb and the area gets battered with more frequent and extreme tropical storms. Myopic development practices that have seen many low-lying neighbourhoods built up for the rich without any consideration of sea level rise, while destroying natural buffers to flooding like mangroves, reefs and wetlands, need to be consigned to the past and rethought before it is too late.

Time is of the essence. Most predict that sea level rise will not be a smooth progression and that tipping points will be reached inducing 'a series of dramatic increments, interspersed with periods of relative stasis'.[6] The problem with the uncertain (read as not 100 per cent proven) science is that it almost always leads to slow and cautious responses, or no response at all. Put alongside political pressures not to create unnecessary fears that might panic residents, put off economic investment or damage real-estate prices, this creates a perfect storm of inaction and silence. This is why until recently few have talked openly about climate change in Florida, with the Sunshine State's Department of Environmental Protection being effectively banned from using terms like 'global warming' in formal communication. Here the long time scales and the urgent need for action do not synchronise well with short-term electoral cycles and rapacious property development that are largely blind to the impending impact of climate change. Business as usual prevails come what may.

This does not mean that some defensive measures are not being put in place to protect against 'known' risks. Sea walls have been built and floodwater pumps installed as Miami and surrounding areas try to engineer out the immediate impacts of climate risk. As Jeff Goodell, author of *The*

Water Will Come: Rising Seas, Sinking Cities, and the Remaking of the Civilized World, notes, the short-term solution seems to be for Miami to build their way out of trouble, but at a certain point in the future this will not be practically or economically feasible.[7]

These kinds of technical interventions, even those where resilience measures are incentivised, will only keep Miami's head above water in the short and medium term. Longer-term planning is much more complicated and yet little has been done to tackle the root of the climate-change problem such as reducing greenhouse gas emissions. This might turn out to be a catastrophic own goal, as some estimates report that if the US stuck to the agreement reached at the Paris climate conference in 2015 to reduce its carbon footprint, then 93 per cent of Florida's 'at risk' homes could be saved. That President Trump effectively ripped up this agreement in 2017 means catastrophe is more than likely being locked into the future of Greater Miami.

Yet, climate-resilience work in recent years has progressed faster than at any point in the past. Miami is at last beginning to take a strategic view of how it deals with inevitable retreat and abandonment of parts of the city because of climate change. In recognising its acute vulnerability to the impact of sea level rise, the City of Miami established a Sea Level Rise Committee in 2015 to advance change to its policies and to increase the city's resilience. Most notably, in 2017 the City of Miami joined forces as Greater Miami with the City of Miami Beach and Miami-Dade County to become a member of the Rockefeller Foundation's 100 Resilient Cities network.[8] The emergent new approach – known as Resilient 305 – has provided a focus on growing the capacity of individuals, communities, institutions, businesses and systems to survive, adapt and thrive in conditions where stressors and shocks (including those linked to a changing climate) are ever present. The hope from being part of this international resilience network is that Miami, and surrounding areas, can be more proactive and learn from the mistakes of the past, using such lessons to devise new solutions to plan a new, long-term future for all Miamians.[9] As former mayor of Miami Maurice Ferré noted of Resilient 305, Miami would again define resilience both in terms of deployment of technical solutions and of community revitalisation to 'make a sustainable, resilient community our legacy'.[10] The city is set to become the poster child of resilience against climate change in order to survive. What happens in Miami will provide a window into the future for other locations facing similar climate Armageddon.

*

In an Australian Senate hearing on global warming in May 2018, it was stated that climate change is no longer an abstract idea that might occur in the future but an 'existential security risk' to Australia, both now and in the future. Here an existential threat was defined as 'one that threatens the premature extinction of Earth-originating intelligent life or the permanent and drastic destruction of its potential for desirable future development'.[11] Specifically, the published committee report argued that climate change threatened health and the viability of communities, businesses and the economy in Australia.

Australia is not alone in making such dramatic statements. Coping with and adapting to climate change in most Western countries is the most urgent crisis of our time, and prominent warnings have been clear and visible for some time. Over a decade ago, at the United Nations Intergovernmental Panel conference in Bali in December 2007, climate change was announced as the defining challenge of our age. This was the first major UN gathering on the subject since the release of the fourth assessment report of the Panel that had left the world in no doubt that climate change was real and happening at pace.[12] At the Bali gathering UN secretary general Ban Ki-moon took up the baton, noting that 'the time for equivocation is over. The science is clear. Climate change is happening. The impact is real. The time to act is now.' In more emotive language, and referring to climate change as 'the moral challenge of our generation', he compelled the world to act in unison: 'Not only are the eyes of the world upon us. More important, succeeding generations depend on us. We cannot rob our children of their future. We are all part of the problem of global warming. Let us all be part of the solution that begins in Bali. Let us turn the climate crisis into a climate compact.'[13]

Many listened and acted, but many did not. As global society continues to hurtle headlong into future crisis, protracted debate goes on about the exact causes of climate change, and doubts are constantly cast on the veracity of the underpinning data and the lowest possible numbers countries need to post to meet emissions targets. As Canadian journalist and activist Naomi Klein noted in her bestselling work on the politics of climate change *This Changes Everything*, 'Faced with a crisis that threatens our survival as a species our entire culture is continuing to do the very thing that caused the crisis, only with an extra dose of elbow grease behind it.'[14] Economic necessity born of neoliberalism trumps environmental protection, notes Klein, in articulating climate change as a battle between deregulated capitalism and the health of the planet. The only solution to a less forbidding future is to *change everything* and to act as if climate change *is* a crisis rather than burying our heads in the sand. The small, incremental changes that have followed global climate agreements since the late 1980s are no longer enough. Transformational change is required to deal with this most urgent of risks. However, how will this be viewed by the market that will likely resist change at all costs?

As illustrated in Miami and exposed in many other places, there is a set of complex past and present decisions, and ways of organising connected to addressing climate change, that, in the cold light of day, can be considered poor or maladaptive. For example, we have seen, and continue to see, many urban planning practices increase rather than decrease vulnerability to the effects of climate change, largely ignoring risk and the urgent requirement for resilience. We have also seen that traditional risk management and neoliberal modes of decision-making cannot be trusted to govern increasingly complex and long-term climate change strategies.

What follows in this chapter highlights the way this transition from merely coping with climate change through short-term mitigation measures to genuine attempts at building resilience and embracing innovation is playing out. This will also showcase how such attempts on the ground in locations at risk from sea level rise have been framed by international policy discussions that are now promoting joined-up and long-term climate-resilience strategies.

PREDICTING AND OBSERVING THE FUTURE OF CLIMATE CHANGE

The year 1988 was momentous in the history of climate change understanding. In this year, the World Meteorological Organization and the United Nations Environment Programme established the politically neutral Intergovernmental Panel on Climate Change (IPCC). Its remit was to use all available scientific information to make evaluations on the impact of a changing climate and devise realistic responses. Coincidentally, 1988 was also the year of ramping up free-market capitalism with the passing of the United States–Canada Free Trade Agreement Implementation Act. The relationship between the growth of neoliberalism and climate impacts should not be underestimated; it has steadily disrupted climate change responses ever since.[15]

Nevertheless, the IPCC work was still a historic start, and in 1990 it produced its first assessment report underlining the importance of climate change as a challenge requiring international cooperation to tackle its impact and longer-term consequences. In this assessment it also made a series of predictions based on state-of-the-art computer modelling that laid out four different scenarios – A, B, C and D. These were linked to greenhouse emissions levels over the next 100 years and possible policies that might be put in place to limit these. Scenarios B, C and D were concerned with conditions where there are different levels of shifting towards renewable energy sources and carbon emissions reductions. These all showcased predictions that would see a stabilisation, or reduction, in carbon dioxide levels in the atmosphere. However, the most powerful picture was painted by scenario A, which was termed 'business as usual' and had an underlying assumption that no interventions, or only minor ones, would be taken to limit greenhouse gas emissions. Modelling this prediction saw greenhouse gas levels in the atmosphere continue to rise alarmingly. In all cases, the scenarios were referred to as 'best estimates', with some acknowledged uncertainty in the projections of greenhouse gas emissions. Nevertheless, the message was clear from all the scenarios: we need to curb carbon emissions to limit the rising of the seas and the warming of the atmosphere.

Since the first assessment report in 1990 outlined the best prediction for climate change, subsequent assessment reports have confirmed its broad findings.[16] But many people took against these predictions given the uncertainty contained within them. While uncertainty in predictions is good science, it was the assessment's Achilles heel: any element of doubt was aggregated into a strong and powerful climate change denial movement. For many years, the movement grew and was emboldened by the lack of tangible proof of the dramatic prophecies of climate change. Where were the sunken cities, long-running droughts or deathly storms that had been predicted? What couldn't be seen might as well not have existed. Then things began to change in the new millennium, as what was formerly predicted became an observable reality on a more frequent basis.

The Fourth Assessment Report of 2007 seemed more certain than those that came before it, with the warming up of the climate system seen as 'unequivocal' and 'very likely due to the observed increase in anthropogenic greenhouse gas concentrations'. The impact of a changing climate on how we can develop sustainably was also stressed, as were the key relations between short-term mitigation measures and longer-term climate adaptation solutions. Some of course would still deny, but the consensus was that climate change was happening and bringing with it the onset of far more unpredictable extreme weather events. This shift from the deniable prediction that characterised earlier IPCC reports towards undeniable observation has restacked the deck in favour of taking adaptive action as a matter of urgency. Seeing is believing. The key question, in Miami and many other locations, is have we left it too late?

As well as drawing together scientific evidence, the IPCC has also played a key role in establishing the key international treaty on climate change, the United Nations Framework Convention on Climate Change (UNFCCC), which was signed off by 165 states in 1992 during the UN Earth Summit in Rio de Janeiro and entered into force two years later. The key objective of the UNFCCC was to 'stabilise' greenhouse gases in the atmosphere at current levels. This was a challenging task given the non-binding targets set and the lack of enforcement mechanisms. The convention was signed by nearly all nations on earth and its signatories (the parties to the convention) have met annually since 1995 at the Conference of the Parties (COP) in order to assess climate change progress. The IPCC has thus succeeded in getting the scientific evidence lined up and building an apparent multilateral consensus over action, but still change has been slow and inaction common. This is what one commentator, in a withering attack on such obdurate behaviour, referred to as 'virtually uninterrupted backsliding . . . fudging numbers and squabbling over start dates, perpetually trying to get extensions like undergrads with late term papers'.[17]

EXIT INACTION, ENTER RESILIENCE

In the early years of the twenty-first century, resilience as a global call for action has gained notable prominence because of the global threat of climate change which has significant local consequences. These are disruptions, caused particularly by flooding, drought and storms, and the increased occurrence and severity of extreme weather events that must be mitigated and managed if catastrophic social and environmental effects are to be avoided. This has been especially the case in our ever-expanding cities that are now, in many cases, on the front line of climate change impacts.

In such a context, enhancing resilience through mitigating and adapting to climate change might include engaging in sustainable design, planning development away from areas at risk such as coastal plains and flood-liable areas, adjusting zoning arrangements or altering building codes and standards to facilitate adaptation. While most of these efforts have traditionally focused on incremental and short-term *mitigation* measures, increasingly issues of *adaptation* and adaptability have come to the fore as the international community seeks a framework of long-term and transformative action. Combined, mitigating and adapting to the effects of climate change is seen as a more integrated way of overcoming existing fragmented and stifled policy responses. The growing frequency and enhanced impact of abnormal weather events has refocused minds. As the UK Royal Society highlighted in *Resilience to Extreme Weather*:

> Climate change will affect the frequency and severity of extreme weather in the future. If emissions of greenhouse gases continue at the current rate, extreme weather is likely to pose an increasing threat to people. Yet even if emission rates are reduced, societies will still need to adapt to climatic changes caused by past emissions. Both mitigation of climate change and adaptation are therefore vital.[18]

It is at this juncture that the discourse of resilience came to prominence as a term that could simultaneously reflect the desire to mitigate *and* to adapt to the impacts of climate change in myriad ways. Climate change adaptation in particular has become an ever more important area of policy since the IPCC scientists published their undisputable assessment findings in 2007. This, however, has not proved an easy task to implement. Developing approaches to deal with the likely impact of climate change requires thinking and acting in new ways. As environmental planners Hartmut Fünfgeld and Darryn McEvoy have highlighted, advancing climate change adaptation has created new challenges for decision-makers who are expected to navigate 'a raft of information generated at different scales, and involving a diverse range of actors in translating these into adaptation options that are socially and politically acceptable despite significant degrees of uncertainty'.[19]

Other global governance bodies, notably UN-Habitat, have further asserted that the response of cities to the challenges of climate change has been fragmented and significant gaps exist between the rhetoric and the realities of action on the ground.[20] However, through the lens of resilience, there are signs of progressive and transformative change occurring with action on climate change transitioning from simply framing the problem and gathering evidence to approaches more concerned with implementation through mitigation and adaptation.

Resilience-thinking has also reframed what we mean by adaptation in this context. In practice there is a big difference between climate change adaptation – that, in many ways, can be seen as a short- or medium-term movement along a pre-conceived path – and the building of adaptive capacity or adaptability that advances a flexible way towards multiple different pathways of possible action. Thus in its current guise, climate change adaptation is still largely about mitigation and can be viewed as reactive, incremental, supportive of the status quo and focused on recovery to a stable position, rather than fundamentally changing established approaches. This is classic bounce-back resilience (and often placed under the umbrella of sustainability or sustainable development) and tends not to encourage innovation of the kind that is arguably needed to tackle the complex and long-term problem of a changing climate. Rather, what is actually required is the mainstreaming of future-looking resilience-thinking into our collaboratively devised and adaptable climate change approaches.

Internationally a range of influential policies focusing on climate change has emerged from national governments and non-governmental organisations attesting to the importance placed on the deployment of resilience ideas to cope with the pressing issues presented by climate change.[21] However, across these policies, resilience is deployed in a loose way, often highlighting the principles of stability and equilibrium associated with traditional risk management approaches that seek a concrete adaptation *outcome*. For example, this might include a community or neighbourhood being seen to be modified, adjusted or adapted to expected changes. Until recently, there has been much less importance placed on the *process* of generating enhanced resilience. This current orthodox approach can be summed up by the fourth IPCC scientific report of 2007, which defined resilience as 'the ability of a social or ecological system to absorb disturbances while retaining the same basic structure and ways of functioning'.

In response to such a conservative approach to climate change adaptation, others have suggested ways in which we might move to 'resilience and beyond' to better address the uncertainty and unpredictability associated with framing and acting on climate change.[22] Because we are nearing dangerous thresholds or tipping points, resilience to climate change must now move towards promoting a longer-term transformation that brings about more radical local change. We need to move from a coping response involving existing ways of working towards responses that seek to reframe the practices and governance of the issue.[23]

This shift in emphasis is reflected in a more recent report by the IPCC, *Climate Change 2014 Impacts, Adaptation, and Vulnerability.* This frames resilience through ideas of learning and transformation. The language of 'adaptive capacity' is specifically used to represent an ability to adapt to the impacts and changing requirements of climate change. It is an approach grounded in the interdependencies and complexities of climate change effects while presenting alternative ways of getting to a desired end point in the future. To this end, the 2014 report further advances the idea of what are termed climate-resilient pathways. Essentially these are possible development trajectories, or scenarios, that combine adaptation and mitigation approaches into long-term strategies, choices and actions that seek to reduce climate change and its impacts. The prospects for climate-resilient pathways are linked into how the world realises climate change mitigation and adaptation actions now, and can be adjusted if interventions are not going to plan. Such pathways, if devised appropriately, are flexible enough to involve significant transformation in the medium and long term if required. In short, climate-resilient pathways present more than just a Plan A option. They can be either progressive or regressive, leading to a more resilient world through adaptation and learning, or to lower resilience because of insufficient mitigation and failure to learn (which can be irreversible in terms of possible futures). Delayed action today will reduce options for climate-resilient pathways in the future.

TOWARDS A TRANSFORMATIVE RESILIENCE AGENDA FOR CLIMATE CHANGE

Cities are at the vanguard of climate change impacts, with many highly exposed and vulnerable to flood risk. Such exposure is often a result of historical decisions and locked-in approaches that make urban areas ill prepared to deal with the increased vulnerability to climate risk and a heightened sense of uncertainty about the future. The sense of trepidation about a future where climate change impacts will ravage cities has spawned terms such as 'climate-resilience', 'climate-resilient development' and 'climate-proofing' with reference to the ways cities are seeking to enhance resilience and futureproof themselves.

Such approaches increasingly seek genuine transformation rather than incremental change. They are about thinking innovatively rather than focusing solely upon technical solutions alongside business-as-usual approaches. While there is evidence of advancement in integrated climate change resilience, more challenging is the ability to achieve this in combination with creating liveable, thriving environments. Encouragingly, we can now see progressive examples emerging internationally that are providing pockets of resilience, which might be upscaled.

In Brisbane, Australia, the impacts of large-scale flooding have been enhanced by rapid urbanisation and poor planning practices. In response, water-sensitive urban design has emerged as the adaptation strategy of choice. Such an approach seeks to integrate the urban water cycle, including stormwater, groundwater and wastewater management, into urban design to minimise environmental degradation and to improve the look and feel of the built environment. Water-sensitive urban design has become an essential element within *Brisbane's Total Water Cycle Management Plan,* which functions as a holistic tool to guide strategic planning and collaboration with the council's partners, providing a 'guide to detailed planning around flood resilience'.[24] *Brisbane's Total Water Cycle Management Plan* is also in line with the broader Brisbane Vision 2030 plan – the long-term community plan for the city, which seeks to ensure that inventive design work is mainstreamed through all city services. Climate change here is seen to provide an opportunity to innovate in adapting the city and making 'the city and its community more resilient to change'.[25]

In further examples, development schemes across Europe are now embodying the principles of resilience in design solutions to climate risks.

After Copenhagen in Denmark was inundated by 100-year floods in both 2011 and 2014, a master plan led by SLA architects was devised using the need to alleviate localised flood risk from 'cloudburst' rain events as an opportunity to advance a series of coherent public spaces that provide a range of additional benefits. Here, a network of sunken basins and water-purifying plants utilises a range of natural processes to provide greater rainwater catchment to alleviate flooding. But the designed solution also offers a vibrant range of community uses to improve residents' quality of life. These flood-resilient measures are embedded within a scenic parkland setting that both deals with anticipated urban risk and contributes to wider social, cultural and environmental quality, and an increasing awareness of local climate change issues.

Similarly, in Rotterdam in the Netherlands, car parks and playgrounds are being incorporated in innovative designs to help make Rotterdam climate-resilient in preparation for heavier rains and rising tides. In a city where 80 per cent of the land is below sea level, traditional techniques like raising the protective dykes are becoming redundant and the city has pledged to work with, rather than against, water. As in Copenhagen, new solutions to stormwater storage have been devised that include double-purpose measures that are presented as opportunities. Notably a number of car parks have been constructed that incorporate a 10,000 cubic metre underground rainwater store, and a number of 'water plazas' – playgrounds and basketball courts under usual conditions but which can temporarily hold water during heavy rain – have been built. This climate-proofing effort is mapped out in a long-term plan called Rotterdam Water City 2035.

In China, sponge-like resilient designs are being rolled out in a number of cities as a result of severe urban flooding. Concrete pavements are being replaced by wetlands, green rooftops, permeable paving and rain gardens, allowing stormwater to be absorbed back into the land. Traditional flood defence schemes are being replaced by innovative green and resilient alternatives, making water work for cities instead of in opposition to them. Shanghai is one example of a metropolis which faces long-term risk from sea level rise, and it has adopted 'sponge city' principles, developing small pockets of resilience to mitigate rapid development.[26] The aim in this city is for 20 per cent of the built area of each pilot district to have sponge city functions by 2020. Sponge city infrastructure also promotes additional benefits. Not only does it soak up water but it also enhances the greening of the urban environment, creating a better quality of life. Importantly, initial evidence argues that the popularity of sponge city principles has changed the mindset of developers who are increasingly keen to adopt them as part of thinking more holistically – resiliently – about future urbanisation.

RESILIENCE HITS GLOBAL GOVERNANCE

In December 2015, the United Nations climate change conference (COP21) took place in Paris, with the objective of advancing an agreement on future climate change adaptation. The ideas of resilience were explicit at the conference and in the eventual pact reached. The third day of COP21 was dubbed 'Resilience Day', where the UN assistant secretary-general on climate change commented at length about the importance of resilience-thinking for approaches to dealing with changing climate. In extolling the merits of resilience it was noted that 'resilience is really important because the climate is already changing, and we need to be able to not just adapt to the changes but actually develop in a way that takes into account that in the future, climate will still change'. This compelled us, he argued, to 'adjust our development process, adjust our economic approach . . . and be more resilient to future changes that will happen'.[27] Then UN Secretary-General Ban Ki-moon further noted at the time of signing the agreement, 'We have entered a new era of global cooperation on one of the most complex issues ever to confront humanity . . . for the first time, every country in the world has pledged to curb emissions, strengthen resilience, and join in common cause.'

The 31-page agreement reached unequivocally recognised the urgent threat climate change represents, and that it requires a long-term, world-wide view.[28] Nearly all the world's biggest polluters agreed to limit carbon emissions.[29] The number of participants and the force of the commitments made the COP21 a landmark event, unprecedented in the field of climate change negotiations.[30] The ideas and practices of resilience in tackling the integrated and complex challenges of mitigating and adapting to climate change were writ large in the eventual pact. The climate agreement made explicit the focus on resilience and how vulnerabilities could be reduced through climate-proofing and climate-resilience measures. Furthermore, Article 7 of the agreement, drawing on the lexicon of resilience, noted,

'Parties hereby establish the global goal on adaptation of enhancing adaptive capacity, strengthening resilience and reducing vulnerability to climate change, with a view to contributing to sustainable development.'[31] The stated purpose of the Paris agreement was to hold the increase in global average temperature to well below 2 degrees Celsius above pre-industrial levels and to ensure that efforts are pursued to limit the temperature increase to 1.5 degrees Celsius.[32] In more practical terms, the accord put forward a framework for all countries to adopt clean energy and phase out fossil fuels to avoid the planet's temperature reaching a tipping point that could bring about irreversible consequences, including rising sea levels, powerful super-storms and crippling heatwaves.

NOT ON MY WATCH

The Paris climate pact was a cornerstone of President Obama's environmental legacy that had authorised carbon-cutting measures to ensure the US could meet its eventual Paris commitments and positioned the US as a leading proponent in fighting climate change. In his speech at COP21 Obama passionately embraced the need for continual action against 'the growing threat of climate change [that] could define the contours of this century more dramatically than any other'. In painting a picture of a possible future – submerged countries, abandoned cities, fields that no longer grow, political disruptions that trigger new conflict and even more floods of desperate peoples seeking the sanctuary of nations not their own – he argued for action 'right here right now' so that the nations of the world could collectively embark on 'an enduring framework for human progress. Not a stopgap solution, but a long-term strategy that gives the world confidence in a low-carbon future.' Quoting an unnamed American governor, he noted that 'we are the first generation to feel the impact of climate change, and the last generation that can do something about it'.[33]

However, Obama's impassioned defence of urgent and continual action on climate change did not last long, being largely ignored once he exited office. On 1 June 2017 his successor President Trump withdrew the United States from the accord despite two-thirds of Americans supporting signing onto an agreement.[34] Standing in the Rose Garden at the White House, the new commander in chief announced that the United States would withdraw from the Paris climate accord, in effect weakening international efforts to combat global warming. The withdrawal argument was based on perceived threats to the US economy and American sovereignty in decision-making by what he labelled a 'draconian' agreement. Bailing out of the Paris agreement was also interwoven with other election promises he made to roll back environmental protection legislation and remove any mention of climate change from federal government websites.

Despite being far from unexpected, the US withdrawal was widely condemned by business leaders, politicians and environmental activists around the globe. In the US, withdrawal from the climate accord led many cities and states to declare that they would continue to pursue climate adaptation policies and meet local commitments with or without federal government backing. The reaction was especially strident in New York State where Governor Andrew Cuomo called the decision 'reckless' and devastating for the planet. The Empire State, he affirmed, was 'committed to meeting the standards set forth in the Paris Accord regardless of Washington's irresponsible actions'. Cuomo, posting on Twitter, further noted, 'We will not ignore the science and reality of climate change which is why I am also signing an Executive order confirming New York's leadership role in protecting our citizens, our environment, and our planet.' In a tag-team action, New York City Mayor Bill de Blasio further announced that the Big Apple would uphold its Paris commitments, tweeting that 'Climate change is a dagger aimed straight at the heart of New York City'.

REBUILDING NEW YORK THROUGH RESILIENCE

New York is a city that exudes leadership credentials when it comes to recent action on climate change. From the wonderfully named 1996 publication *The Baked Apple? Metropolitan New York in the Greenhouse*, through the 1999 report entitled *Hot Nights in the City: Global Warming, Sea-Level Rise and the New York Metropolitan Region* and 2001's *Climate Change and a Global City: Potential Consequences of Climate Variability and Change* to a series of reports post-2008 by the city's Climate Change Adaptation Task Force, New York for over two decades has amassed a distinguished history of attempts to stop the worst elements of climate change coming to pass.[35]

More recently, in the immediate wake of the launch of the fourth IPCC assessment report in February 2007, Mayor Bloomberg unveiled *PlaNYC:*

A Greener, Greater New York, heralded as the long-term sustainability plan for the city. PlaNYC comprised a set of proposals that would allow New York to meet the challenges faced as the population grew by nearly 1 million by 2030. While PlaNYC had compelling sections on, for example, brownfield remediation, housing, transport, open space, infrastructure, energy, water and air quality, written through all of these policies was the 'increasingly urgent challenge' of climate change – the 'definitive challenge of the twenty-first century'. As PlaNYC noted:

> It is an issue that spans the entire planet, but New Yorkers are already feeling the effects. As a coastal city, New York is especially vulnerable. Our winters have gotten warmer, the water surrounding our city has started to rise, and storms along the Atlantic seaboard have intensified. And so we took a close look at the potential impacts of climate change on New York City, and our own responsibility to address it.

PlaNYC made 127 pledges, which were to be carried out across *all* city agencies. These included reducing greenhouse gas emissions by 30 per cent by 2017, engaging all stakeholders in community-specific climate adaptation strategies, launching a citywide strategic planning process for climate change adaptation and amending building codes to address the impacts of climate change. Also included were promises to update flood maps for the city and ensure flood insurance was affordable for all.[36]

Having a coherent plan is one thing. Implementing it is altogether more difficult. Many places are plan-rich but delivery-poor. In terms of taking PlaNYC forward and ensuring it did not fall into an abyss (or was placed on a shelf to collect dust), the plan committed to creating an inter-agency task force to expand the adaptation strategies beyond the protection of the water supply, sewer and wastewater treatment systems to include *all* essential city infrastructure. This key group was launched a year later, in August 2008, as the Climate Change Adaptation Task Force, which was tasked with helping to drive forward a strategic future vision of how to secure the city's critical infrastructure against the sea level rise, higher temperatures and fluctuating water supplies projected to result from climate change. Resilience demands collective and integrated action, and echoing this, the Task Force established impressive stakeholder engagement consisting of 40 city, state and federal agencies, regional public authorities and private companies that operated, maintained or regulated critical infrastructure in the region.

The task force was guided by the New York City Panel on Climate Change (NPCC), established at the same time as the Task Force. This expert panel included scientists and legal, risk and insurance experts, and provided a strong local knowledge base that supported the Task Force in identifying climate change risks and opportunities for the city's critical infrastructure. The NPCC would in time also assist in developing coordinated adaptation strategies and produce a set of climate projections specific to New York City. Notably, in 2010 the NPCC reported on progress against targets in *Climate Change Adaptation in New York City: Building a Risk Management Response.* This report is noteworthy as it provided a detailed assessment of climate vulnerability and adopted a 'flexible adaptation pathways' approach as its guiding principle in order to ensure that adaptation and mitigation fitted into a common framework. The pathways approach was steered by climate change scenarios, with focus on the 2020s, 2050s and 2080s. It recognised that risk management strategies need to evolve through time in response to continuous climate risk assessment.[37] A key emphasis within this process was to identify tipping points and impact triggers, which could help prioritise when, and how, to adopt different types of mitigation and adaptation measures. Near-term, low-cost actions – low-hanging fruit – were identified as short-term objectives that could assist long-term goals. The process was also intended to identify interdependencies among, and within, infrastructure sectors and to emphasise the importance of mainstreaming such a flexible approach across all sectors.

The achievements of New York City in mobilising and gaining consensus around how to approach long-term climate adaptation in a holistic and integrated manner should not be underestimated. The Task Force and NPCC had laid the groundwork for anticipating the future. However, prediction and preparation are one thing. When Hurricane Sandy bore down on the city in October 2012 climate change devastation became a reality for New Yorkers and catalysed even greater levels of action in the cause of becoming more resilient.

The impact of Sandy focused attention on elements of the climate adaptation plans that had *not* been completed. Flood maps (and associated insurance rate maps) that had last been produced in 1983 were only in the process of being updated when disaster struck. The city had also just passed Local Law 42 in September 2012, which established the NPCC as an ongoing body. The city subsequently convened a second and enlarged New York City Panel on Climate Change (NPCC2) in January 2013 that provided scientific input into the Special Initiative on Rebuilding and Resiliency's report on *A Stronger, More Resilient New York* in June 2013. This report, released as a PlaNYC publication, made it clear that mitigation and adaptation to climate change had to be elevated to a new level of urgency.

CLIMATE-PROOFING THROUGH DESIGN AND RESILIENCE

When in October 2012 New York City was hit by a devastating storm surge, propelled by Hurricane Sandy and driven by record-breaking summer temperatures in the atmosphere and the oceans, there was widespread flooding of streets, tunnels and subway lines, and significant loss of power. The city's coping capacity was pushed to its very limit as hundreds of thousands of homes were damaged or destroyed and many critical infrastructures incapacitated. Nearly 200 people were killed and over $60 billion worth of damage caused.

Critically, many of the impacts of a storm of this scale and magnitude were predicted in prior reports, but warnings had not been heeded or were simply not prepared for. Sandy starkly highlighted the vulnerability of the city's assets, the inaccuracy of out-dated quantitative flood maps and, in particular, the poor siting of critical infrastructure. A 1969 study by Ian Char, which attempted to identify the 'suitability of land for urbanization' using topographic and geographic analysis, almost perfectly predicted the flood locations of 2012.[38] Furthermore, this study suggested that areas 'unsuitable for urbanization' should instead be used for passive recreation and nature conservation, while recommending the construction of new 'barrier islands' to protect the city from storm surges. Such ideas, as we will see, became *en vogue* in the wake of Sandy.

Hurricane Sandy illuminated on the global stage the power of, and requirement for, resilience against climate change. The major flooding that resulted from an unprecedented storm surge of over 4 metres sent vivid images around the world of a global city decimated by a climate disaster and struggling to function normally. Many homes and businesses were flooded out and a failure of critical infrastructures cascaded through the city. In Manhattan poorly located electricity substations were incapacitated, leaving nearly eight million households and businesses without power and forcing hospitals to be evacuated. This combined with the closure of public transport networks and gasoline shortages to significantly disrupt the mobility of New York citizens.

Sandy was a wake-up call for New Yorkers, forcing them to confront the realities of extreme weather brought about by climate change. As one media outlet suggested, 'It provided violent and tangible evidence, if ever it were needed, that extreme weather is here, sea levels are on the rise and that cities must adapt more urgently than ever before.'[39] In the wake of Hurricane Sandy, new logics of risk management emerged centred on the discourse of resilience, which saw $50 billion worth of funding immediately invested in resilience initiatives. This propelled New York onto the leadership stage as an exemplar for urban resilience by enacting a host of innovative and transformative initiatives.

In the post-Sandy recovery period, a 'building resiliency task force' was set up by the mayor's office to identify measures to protect the city against similar events. Subsequently, this task force proposed improvements to the state's building codes and better zoning and planning to ensure that developments were located in suitable locations. The pressing need for future-looking risk mitigation and adaptation strategies also led to the creation of New York State's 2100 Commission and the enactment of long-term planning proposals, based on preparedness, adaptation and, most critically, resilience-building. The subsequent report, *Recommendations to Improve the Strength and Resilience of the Empire State's Infrastructure*, published in 2013, focused on how to contend with future extreme weather that was seen as the 'new normal', and on the best ways to make the state's infrastructure more resilient.

Resilience here was seen as the need to 'create diversity and redundancy in our systems and rewiring their interconnections, which enables their functioning even when individual parts fail'. This quite technical description of resilience had a number of key characteristics, including spare capacity, flexibility and constant learning. Moreover, the commission report outlined a number of 'challenges' for the state that would be taken up in due course, emphasising the need to 'rebuild smarter' and consider the appropriateness of land uses in relation to risks and vulnerabilities; to increase the use of green infrastructure including permeable surfacing and the re-establishment of soft shorelines; to ensure the implementation of 'integrated planning'; to increase 'institutional coordination', including the establishment of a state-level 'risk officer' to put in place a strategic framework for risk management; and, finally, to establish sufficient 'incentives' for building resilience and education programmes.[40]

Stimulated by the desire to avoid further significant impacts from extreme weather events, New York City was seeing additional important resilient design initiatives emerge. This represented a progressive agenda for urban development through the bringing together of hazard mitigation and holistic design practice. In New York's case, this was facilitated by President Obama's executive order, which set up the Hurricane Sandy Rebuilding Task Force and compelled multiple federal agencies to collaborate, reduce regulation and get rebuilding as soon as possible. The Rebuilding Task Force also developed infrastructure resilience guidelines in 2013 to ensure that federal agencies incorporated key principles of resilience into their actions and investments related to Sandy rebuilding.

The impetus given by the Rebuilding Task Force and New York's own Building Resiliency Task Force[41] gave birth to an open-ideas competition called 'Rebuild by Design', launched in June 2013. This sought to combine innovative design with local community understanding in order to develop solutions to the impacts of climate change that could be implemented in New York and replicated elsewhere. The 'Rebuild by Design' competition was revolutionary in its outlook. As architect Henk Ovink, principal for the competition, noted in *Too Big: Rebuild by Design: A Transformational Approach to Climate Change*,[42] 'Rebuild by Design' was an unprecedented exercise in collaboration and innovative thinking at the federal level. Ovink also emphasised that the competition was deliberately 'by design'. This did not just refer to the innovative physical designs that were proposed but, more importantly, also to the *process* of design. Here design thinking was seen as different from restructuring or planning in the traditional sense. It represented a distinct way of knowing and engaging with the world, providing a critical space by which decision-makers can think about and plan changes to their current ways of working as a response to fluid contexts. Design thinking was seen to offer new and creative ways of solving problems, providing the glue that holds divergent viewpoints and ways of working together. Design, as Ovink states, 'should create a narrative that can seduce and convince people . . . uniting them around complex decisions that can lead to action'.[43]

Eventually, the competition saw six winning entries developed towards potential implementation, while gaining widespread media coverage and critical praise for the process itself. Despite the wide-ranging remit and architectural focus of the competition entrants, all designs utilised some form of green infrastructure. This was exemplified by Scape Design's Living Breakwater project for Staten Island, an area badly damaged by Hurricane Sandy and located on a coastline that has been increasingly vulnerable to flooding because of years of inappropriate development. Taking inspiration from the region's historic oyster beds, the aim of the project was to create new barrier islands and breakwaters to protect the edge of Staten Island from the wave action and storm surges that devastated it in 2012.

However, the project that has attracted most attention is BIG Architecture's BIG U (or Dryline) that was awarded $335 million and will start construction in 2019. Apparently inspired by the Highline in New York City, it aims to convert the 10 miles of Manhattan's hard shoreline, with its bridges and infrastructure, into a continuous network of landscape buffers and 'protective parks'. The BIG U approach was based on extensive analysis of Manhattan's vulnerabilities and exposure to flood, as well as studies of historic land use that show how the development of Manhattan has encroached onto the shoreline that once buffered against such events. The proposed design incorporates a system of levees, dams and floodwalls that will improve resistance to flood events, integrated within a linear public park that finds imaginative uses for the resultant spaces. This includes tennis courts, soccer fields and basketball courts.

While none of the proposed elements are revolutionary in isolation, the BIG U represents an increasingly important relationship between landscape and critical infrastructure, developed with an understanding of localised risk but weaving in new social and environmental benefits. The BIG U challenges the assumption that flood infrastructure has to be detrimental to urban character, and highlights the co-benefits of considering issues of urban design and enhanced resilience in unison.

MAINSTREAMING RESILIENCE BY DESIGN

Embedding resilience-thinking into how New York organises itself to tackle climate change has taken time but has been dramatically advanced by the impact of Hurricane Sandy and the realisation that this might not be an isolated incident. As Henk Ovink has noted, 'Sandy wasn't the exception; Sandy was the announcement of a new standard.'[44] Facilitated by the emergency responses required after Hurricane Sandy together with some recent scenarios, which suggest that storm surges of a similar magnitude to Hurricane Sandy (broadly a one in 100-year event) could occur every three to 20 years, planning for resilience is rapidly becoming increasingly part of the DNA of New York. The mainstreaming of climate-resilient leadership can be readily seen in two documents released by the city in in 2015. The first was released by the New York City Panel on Climate Change in the February – *Building the Knowledge for Climate Resiliency* – and for the first time provided climate projections for the remainder of the twenty-first century. It was recognised in this report that as climate risks play out in the future there is a need to update the knowledge base and policies and programmes. In doing so, the NPCC continued to emphasise a flexible adaptation pathways approach to guide the city in developing greater resiliency. The push for resilience here emphasised *improvement* of city systems in contrast to their simple restoration. This was about encouraging bounce-forward rather than bounce-back resilience.

The release of the city's resilience blueprint *One New York: The Plan for a Strong and Just City* (OneNYC) in April 2015 was also highly significant. This strategy was released as New York's commitment to the Rockefeller-funded 100 Resilient Cities campaign and was a 332-page update and successor plan to the last PlaNYC release in 2011. The scope of this renewed document served to embed resilience into everything the city does. Of its four key visions, one is entitled 'Our Resilient City', where neighbourhoods, the economy and public services will be ready to withstand and emerge stronger from the impacts of climate change and other twenty-first-century threats. The issue of social justice was also centrally important here, and was written through the document. Sandy had demonstrated a truism that we see in many disaster zones: the impacts hit the poor and vulnerable the hardest. That this enhanced vulnerability is largely a product of prior policy decisions should not be ignored. What OneNYC articulated was a vision for this often maladaptive decision-making process that should now include multiple community voices to ensure that resilience interventions, and programmes that are designed, are equitable and do not discriminate. OneNYC sought resilience for all by all.[45]

In a strategy update in 2018 (for 2019 implementation), the city's OneNYC director and chief climate policy advisor, Daniel Zarrilli, reflected on the success of the policy, noting: 'The challenges of the 21st century are upon us and cities like New York are at the forefront of solving them. That's why it's so critical that we deepen the work of OneNYC and help bring the climate and resilience lessons of New York City to the rest of the globe.'[46] Such a deepening approach also has concrete form in new climate-resiliency design guidelines, making New York the first US city to integrate multiple climate risks into its capital programme. Launching the guidelines in April 2017, Mayor Bill de Blasio reasserted New York's climate and resilience leadership role, noting: 'New York is meeting the challenge of climate change head-on, and in the process we are building a better city. These guidelines are another national first, and will make the city's buildings and infrastructure more resilient in the face of rising seas, extreme heat, and storms.'[47]

LEARNING TO ADAPT TO PERMANENT RISK

The extreme risk of climate change has led to various mitigation and adaptation measures that further focused attention on the *process* of resilience building and guided us towards embracing increasingly holistic and collaborative ways of working across multiple systems, networks and scales from the local to the trans-national. These can be increasingly progressive and proactive ways of thinking that work for the long-term future. This further requires us to move beyond a narrow range of options based on the past and develop a range of more adaptable solutions, or pathways, into the future in response to contemporary and future 'unknown' risks brought forth by a changing climate.

Surviving and thriving in the age of climate change is going to require more than mere protection and coping mechanisms. It will demand that we are bold and innovative, and that we embrace uncertainty and commit to transformation. The illustrations from Miami, New York and elsewhere confirm our worst theoretical nightmares. That all the social, environmental and economic systems are deeply interconnected and layered over by partisan politics means our approaches to the challenge of climate change must see the solutions as necessarily complex and fluid. Real and anticipated climate change impacts implore us to ask some fundamental questions of ourselves. What if we reach the tipping point? Are we prepared for the collapse of civilisation that the worst excesses of climate change will likely bring? All of this prompts a re-evaluation of past and present approaches and forces us to look into the uncertain future and think through how we are going to respond in the long term. Even though we have suspected for a long time that climate change was an unmatched existential threat, our responses have been slow and encumbered by doubt, fractious politics and an unwillingness to change. However, as Naomi Klein has bluntly put it, the complex realities and scale of climate change *changes everything*: 'It changes what we can do, what we can hope for and what we can demand from ourselves and our leaders . . . And for a brief time the nature of that change is up to us.'[48]

However, there are no quick fixes to the challenge of our age. Technological silver bullets alone cannot save us. 'Complexity is the new normal. It challenges us to change and seek real innovation,' writes Henk Ovink in his impassioned plea that we collectively look to the uncertain future rather than the historic past. For decades climate change has been viewed as a 'wicked' problem that has proved difficult to address or impossible to solve because of partial and ever-changing requirements that are often difficult to recognise. We must, Ovink continues, demand 'a new approach, one that steps outside existing frameworks and agreements made on the assumptions of the past.'[49] Such change is, of course, not easy and will be resisted by some. In other circumstances, prior decisions that in the cold light of day have turned out to enhance climate vulnerably are still locked into our decision-making frameworks or designed into our environments. Finding innovative workarounds to these apparently obdurate conditions is essential. This will necessitate much experimentation and learning and a cultural shift that allows us to learn from failure – a move from a fail-safe risk-averse world towards one that embraces the ideas of safe-to-fail.

Through the rubric of resilience, we have seen a number of innovative approaches emerge that might hold the key to future solutions. These are often process-, rather than outcome-, based. They focus on the big picture and on holistic approaches that seek coordination and collaboration in assessing risk, compiling knowledge, analysing challenges and preparing solutions. We can call it design thinking but really it is about creating inclusive dialogue between everyone with a stake in adapting to climate change. It is also about ensuring we have the agility and flexibility in decision-making processes to change course if required, if something unexpected happens and as our knowledge grows.

We must enhance the adaptive capacities of all interlinked systems and, in order to do this we must treat climate change as a learning process. Our current adaptive measures are predominantly short-term fixes and are not good enough. We urgently need to shift towards approaches that prepare us for an unknown future. We should not wait for extreme events to hit in order to enact necessary reform. We should plan ahead. As demonstrated by New York's flexible adaptive pathways approach to climate change adaptation, it is possible to do this in ways that synch knowledge, resources, political and institutional buy-in and available technologies in a way that both mainstreams resilience-thinking into long-term plans and also gives the flexibility to change course if required.

Band-aid solutions to climate change are no longer viable and it is time for true resilience-thinking to be deployed more widely. Through the narrative of resilience, we can also seek to address political questions as to how to create governance institutions to tackle these challenges in a collective and socially just way. Ultimately, climate-resilience means planning now rather than having to cope in emergency conditions later.

4

RESPONSIVE CRITICAL INFRASTRUCTURE LIFELINES

Business and society operate in an increasingly complex world marked by interconnection and interdependence across global networks. This complexity requires that owners and operators of critical infrastructures manage their operational risks in an all hazards environment across the full spectrum of prevention, protection, response, recovery, and reconstitution activities.

US National Infrastructure Advisory Council, 2009[1]

The basic physical and organizational structures and facilities (e.g. buildings, roads, and power supplies) needed for the operation of a society or enterprise.

Oxford English Dictionary, definition of infrastructure

Shortly after 2 p.m. Eastern Time on 14 August 2003, a minor fault occurred on a high-voltage power line in Ohio that had been softened by the high summer temperatures and subsequently sagged into a tree. While ordinarily this would have tripped an alarm in the nearby control room, on this occasion this failed to happen, leading to panic among those who were trying to ascertain what was wrong. As a resolution was being sought further power lines collapsed into trees. Over the next hour and a half, as system operators tried to understand what was happening, three other lines switched off, obliging other power lines to transmit the extra power. Ultimately, in a short space of time this extra flow of power overburdened and tripped the system, leading to a ripple effect throughout the grid of southeastern Canada and eight northeastern American states. The result was the largest blackout in North American history that left 50 million people without power for up to two days. The event directly, or indirectly, caused at least eleven deaths and cost around US$6 billion.

Many saw this 'cascading' event as inherently designed into the grid's complex structure, because of interconnections between the main parts of the system that transmits electricity from generating plants to local utility companies who then distribute power to homes and businesses. While this inter linked system allowed some level of compensation by allowing different parts to act differently to account for local variation in power generation, it also laid out a larger system into which failure could spread like a contagion when something went wrong. Post-event assessment showed that the event in Ohio was principally caused by a technical failure and a lack of adequate risk assessment. It not only illuminated how different parts of the same electrical system did not always work in synch but also how grid infrastructure tends to focus on protecting *itself* and largely ignores other related critical infrastructure systems that rely on it.

We know from a large number of recent experiences that complex and integrated systems can facilitate what has been referred to as a black swan event: low probability of the event occurring but a high impact when it does. The 2003 blackout caused not only widespread inconvenience and loss of power to many homes and businesses but threatened the safety, lives and economic well-being of many citizens. The effects were felt most in large urban areas where denser networks of interconnected infrastructures were found. New York City was brought to a virtual standstill for a day and a half. The closure of the subway and airports left thousands of passengers stranded. Many high-rise buildings lost water supply as well as power when electric pumps were disabled. Emergency services were severely compromised when reserve battery-operated systems also lost power periodically. Hospitals remained open but without full power, as backup generators failed to function. Many operations were conducted in suboptimal conditions without air conditioning. As David Rosen, president of Jamaica Hospital in Queens, told the *New York Times*, 'Everybody is blowing generators. I'm shocked at what I'm seeing. And I'm troubled. For all the yelling and screaming that everybody did after 9/11, there is nothing forthcoming to help us shore up this infrastructure.'[2] The number of fires reported in New York during the 2003 blackout was over 200 per cent greater than the norm because of malfunctioning generators, with many residents resorting to burning candles. Millions of gallons of raw sewage overflowed into the waters around the city as generators at sewage plants failed. There was a resultant spike in emergency room admissions for diarrhoea. Economic losses from the blackout exceeded $1 billion in New York City alone.

*

The infrastructure failure that was triggered in Ohio is the embodiment of what we have previously termed robust-yet-fragile design. This defined a system where rigidities were built up and vulnerability intensified by an inability to adapt to demand caused by a change in the weather. While the grid was exceptionally robust (or resilient from an engineering perspective) in normal operating conditions, and could keep power coursing through its wires at an even rate, it failed to cope with the unexpected heatwave conditions and, subsequently, the spike in demand. It could not self-regulate or adapt. It lacked resilience.

Cascade, or cascading failure, of the type illuminated during this grid breakdown further highlighted what architect Thomas Fisher in *Designing to Avoid Disaster* argued was a fracture-critical design that plagues the modern world: 'structures and systems have so little redundancy and so much interconnectedness . . . that they fail completely if one part does not perform as intended'.[3] Fisher demonstrated his fracture-critical thesis by drawing on transport infrastructure, particularly inadequate bridge design. He focused his attention on the collapse of the I-35W Bridge in 2007 that was initially constructed as part of the interstate highway system around the city of Minneapolis. The I-35W Bridge, which had been built only 40 years previously and had long been known to be structurally weak, collapsed suddenly when one critical element failed. There was no spare element to take the load. The eight-lane, 300-metre-long deck of the 580-metre-long bridge fell into the Mississippi River within seconds. Thirteen people were killed and nearly 150 injured. Damage and a replacement bridge would cost over $300 million.

Fracture-criticality, for Fisher, was seen to have four main characteristics: lack of redundancy, interconnectedness, efficiency and high sensitivity to stress – all of which were at play when the I-35W Bridge came tumbling down. A lack of redundancy was demonstrated by the failure of the bridge's undersized gusset plates that joined steel elements of the bridge together. These were insufficient to carry the structural load of the bridge with no spare components to assist. At the time of construction, such redundancy was seen as an unnecessary and wasteful expense. The I-35W Bridge also had high levels of interconnectedness and efficiency that didn't work so well when great levels of stress were applied. When the gusset plates begun to fracture this overstressing spread to other interlinked structural elements, inducing serial collapse. Fracture-critical design was further seen by Fisher to equate with resilience ideas, which 'warns us that we need to replace such structures with designs that are less connected, less efficient, more resilient'.[4]

While the I-35W is a tragic example, hundreds more bridges across the US and thousands worldwide have the same engineered-in faults that were showcased by the I-35W collapse. More crucial, perhaps, is the fact that the maladaptive design principles embodied in the I-35W Bridge are common across many infrastructure sectors since the post-war infrastructure and development boom. This bridge collapse is an omen, not only foretelling what might happen in the future, but also teaching us unequivocally about the risk we are storing up when we design critical infrastructures to be ultra-efficient and able to deliver optimised services with no slack or spare capacity. It also warns us that we need to design our infrastructure to be more resilient and adaptable.

As if more examples were needed, on 14 August 2018 a 1,100-metre-long bridge spanning a viaduct collapsed in the city of Genoa, Italy, killing 43 people. The Morandi Bridge, built in the 1960s, was a key transport link and a source of civic pride in this vibrant port city and its collapse has opened up serious questions about cause and responsibility. At the time of writing it is still under investigation but it seems clear that maladaptive construction, poor maintenance and an unwillingness to act on warnings were again to blame. Tests in 2017 had found troubling signs of corrosion on the supporting structures of the bridge and recommended permanent sensors be fitted so as to monitor the situation. Such retrofitting was being considered but was held up by bureaucracy, a lack of budget at the national Ministry of Infrastructure and the privatisation of much of Italy's transport infrastructure. Some have further alleged that corruption and organised crime was to blame for holding up essential maintenance.

The failure of these vital supports looks to have triggered huge dynamic loading on the remaining structures that collapsed under stress in a matter of seconds. When it was constructed the design of the bridge was seen as simple and elegant but, over time, engineers came to recognise that this pared-back design lacked a sufficient number of crucial supports, meaning that if one failed whole sections of the bridge would crumble. This was typical of construction methods in the 1960s. The bridge lacked robustness and redundancy and therefore did not have the capacity to redistribute crucial forces when stressed.

CONNECTING TO OUR CONNECTEDNESS

The enhanced interconnectivity of natural and built systems, and their further coupling with social and economic life, can cause complex failure and cascading impacts.[5] The frequency and severity of recent crises, disruptive challenges or disasters have channelled attention into adapting critical infrastructure or lifelines systems (generally considered to be energy, water, transportation and communications). These are vulnerable systems whose incapacitation or destruction have the potential to significantly affect public safety, security, economic activity, social functioning and environmental quality. Such vulnerability has driven various Western governments and operators to attempt to enhance the security and resilience of such vital infrastructure systems as a matter of priority.

According to the US National Association of Counties,[6] such 'lifelines' have a number of key common characteristics that make them vulnerable to disruption. First, in terms of supply, they provide necessary services and goods that support the majority of homes and businesses. Second, disruption has the potential to give rise to life-threatening situations. Third, lifelines are generally entangled in complex physical and electronic networks that are interconnected within and across multiple sectors. Fourth, and in terms of interconnectedness, a disruption of one lifeline has the potential to affect or disrupt other lifelines in a cascading effect. In essence, critical infrastructures do not operate in isolation (or in what public administrators might call a silo); rather they are closely linked and dependent on one another (interoperable). It is this interconnectedness, complexity and 'system of systems' networking that demands attention in order to address the security and reliability – or resilience – of various lifelines. This is work that should be undertaken collaboratively across multiple critical infrastructure networks, considering not just technical or engineering issues as is conventionally the case, but also the wide-ranging social and economic impacts of lifeline disruption.

In the new millennium, concerns about the security and disruption of critical infrastructure lifelines has led to a progressive change in thinking about how infrastructure operators, governments and society can best respond to complex future challenges. In the late twentieth century, driven by privatisation and deregulation, networks of critical infrastructure tended to be optimised for efficiency rather than for being resilient and adaptable. In the new millennium, and in the wake of 9/11, there was a further focus within emerging security policy and associated federal grants on what was termed 'critical infrastructure protection'. In such an approach, conventional risk management principles and security strategies continued to dominate discussion. The resulting protective measures that were deployed largely focused on single critical infrastructure sectors or, occasionally, across a number of easily compared critical infrastructure sectors in isolation, emphasising toughening system components against failure.

This approach, although reassuring for many in a heightened climate of fear of attack in the wake of 9/11, did little to address the complex types of risk that were being stored up in an ever more elaborate, and hence vulnerable, infrastructure network. As disaster expert David Alexander and colleagues have noted, events such as the eruption of the Eyjafjallajökull volcano in Iceland (2010), the Tohoku earthquake and tsunami (2011) and Hurricane Sandy (2012) starkly illuminated a new kind of interlinked threat that required alternative forms of intervention to be put in place. Notably, such events shone a light on the need to actively consider 'cascading' disasters and their effects on a highly networked society. While this kind of phenomenon was relatively well known, its incorporation into risk management plans was limited to simple discussions about linear cause and effect.[7] Simple cascade effects had conventionally been viewed similarly to toppling dominoes, where disruption would have known knock-on effects. The acknowledgement of a much more complex and unpredictable set of consequences of failure and disruption of one infrastructure to other parts of the network has reframed how operators and managers must now think about risks. This increased attention given to complex and intertwined risk, and by extension the cascading effects of a breakdown in one system on other networked systems, is now leading to a prioritisation to enhance critical infrastructure resilience.[8]

In contrast to defensive and protective approaches to infrastructure, approaches informed by resilience offer a proactive response to risk management and are increasingly used to assess the ability of complex infrastructure systems to maintain function safely, adapt, and recover from disruption as quickly as possible. As German engineering giant Siemens noted in relation to urban infrastructures, 'Resilience is the ability of a system to survive and thrive in the face of a complex, uncertain and ever-changing future.' Here resilience can be seen to encompass elements of defence but also adaptation that are deployed at various points during a disruption or crisis. Resilience therefore represents a change in mindset and 'is a way of thinking about both short term cycles and long term trends: minimizing disruptions in the face of shocks and stresses, recovering rapidly when they do occur, and adapting steadily to become better able to thrive as conditions continue to change.'[9]

Across infrastructure sectors, resilience ideas are shaping the ways providers deal with complex risk and the transition from protective-based risk management towards adaptive-based resilience. In short, this is a way of promoting more integrated ways of assessing and managing risk responses simultaneously across multiple systems, networks and scales. The remainder of this chapter will test how operators and managers of critical infrastructure lifelines are *actually* shifting their approaches to risk, from emphasising protection and the adoption of security models towards integrated approaches to enhancing resilience. Implementing such changes has not been an easy process but is essential to maintain the future operation of such lifelines at current levels. As will be further illuminated, it is now vital that critical infrastructure operations begin to adapt to the challenges of uncertainty and system interdependences in a future where there is less emphasis on efficiency and the lowest possible cost and where the ability to be resilient and adapt quickly to disruption is privileged.

PROTECTING LIFELINE INFRASTRUCTURES

It is one of the great paradoxes of our time that while human progress increasingly seeks to shape environmental conditions, the ability to do this in a conscious and deliberate way is hampered by an inability to tackle the complex interactions and interdependencies involved, and thus the true nature of risk to global society. Think of the of miles of roads, rail tracks and waterways that criss-cross most countries and then consider the thousands of stop-off points in this vast and complex network – the ports, train stations and airports that provide key nodes in the network. Think too of the thousands of drinking and wastewater systems that flow through town and country and the vast energy supply network that keeps society powered and facilitates our vast communications networks. Then consider how these lifeline systems are knitted together in ever more intricate ways and managed by an increased array of owners and operators. What might happen if one small section cannot function? This could be the result of a catastrophic disaster event or a malicious cyber-attack. It is more likely, though, to be the result of a simple component breaking under stress, because it has reached its sell-by date or has been poorly maintained. Either way, when something goes wrong the disruption has a tendency to ripple out everywhere, affecting other critical infrastructure systems and impacting on the way society functions and markets perform.

Take, for example, the case of Auckland, New Zealand, in the summer of 1998 where electricity cable failure plunged the city into a five-week power outage. The power cables were past their replacement date and were experiencing a surge in demand due to extra requirements for air conditioning in the central business district during unusually hot weather. When one of the major power cables failed, extra stress placed on the others caused further failure. These cables had been considered so reliable that risk assessments had not even contemplated their malfunctioning. This was both a breakdown of contingency planning and poor cable maintenance. Many also saw this inattention to the condition of the infrastructure as a result of the recent deregulation of New Zealand's electricity sector.

The resulting outage had significant consequences for the public and businesses, leaving most of the central area of the city without power. When the lights went out, people were caught in lifts, traffic signals became intermittent, air conditioning stopped, water pumps didn't work affecting the water supply in high buildings, fuel couldn't be dispensed from garage forecourts, food was spoiled as refrigeration units failed, telecommunication systems, including mobile networks, experienced problems with their capacity, and cash registers stopped ringing. The central business district, whose lifeblood was electricity, struggled to operate. This resulted in backup generators being swiftly brought in to power essential services, as temporary overhead cables were looped onto hastily erected concrete pylons along corridors into the central business district. This further led to energy being rationed and to a lengthy period of unpredictable supply. For five weeks, until reliable power was restored, most business personnel worked from home or were relocated to other cities. Over 6,000 city-centre residents had to find alternative accommodation. The retail and restaurant trade slumped by 90 per cent. Angry protesters affected by the power cuts demanded more say and greater accountability from electricity companies.

It is the impact of disruption to these essential linked systems that puts critical infrastructures in the crosshairs of the Anthropocene – the age of persistent uncertainty. The inherent difficulty of protecting lifeline systems and infrastructures amid growing complexity illuminates the most famous expression of chaos theory – the butterfly effect, where small changes in one part of a complex system can have far-reaching impacts on the overall system. This observation has catalysed a growing interest in utilising the concept of resilience for critical infrastructure assurance.

Critical infrastructures are now so interwoven into the fabric of everyday life that ensuring they continue to function has become a political priority. Here, resilience-thinking is radically changing how some nations and infrastructure sectors are preparing their key services for the challenges of disruption. As Brad Evans and Julian Reid noted in their critically acclaimed book *Resilient Life*, 'Critical infrastructure is now central to understanding living systems and politically, the combined lifelines deemed necessary for security, survival, and growth.'[10] Others have further argued that conventional approaches to designing critical infrastructure lifelines leave too many decisions to the market to determine and are fundamentally flawed, requiring policy-makers to make far-reaching interventions if they are to avoid major disasters in the future.

If ensuring critical infrastructures continue to function is a major political issue, it has been further enveloped by the push towards free-market principles from the 1980s onwards which saw the breaking up, and fragmenting of, national monopolies that ran and maintained conventional infrastructure systems. As we saw in Auckland, and more recently in Genoa, such splintering of responsibility not only makes a collective response to disruption far more complicated, and in many cases impossible, it can also lead to inequitable and ethically dubious practices taking hold. Here catastrophe can be the result not only of a combination of natural hazards and infrastructure breakdown but can also be induced by the manipulation of service supply for political purposes or financial gain. Since the 1980s, the deregulation and privatisation of many utility sectors (notably gas, water, electricity and transport) and the shift of ownership from public to private hands has meant that publicly run systems, which once ensured that reserve supply was available to cope with peak demand spikes, have been abandoned to market forces. Prices have gone up and private companies have been able to limit supply in times of high demand. The California electricity crisis of 2000 and 2001 is emblematic of the trend where a shortage of power is caused by market manipulation and the drive towards profit, resulting in multiple large-scale blackouts and capped retail electricity prices. Here, increasing the gap in supply and demand was a deliberate strategy of a number of large energy companies operating in the marketplace, such as the now disgraced Enron who deliberately induced shortages (by for example taking generating plants offline at peak times), thus giving themselves the opportunity to sell power at massively inflated prices.

Political motivations have also led to energy crises, revealing once again the vulnerability of existing infrastructure systems. Most starkly, Russian gas supplier Gazprom literally turned off the tap of its gas supply to Ukraine in 2009 when its contract to supply its neighbour ended. This was also linked to a broader political dispute between the two countries. A similar disagreement in 2006 had restricted gas supplies not only to Ukraine but also to a number of other European countries including Germany and Hungary (pipelines crossing Ukraine carry about 20 per cent of the EU's gas needs). In this sense, critical infrastructure also emerges as a key aspect of state power through which control of others' utility needs might be exerted.

THE DRIVE TO PROTECT INFRASTRUCTURE

We are all familiar with stories of the US National Guard rushing to protect critical infrastructure in the immediate wake of the 11 September 2001 terrorist attacks, with thousands of troops mobilised to protect energy-producing facilities, domestic water supplies, bridges and tunnels. In this understandable climate of fear, prioritising the protection of critical infrastructure emerged in the wake of 9/11 as a key political priority. Initially, such approaches were characterised by measures that focused on highly technical considerations within a single critical infrastructure sector, be that energy, water or transport. As noted by engineer Richard Little at the time, such an approach was not integrated and hence inherently flawed: 'Typically, hazard mitigation strategies for infrastructure have generally addressed first-order effect – designing robust systems to resist extreme loads imparted by natural events or malevolent acts such as sabotage and terrorism. However, because these systems do not operate independently, strengthening a single system is seldom effective at preventing outages.'[11]

At this time, the tools of choice for conventional critical infrastructure protection were based on relatively static risk-based frameworks and methodologies, such as probabilistic risk assessment that calculated the likelihood of an event occurring against its impact. Typically, the risk analysis undertaken on infrastructure systems fed into computer simulation models governed by complex mathematical equations that have proved difficult to calibrate against real-world experiences or for unknown and unexpected threats. Such approaches also tended to focus on enhancing the physical characteristics in a system such as the inherent strength or resistance (robustness) to withstand external demands without degradation or loss of function. For example, can the resistors at a power plant take increased loading or can the flood defences in place around a river withstand the forces from more water being stacked up behind them? Such approaches also focused on how quickly disruption could be overcome and safety, services and stability restored.[12] The technical emphasis of these critical infrastructure qualities of robustness and rebound understood resilience primarily as resisting and recovering from 'known threats' in ways that can secure and stabilise an infrastructure system. The unintended consequence of the drive towards protection was that it made it more difficult to cope with dynamic changes in infrastructure need (such as huge surges in demand) as well as with the new and emerging threats that might cut across a number of different infrastructure networks. By focusing on the protection, preservation and recovery of single critical infrastructure systems or facilities, and against specific types of threats, efforts to protect often systemically failed to account for cascading effects, unexpected events or the more holistic underpinnings of critical infrastructure assurance. Working in isolation might be a good defensive strategy but, in the long term, ignoring the complexity of interlinked infrastructure networks can store up additional vulnerability.

There has been widespread comment about the limitations of such protective approaches, including the lack of meaningful social and organisational considerations, that these technical-focused initiatives discourage necessary adaptation and that they are based on a false idea of equilibrium and stability.[13] Such protective approaches are, fundamentally, a reaction to a limited range of 'known' risks, and their success, or otherwise, can only be measurable *after* a disruption. The future, as we have seen, should no longer be predicted using traditional foresight and risk assessment methods. Optimal planning using a single 'most likely' future (often based on the extrapolation of trends) might produce acceptable outcomes in the short term, or temporarily stable conditions, but will need to be ripped up if the future turns out differently.

To build such future contingency into plans, more recent approaches to embedding resilience-thinking into the operation and functioning of critical infrastructures have sought credible approaches grounded in sound engineering principles and informed by social, organisational and policy imperatives.[14] Through a resilience lens, multiple threats to aligned infrastructure lifelines can be considered, diverse situations or scenarios planned for and a focus given to building adaptive capacities in the operating environment. In short, this has meant designing the flexibility to act in different ways and the addition of spare capacity – redundancy – into the physical components of the infrastructure. This further includes a fundamental shift in the philosophy of operations where encouraging optimised, fail-safe operations that are calibrated for known threats and the preservation of the status quo (within acceptable limits) are being replaced by a safe-to-fail approach where experimentation and learning are encouraged.

At the crux of the move from *critical infrastructure protection* towards *critical infrastructure resilience* has been a struggle between what innovation analyst Lewis Perelman has referred to as the hard and soft paradigms of security.[15] Here the hard pattern represents the path of conventional and protective security policies and practices associated with prevention and resistance. By contrast, the soft pattern is associated with adaptation and resilience. The latter moves away from a technically focused approach and towards a more socially grounded and transformative approach that seeks to soften the brittleness of conventional infrastructure systems. In his work, Perelman cited the influential American physicist Amory Lovins's studies in the 1970s on future energy demand, which highlighted the advantages of the soft resilient path over the hard brittle path:

> The soft path appears generally more flexible—and thus robust. Its technical diversity, adaptability, and geographic dispersion make it resilient and offer a good prospect of stability under a wide range of conditions, foreseen or not. The hard path, however is brittle; it must fail, with widespread and serious disruption, if any of its exacting technical and social conditions is not satisfied continuously and indefinitely.[16]

A protection-based approach to critical infrastructure is, in large part then, a legacy of ingrained engineering-focused methods of risk management, which dealt with discrete, concrete and fixed assets. This was an approach with a strong focus on ordering and probability, on optimisation, toughening and control, and a near exclusion of social and human factors. It was a viewpoint where short-term fixes were seen as an appropriate response. As it has become clear that such approaches are outdated, and in many cases enhance vulnerability, ideas of resilience and resilience management have been increasingly adopted. This is a new type of approach that goes beyond conventional risk management to address the complexities of large integrated systems and the uncertainty of future threats in the long term through attempts to enhance the responsiveness and flexibility of infrastructure.

THE RESILIENCE IMPERATIVE

In the last 20 years critical infrastructure assurance has been progressively moving away from a focus on protection towards emphasising resilience. This has occurred as the critical infrastructure sector has become a larger, more complex and increasingly interconnected amalgamation of social, technical and economic networks and where the risk of breakdown has been rising. The failures of infrastructure during disaster events starkly demonstrate the vulnerability and potential weaknesses of our critical systems, and how such failures often have common roots, particularly around institutional failings. Such weaknesses have catalysed the emergence of resilience as a way to assess the complex challenges that critical infrastructure faces as well as providing a potential framework by which to respond. The growing interest in applying resilience methods in securing critical infrastructure has grown as traditional risk management methodologies have proved ineffective in the face of growing complexity and threat. Protection and the need for security has been recast as resilience, given the requirement to assure the functioning of critical infrastructure against a range of known and unknown disruptions.

While on the surface conventional risk management and new resilience approaches share a lot of similarities in terms of avoiding negative impacts, assessing system vulnerabilities and putting in place mitigation plans, there are important differences of note. Most importantly, given the increasingly uncertain world we now inhabit, we can see that while risk-based approaches focused a lot on assessing individual components of systems and assessing them for their potential to degrade the system based on past experiences, this approach is seen as inflexible. By contrast, resilience focuses increased amounts of attention on unknown and unexpected disruption in the future. Fundamentally, risk and resilience assess the future – and in particular ideas of uncertainty – differently. Low probability but high impact risks that have tended to be largely ignored by conventional risk planning are the food of resilience. Resilience operations place a greater emphasis on 'what if' questions based on overall system effectiveness, the effect on a system of component failure and the need to adapt and adjust the entire system to changing circumstances both in the short and long term. As Igor Linkov and José Manuel Palma-Oliveira have highlighted in their edited book, *Resilience and Risk*, such subtle differences are essential in today's interconnected and complex operating environment where resilience is about the 'ability of the impacted organization, infrastructure, or environment to rebound from external shocks, recover and adapt to new conditions'. In other words, resilience seeks to 'offer a soft landing for the system at hand', whereas traditional risk approaches 'seek to harden a vulnerable component of the system based upon a snapshot in time'.[17]

Resilience-thinking is thus increasingly forcing operators of infrastructure to work with unknown risk and uncertainty, to devise a range of alternative visions of the future and to seek adaptation through improving flexibility and agility. Infrastructure resilience, here, calls for advancing a collaborative process and developing a long-term strategy rather than focusing on performing complicated risk assessment. The application of the dynamic resilience perspective suits the characteristics of these complex infrastructure systems, with multiple interdependencies, a broad variety of hazards and threats and the presence of multiple organisational and human factors, which during severe disruptions must all work harmoniously.

ADOPTING INFRASTRUCTURE RESILIENCE

As with all sectors into which resilience has been parachuted in the twenty-first century, in critical infrastructure it took time for its principles to be adopted. The US was among the first nations to develop a national strategy for the identification, management and protection of critical infrastructure through the 1997 President's Commission on Critical Infrastructure Protection (CCIP) and has been at the forefront of the shift from 'hard' protection to 'softer' resilience approaches. The impact of the 9/11 attacks prompted a further addressing of vulnerabilities in the nation's critical infrastructure preparedness. In 2002, the US Congress funded the creation of the Critical Infrastructure Protection (CIP) project to undertake applied research on critical infrastructure and to anticipate and reflect changes in the national risk environment. This work subsequently led to a new approach being adopted for perceiving and prioritising threats, vulnerabilities and consequences to critical infrastructures based on ideas of resilience. This approach was put in train in early 2006 when, in a presentation to the Homeland Security Advisory Committee, the Critical Infrastructure Task Force recommended 'critical infrastructure resilience as the top-level strategic objective to drive national policy and planning'.[18] This was defined simply as the 'ability to anticipate, absorb, adapt to, and/or rapidly recover from a potentially disruptive event'.

More recently the 2013 Presidential Directives on 'National Preparedness' (PPD-8) and 'Critical Infrastructure Security and Resilience' (PPD-21) sought to promote an all-hazards approach which stressed the importance of anticipating cascading impacts and highlighted the shared responsibility of critical infrastructure protection and resilience to all levels of government, the private sector and individual citizens.[19] As President Obama's policy briefing noted:

> The Nation's critical infrastructure provides the essential services that underpin American society. Proactive and coordinated efforts are necessary to strengthen and maintain secure, functioning, and resilient

> critical infrastructure – including assets, networks, and systems – that are vital to public confidence and the Nation's safety, prosperity, and well-being . . . U.S. efforts shall address the security and resilience of critical infrastructure in an integrated, holistic manner to reflect this infrastructure's interconnectedness and interdependency.

Reducing the vulnerabilities of critical infrastructure, and increasing their resilience, has also been one of the major objectives of the European Union. Here critical infrastructure is viewed as essential for the maintenance of vital societal and economic functions, with damage and disruption likely to have a significant negative impact for the security of the EU and the well-being of its citizens. The European Programme for Critical Infrastructure Protection, established in 2006, sought to provide an all-hazard, cross-sectoral approach which led to a 2008 Directive on Critical Infrastructure that established a common approach for assessing the need to improve protection. In line with a broader turn towards resilience concepts within the EU, such concerns are now being focused on how resilience ideas are shaping the ways in which critical infrastructure providers deal with complex risk.

Similarly, Australia has adopted an 'all-hazards strategy' that provides a foundation for collaboration and organisational resilience building within the infrastructure sector rather than different probability-based risk management frameworks operating in adjoining sectors. The move towards resilience is premised on the idea that this integrated approach better enables owners and operators to prepare for, and respond to, a range of unpredictable or unforeseen disruptive events. Australia's approach to advancing resilience in critical infrastructure is underpinned by two core objectives that treat foreseeable and unforeseen risks differently. The first adopts a mature risk management approach to foreseeable or 'known' risks on a sector-by-sector basis. This focuses on the continuity of operations in almost identical ways to processes that underpinned prior critical infrastructure protection programmes. This ensures risk-based information can be effectively shared so that known risks can be correctly managed. The second key objective extends this into an approach focused on resilience so that for unknown and complex risk the owners and operators of critical infrastructure can build response capacity within their organisation. This will be invaluable for when there is insufficient information available or when unforeseen or unexpected events occur that might affect the ability of infrastructure to continuously function. Specifically, focus is placed on enhancing 'adaptive abilities' that will improve organisational resilience and allow operators and managers to better cope with complexity.[20]

GHOSTS IN THE MACHINE

While strategic plans to enhance the resilience of critical infrastructure have evolved in many countries since 9/11, in more recent years lifeline services are increasingly having to contend with the new threat of cyber-attack that exposes the inherent vulnerabilities in critical systems.[21] Digital connectivity has been so well embedded in highly networked infrastructure that it has become the source of vulnerability rather than strength. Cyber threats appear every day and vulnerabilities typically occur due to weaknesses in computer codes that allow hackers to gain access to infrastructure control systems. During such incidents, critical infrastructure can be brought to its knees with many old and outdated infrastructure control systems lacking the ability to resist such efforts.

Perhaps the first significant cyber-attack against critical infrastructure occurred in April and May 2007 in the small country of Estonia, one of Europe's most wired countries. Here hackers crippled dozens of government and corporate sites when the online services of banks, media outlets and government bodies were taken down using thousands of computers in a coordinated attack that caused unprecedented and unsustainable levels of Internet traffic. This so-called 'distributed denial of service' (DDoS) attack was an attempt to make online services unavailable by overwhelming the Internet with traffic from multiple sources. In this case, massive waves of spam were sent by botnets[22] and huge numbers of automated online requests swamped servers. Estonian authorities suggested this attack had been orchestrated by Russia, as it followed Estonia's decision to move a Soviet Second World War memorial from central Tallinn in late April 2007. This sparked protests from Russian officials and some civil disruption among the country's ethnic Russian minority.

The attack had far-reaching consequences in Estonia and beyond, prompting global organisations such as NATO and the EU, as well as many nations, to seek to enhance cyber-security capabilities.[23] After the Estonian attacks, cyber-attacks were often seen in terms of state-sponsored cyber-terrorism and elevated to warfare status, with critical infrastructure seen as especially under threat. Power grids comprising many interconnected systems appeared particularly vulnerable and in subsequent years were targeted. The first confirmed takedown of a large power grid occurred in December 2015, as hackers took control of the grid in western Ukraine, plunging 230,000 residents into darkness for up to six hours. In a highly planned and stealthy attack, the perpetrators successfully immobilised 30 substations and two power-distribution centres. Adding further to the ensuing panic, they also deliberately disabled power-backup systems by hacking into the SCADA (Supervisory Control and Data Acquisition) network that controlled the grid, gaining access to vital control systems. Only a year later, a similar but less devastating cyber-attack took out power to the northern part of the Ukrainian capital, Kiev, for a few hours after a single transmission substation lost power. This was followed, in June 2017, by a further attack on Kiev where a number of financial institutions and power distribution companies were affected. These instances of sabotage, or cyber-warfare, targeting critical infrastructure, took place amidst growing political tensions between Kiev and Moscow. In their wake experts have attributed the hacking to groups with suspected, although unclear, connections to the Russian government.

Whatever the cause and whoever the perpetrators, these incidents in Ukraine represent a growing category of attack intended to sabotage critical infrastructure and have foreshadowed more recent attempts to hack into vital infrastructure utilising embedded cyber vulnerabilities. In 2017 fears of major attacks against energy grids in Europe and the US intensified due to the re-emergence of the well-known cyber-hacking group Dragonfly. The group first came to global attention in 2011 and was implicated in the Ukrainian power disruptions and similar attempted attacks in other European countries, together with concerns that nuclear facilities in the US could have been compromised.[24] In 2017, the security tech company Symantec, who had been tracking the Dragonfly group, reported a noticeable upsurge in hacking campaigns using customised malware and other 'trojanised' software delivered by email – what they termed Dragonfly 2.0. This, they speculated, could have provided the group with access to the operations systems of infrastructure. If this is the case, it might be possible to take control of the interfaces operators use to send real commands to vital equipment, such as circuit-breakers. This would give hackers the ability to induce power grid blackouts with the flick of a switch.[25]

In April 2018 the US and UK governments further issued an unprecedented alert accusing Russia of conducting a malicious Internet 'hacking' campaign that was not only aimed at conventional espionage activities but also part of a build-up towards a full-scale attack on critical infrastructures across the globe. One fear was the prospect of another massive cyber-attack against Kiev in the build-up to the Champions League Football final to be held in the city in May 2018. Such attacks would be targeted towards the dense interconnected, robust-yet-fragile infrastructure systems that underpin critical lifeline services. These complex networked systems are very vulnerable to the failure of individual components that can compromise the broader network. Notably, new generation control systems are seen as particularly vulnerable and expose the providers and operators of infrastructure to a host of cyber-security risks that are only just beginning to be comprehended.

Just as with traditional lifeline infrastructures, those responsible for the security and protection of cyber-enabled infrastructures are looking to resilience as a cure. In response to such 'designed in' or over-engineered vulnerabilities, traditional approaches to protecting a network from cyber intrusion – the use of perimeter devices that seek to secure the network externally – are increasingly giving way to more nuanced discussions about cyber-resilience. This is an emerging concept that seeks to draw together the areas of information security, business continuity and organisational aspects of resilience into a holistic approach. The key aim of such strategies is to maintain the ability to deliver the intended service continuously as well as to change or modify these delivery mechanisms if needed in the face of new risks. In essence, it is an attempt to deliver an approach that ensures short-term stability and encourages long-term adaptability.

Cyber-resilience will continue to evolve as cyber-attacks on infrastructure remain a top-level national and international priority as part of broader cyber-security strategies. For example, in May 2018 the US Department of Homeland Security unveiled a new strategy, highlighting that cyber-threats are capable of disabling infrastructure sectors and the nation.[26] Noting the seriousness of this challenge, DHS chief Kirstjen Nielsen said in a statement that the government 'must start to think beyond the defence of specific assets – and confront systemic risks that affect everyone from tech giants to homeowners'. Specifically linked to this top-level cyber strategy, the US Department of Energy launched a five-year plan for defending the US power grid from hackers through the boosting of what they call cyber-preparedness in the energy sector. While such work is not new, the DoE is doubling down on these initiatives, citing growing risks posed by today's interconnected world where cascading failure is a very real possibly. The future endgame of the DoE efforts is, they note, a more resilient energy grid that is better able to respond to and recover from disruption in energy supply caused by a cyber incident.

Just as critical infrastructure resilience has become an extension to critical infrastructure protection, so cyber-resilience has emerged out of the need to move beyond traditional methods of cyber-security that have sought to protect systems, networks and data from cybercrimes. This has meant having to think differently and being more agile and adaptable in handling complex cyber-attacks that can have multiple and long-term impacts. That a major attack on a country is seen very much as a matter of 'when, not if' is focusing minds, but there are accusations that the expectations of delivering cyber-security and resilience are hampered by a lack of resources and the 'wicked' nature of the problem. This reflects the constantly evolving nature of the threat, meaning that the threats we perceive today weren't envisioned when many of the systems were originally designed, leaving them increasingly vulnerable to attack.

RESILIENT AND ADAPTABLE LIFELINES

While it is imperative that we protect against disruption and defend against attacks on critical infrastructure lifelines, it is equally important that we devise future plans in order to cope with the enhanced risk of disruption. To this end, resilience-thinking has become a necessary component of reliable infrastructure operations. In this context, resilience is considered as the capacity of a critical infrastructure and its operative environment to combat in a preventative and adaptive manner adverse conditions resulting from a disruption or disaster, to mitigate possible impacts and to recover itself largely independently from the negative effects of the disturbance. Critical infrastructure resilience therefore emerges as a transformative, cyclical process that is an extended form of risk management. Here, increasing priority is placed on agility, responsiveness and flexibility over optimisation and efficiency, alongside encouraging stakeholders to enhance the adaptive capacities and resilience qualities of these complex systems, both organisationally and technically.

The transition from protection towards resilience of critical infrastructure operations can be represented as a continuous process of change but it has proven to be difficult to implement given long-standing conventional practices. The application of risk management for critical infrastructure is traditionally premised on a command and control approach from national government or a central operator that privileges a static and often short-term approach to governing complex systems. This is what classic ecological resilience theory identified as a 'rigidity trap', where such management practices can lead to institutions lacking diversity and becoming highly connected, self-reinforcing and inflexible to change.[27]

By contrast resilience ideas of 'adaptive management' are now seen as necessary to enhance the responsiveness in interconnected systems and are being increasingly adopted in the critical infrastructure sector as a way to futureproof decision-making. Central to such adaptive approaches is considering and planning for unknown risks by advancing a range of scenarios as a response to deep uncertainties about the future. As with climate change, working through adaptive pathway approaches has provided operators with information on the function and future functioning of the infrastructure, as well as the linkages to other infrastructures and contextual factors that could impact on future service delivery. This provides a more comprehensive, holistic and resilient approach for large-scale, long-lived and costly infrastructure services and projects by providing a useable framework for decision-making under uncertain conditions. It further means decisions can be modified according to changing conditions.

Central to this approach is an underlying philosophy that focuses on advancing the processes best suited to a particular context rather than based on infrastructure planners taking decisions on a purely scientific basis.[28] Context-first approaches encourage decision-making related to the adaptation problem itself rather than with modelled projections. The focus on the problem at hand allows space for considering the interactions of other risks and infrastructural priorities alongside the adaptation problem. Moreover, working in this way can encourage more joined-up and often mutually beneficial strategies to emerge. From here, a range of appropriate adaptation pathways or route maps can be devised and linked to plausible change scenarios that could be seen in the long term.

ADAPTING CRITICAL INFRASTRUCTURE PLANNING IN AN UNCERTAIN WORLD

In the UK, a large-scale and high-cost (up to £9 billion) water infrastructure project – the Environment Agency's Thames Estuary 2100 project (TE2100) – has, since 2010, sought to utilise a pathways or route-map approach to advance more resilient future-looking infrastructure. This was stimulated by growing concern over how tidal flood risk is likely to change in response to future changes in climate and development in the Estuary's floodplain. The ageing of existing flood defences and barriers meant replacement interventions would likely be needed in the medium to long term. As the 2012 plan for the Thames Estuary noted, 'It was time to plan for the future and make recommendations on what actions were needed to adapt to a changing estuary.'[29] Notably, it was important to assess the future use and function of the Thames Flood Barrier, which has been operational since 1984 and which currently stops a large part of London from being flooded by storm surges moving up the North Sea.

This type of adaptive approach was a proactive response to the uncertainty over what the most appropriate policy measures should be, itself complicated by uncertainty over the underpinning scientific evidence and models for climate change and the scope and scale of ongoing development on the floodplain. As scientists working for the UK Environment Agency noted:

> These types of investments tend to be difficult or costly to reverse, are high-stakes and their design is dependent on what assumptions are made today about the climate over its lifetime. This means that if forecasts are incorrect today, the project can become maladapted to climate, exposing society to greater risks, wasted investments or unnecessary retrofit costs.[30]

In TE2100, where the main concern was coping with extreme water levels, flexibility was incorporated by arranging the implementation of different interventions over time, with options being left open to deal with a range of different future possibilities through a simple route-map or adaptation pathways decision analysis method.[31]

The TE2100 project has utilised a context-first approach in progressing a number of key steps in adaptation planning.[32] Initially this involved thinking through the problem at hand and involved an assessment of current vulnerabilities, the potential ranges of risk impacts (in this case low and worst-case water level rises) and assessment of key thresholds (how and when the worst-case scenario might occur). It also involved assessing other features (such as development on the floodplain) that might influence planning decisions, and began to advance high-level ideas for what adaptation options might be feasible. Following this, possible solutions or pathways were appraised in terms of cost and benefits, as well as the impact on other relevant criteria of different changes in extreme water levels. Eventually, a preferred pathway emerged which is now constantly monitored using key variables to determine if, and when, a switching to a different path might be required in the future.

For each pathway, or adaptation route, the TE2100 project evaluated the extreme water level at which that option would be required, the likely lead-time needed to implement that option and, therefore, the estimated decision point to trigger that implementation.[33] For example, if sea level rise were much higher or lower than expected this would lead to a speeding up or slowing down of the programme of actions. Similarly, if erosion rates of existing defences increased then this would hasten the upgrading of defences. Current estimates for the TE2100 project expect key decision points to emerge around 2050 when an appraisal of the most appropriate pathways option to take will be determined, aided by an extra 40 years of climate data. This will dictate, for example, if a new Thames barrier will be required or whether the existing scheme can be safely upgraded. Essentially, the route-map or adaptive pathways approach has allowed better and more flexible decision-making through the identification of key decision points conditioned on future sea level rises. Agility in making informed decisions and investments in the medium- to long-term future has replaced inflexible short-term decision-making based on analysis of past events.

THE DUTCH ADAPTIVE DELTA MANAGEMENT APPROACH

The Netherlands has a long and celebrated history of flood protection but, as in London, it has become increasingly concerned about managing its water infrastructure in the era of climate change. Launched in September

2008 and officially adopted in February 2010, the nationwide Delta Programme seeks to maintain the Netherlands as a safe and attractive country today and into the future, and brings together central government, provincial and municipal authorities and local water boards comprising civil-society organisations, the business community and organisations with specialised water expertise. Within the Delta Programme, a philosophy known as 'adaptive delta management' (ADM) has been prominently used in an attempt to make infrastructure more climate-resilient and more water-robust. ADM is seen as a 'phased decision-making [process] that takes uncertain long-term developments into account explicitly and in with transparency towards society [and that] encourages an integrated and flexible approach to land and water management'.[34] Unlike many existing international approaches to protecting and shoring up vulnerable infrastructure, ADM is a long-term vision (up to 100 years) which engages with local communities and has support across many government departments. ADM is directed towards safety and economic targets and at the same time tries to build flexibility into how and when to implement management interventions. In essence, ADM is required to 'anticipate' future conditions and stop 'tipping points' being reached.

As with TE2100, the ADM approach uses 'adaptation pathways' that have been developed as alternatives for the traditional 'end point' scenarios, to support robust decision-making that allows adaptation to new conditions. In the Netherlands, the formation of adaptation pathways is linked to the acknowledgement of uncertainty in climate change and thus bases much of its thinking on a scenario matrix based on various climate change predictions. Working through this process seeks to make infrastructure planning more resilient, by not only anticipating the future but in selecting the most appropriate set of measures in the short, medium and long term. This crucially leaves room for policy processes and outcomes to adapt as the future unfolds. This further involves an assessment of whether a policy transition is required or not, and ensures a proportionate approach to risk; that is not doing too little too late or too much too early.

The proactive Dutch ADM programme is in its infancy but its adaptive, pragmatic, flexible and anticipatory philosophy has seen the approach utilised around the world, notably in Bangladesh, Indonesia and Vietnam, but also in New Orleans where the Dutch Dialogues (a series of US–Dutch workshops) helped shape the post-Katrina comprehensive water management strategy.[35]

INTEGRATING RESILIENCE INTO FUTURE INFRASTRUCTURE OPERATIONS

The complex interconnectedness of infrastructures, governance, economic growth and social need gives rise to risk. In response, the drive for resilient infrastructure requiring redundancy, diversity of approach and more than just a Plan A, underpins the maintenance of services that are essential for everyday life. It is here that resilience ideas have gained prominence as one method of securing critical infrastructure lifelines from the likely, but uncertain, impact of multiple vulnerabilities. Resilience is the way in which the promoting of adaptive capacities is currently sold to the providers of potentially vulnerable critical services. Such vulnerability increasingly characterises the volatility of the contemporary world and must be mitigated and adaptively managed if catastrophic social and environmental effects are to be avoided. Most recently, within the realm of cyber-security, resilience-thinking has further achieved a high degree of prominence due to open and interconnected technology environments that are embedded in the control centres of critical lifeline services.[36]

In the majority of infrastructure operations, resilience and the need to adapt is emerging as the preferred strategy to address change and uncertainty. Here, resilience serves to complement, not replace, conventional risk management approaches. It aims to facilitate more integrated visions of how infrastructure sectors might collaborate and respond to disruption caused by breakdown, disaster, cyber-attack or cascading failure.

While there is a lot of talk of resilience surrounding critical infrastructure operation – as a way of coping with the complexities of large integrated systems and adapting to the uncertainty of future threats – there is a noticeable gap in how such ideas are implemented in practice. As in other areas of life where resilience is becoming noteworthy, the extent to which resilience-thinking is actually changing the often deeply ingrained practices of critical infrastructure protection is debatable. Current practice in resilience assessment and promotion for critical infrastructure is too often limited to specific, technical factors linked to hardening or making more robust the system component, or to conservative bounce-back or rebound models that seek to quickly restore a system to pre-disruption levels.

It can be seen from the foregoing discussion that there is a pressing need to address the shortcomings of traditional 'siloed' thinking and more 'traditional' views of 'hard' critical infrastructure protection that seeks bounce-back to a pre-shock state. Unlike protection, resilience is not yet readily definable across all infrastructures nor is it easily measurable. Information sharing between infrastructure operators and agencies also needs to improve and be integrated in current assessment tools and methods, a task made more difficult by ongoing privatisation of infrastructure networks that can fragment systems and limit cooperation across organisational boundaries. The longer-term financial benefits of moving from a risk management method to a resilience approach need to be made clear and regulated for, or incentivised, if required. One strategy commonly deployed to cope with deep long-term uncertainty in decision-making is to incorporate flexibility into adaptation measures from the start but often this can mean greater costs (e.g. the larger or more resistant protective features, or the need for backup systems) or reduced productivity. As previously noted, to create resilience in critical infrastructure systems means operating in a less than optimal way and leaving some slack or redundancy in the system that allows reorganisation and adaptation when disruption hits. Here the need for a long-term approach that operates within acceptable limits rubs up against maximising efficiency and cost.

The transition towards critical infrastructure resilience requires a willingness to transform existing administrative or engineering practices in order to lock in the adaptability and flexible thinking required to cope with volatile infrastructure disruption in the future. This necessitates pushing for more evolutionary 'bounce-forward' approaches more applicable to coping with increasingly complex, networked and digitally enabled infrastructure systems. In practice, the adoption of approaches to critical infrastructure resilience is occurring slowly, and often through adaptive pathway approaches. As we have seen, this strategic approach has been used by the UK Environment Agency in developing a long-term tidal flood risk management plan for London and the Thames Estuary, as well as for water management in the Netherlands to tackle the threat from climate change. Pilot studies are also ongoing in other parts of the world including the US, Australia and New Zealand, where a relatively strong evidence base exists that allows a range of scenarios to be planned for. In these cases, the utility of the adaptation pathway approach has been to drive forward adaptation planning in the short, medium and long term, to promote the virtues of resilience and to recognise the uncertain nature of future risk. Such approaches also enable the widespread adoption and subsequent adjustment of adaptation strategies in response to new information and changing circumstances. This also promotes decision-making as a collaborative affair, taking into account viewpoints from the multiple stakeholders involved. This should not only involve a particular critical infrastructure but the entire network of critical infrastructures in a given location. Adaptive pathways thinking further requires that changes are made in the way risk is assessed and used in decision-making. Highly technical risk analysis based on known risk and past data should be complemented by decision frameworks based upon acceptable and unacceptable levels of risk for different issues. A range of scenarios should be produced that inform future actions while encouraging dialogue between a range of stakeholders to identify when tipping points on any one pathway are likely to be reached and where severe impacts and irreversible change might occur.

Advancing a coherent and integrated approach to meeting the requirement of building resilient infrastructure is a significant challenge confronting the operators of infrastructure not just in the Western world but also globally over the coming decades. In the UN's Sustainable Development Goals released in September 2015, the rubric of resilience was utilised to highlight how we might collectively operationalise a joined-up response and build resilient infrastructure, promote inclusive and sustainable industrialisation and foster innovation (Goal 9). This holistic integration of how infrastructure provides not only the lifeline services required for survival, but also the conduits through which human progress can thrive, reinforces the centrality of complex and interconnected infrastructures to contemporary life. More importantly, it demonstrates why we need to make such networks more resilient and better able to adapt to shocks and stress in the long term.

5

SECURITY, RESILIENCE AND PREPAREDNESS

By failing to prepare, you are preparing to fail.

Attributed to Benjamin Franklin

[The current terrorist threat] requires that we all acquire a mind-set of community security and resilience . . . where security and resilience is designed in and is part of the city's fabric, and where everyone who lives and works here sees security and resilience as their responsibility just as much as it is for the emergency services and civic authorities.

'London's Preparedness to Respond to a Major Terrorist Incident', report[1]

In August 2016 *The Economist* announced that, according to their index, Melbourne, Australia was the world's most liveable city for the sixth year in a row.[2] Although such quality of life calculations take on board many factors, low rates of crime, terrorism and warfare, and high-quality, vibrant public spaces, are essential to score well in this survey. In this regard, Melbourne had Federation or 'Fed' Square, a modern piazza that was promoted as the heart and soul of the city and home to major cultural attractions, world-class events, tourism experiences and retail stores. Since its opening in 2002, Fed Square has seen more than 100 million visits and is recognised internationally as a contemporary world site and inspirational public space that showcases Melbourne's civic and cultural strengths. However, since its opening it has also been seen as a potential target of international terrorism and, as a result, has sought to become more resilient, a situation that attracted a greater degree of urgency in the months following the 2016 announcement crowning it as the world's premier liveable city. The upsurge in international terrorism targeting Western cities made making Fed Square and Melbournians more resilient a key priority as new security and resilience plans were developed apace.

On 20 January 2017, just after midday, a local man, Dimitrious Gargasoulas, drove at speed towards Melbourne's central business district. His car accelerated, hurtling through a number of intersections before careering into pedestrians in the busy Bourke Street Mall a few blocks from Fed Square. Six people were killed and 37 critically injured. While it quickly emerged that this wasn't a terrorist attack of the kind that just a month before had seen over 50 people mown down by a lorry at a Berlin Christmas market, the reaction from the prime minister of Australia, public officials and the mass media immediately referred to 'an attack' and sought a quick and high-profile security response. Making Fed Square more resilient to disruption or attack by limiting hostile vehicle access was the order of the day.

Spurred into action by further vehicle-as-weapon attacks in London and Stockholm, as well as other potential attacks against the square itself, on 9 June 2017 the heightened threat level led to over 150 temporary concrete anti-terror blockers being placed in and around key public places in Melbourne, including Bourke Street Mall and Fed Square. The planned security interventions also followed hot on the heels of Australian national government advice on the protection of crowded places from terrorism that aimed to 'protect the lives of people working in, using, and visiting crowded places by making these places more resilient to terrorism'.[3] It also followed the allocation of $10 million in the Victoria state budget to increase security measures across its jurisdiction. In addition to concrete blockers and steel barriers, CCTV cameras and loudspeakers were installed to aid the monitoring of the location and its possible evacuation when required. Time was of the essence. As the State of Victoria premier noted, speed of response was crucial, despite the ugly appearance of the concrete blockers: 'We weren't going to wait around for six months or twelve months while planter boxes are built so they look better.'[4] In Melbourne resistance to such draconian security followed and a counter-protest to the placement of blockers and bollards was organised and went viral on social media with the hashtag #bollart. Here the concrete blockers placed around pedestrian hotspots were artistically decorated as a reaction against what many saw as an unnecessary eyesore that risked turning the world premier liveable city into a fortress.

The visible enhancement of security in downtown Melbourne was not enough to stop a further attack in early November 2018. Here a single attacker went on the rampage with a knife after the vehicle he was travelling in, and which was packed with 'barbecue-style' gas cylinders, crashed and caught fire. One person was killed and two others injured. The Islamic State (IS) group claimed that one of its 'fighters' was responsible. The incident came as Dimitrious Gargasoulas was on trial for his 2017 attack on the same street.

*

The concepts and practices of resilience have become a staple of international security discussions over recent years and are now firmly embedded within numerous government documents, replacing and updating policy ideas based on risk. As in many policy arenas where it has taken hold, in relation to international security, resilience has metamorphosed out of a fixation with future security challenges and a focus on pre-emption and risk scanning. As criminologists Sandra Walklate and Gabe Mythen have noted, this has combined with 'a preoccupation that has been concerned to reduce wider societal exposure to places, people and situations deemed "risky"'.[5] In other words, policies of resilience have led to a reappraisal of who, what and where is vulnerable to terrorism and how people, places and processes can be made more resilient. The upsurge in terrorist attacks over the last few years has led to further proclamations that enhanced resilience is an antidote to the impact of such assaults, both in terms of how our cities look and feel, but also in terms of how society can cope with terrorism as well as assist with broader national or homeland security. The response to terrorist threat in Melbourne, as noted above, has been central to both global media discourse that illuminates the risks still faced by terrorism but also government aims that seek to make urban areas and communities more resilient to such events. What is currently happening in Melbourne is not unique but showcases how ideas of resilience have come to the fore in security policy in the wake of 9/11 and subsequent attacks, and how over time, more adaptive responses have been sought.

Acts of terrorism and the need for national governments to show they can stop them occurring, be prepared if they do occur, and quickly put in place visible security measures to assure the public they are doing all they can to keep them safe, have sadly become all too common in the twenty-first century. Despite the statistical evidence highlighting that you are more likely to die as a result of falling off a ladder or slipping in a bathtub than from a terror strike, as Dan Gardner notes in *Risk: The Science and Politics of Fear*, international terrorism is the *bête noire* of our age. Moreover, amidst doomsday warnings of existential threats, counter-terrorism has also systematically siphoned up an increasingly large proportion of government emergency budgets. In particular, Gardner highlighted what risk researchers refer to as 'signal value'; that is how much an event is seen as a predictor of future dangers – which was off the chart after 9/11 and has remained high ever since, at least according to government threat assessment scorecards.[6]

In today's so-called age of terrorism, and given the unpredictable nature of the terror threat, we should not be surprised by the increased attention given to reducing its impact. Given the vast array of targets, strategies and technologies available to would-be terrorists, traditional security approaches are no longer suitable. This has meant that we are required to adapt to new realities and provide increasingly agile and flexible responses to address multiple new threats as they emerge.

Such a twenty-first-century requirement has increasingly seen security recast through notions of resilience with a focus on the need to better anticipate, and be adaptable to, known and unknown threats. In the contemporary period, the response to terrorist risk usually poses the question 'Are we prepared?' rather than 'Can we prevent it?' National security policy has become increasingly focused on how to restrict further 'inevitable' attack and embed resilience into physical defensive measures and local populations, foretelling the need to adapt to a changing landscape of terrorist risk. It is, we are told, not a matter of *if* but *when* an attack will occur and we need to get ourselves ready. In this view of the world, risks from terrorism can only be managed and prepared for but never completely eradicated.

While this shift towards resilience has forced security policy to adopt proactive and pre-emptive solutions, in many ways these have often amounted to little more than extrapolations of previous security trends, dating from the latter decades of the twentieth century. For some this signals 'resilience creep' and has seen resilience-centred counter-terrorism gradually expand in scope and scale since 9/11.[7] However, in actuality this process has been more of a series of surges, catalysed by various moments of devastating terror that provide the signal moments for changing course, ditching conventional understandings and adopting new approaches to counter-terrorism under the rubric of resilience. 9/11 notably proved a catalytic event for the mass introduction of hi-tech surveillance systems with the intensification and expansion of existing systems and the adoption of ever more refined technologies to assist in risk-scanning activities. Similarly, after home-grown terror attacks in London on 7 July 2005, communities have become increasingly engaged in the surveillance effort and asked to report suspicious activity as part of enhancing 'community resilience' and being a responsible citizen. Moreover, across the globe, fortress architecture has become *en vogue* as residential and business communities seek the sanctuary of purpose-built enclosures. Likewise, there is an increasing sophistication and cost to contingency planning undertaken by many types of organisation, with the intention of decreasing vulnerability to attack and increasing preparedness to 'bounce back' and maintain business as usual in the event of a terrorist strike.

These new 'resilient' security approaches have had significant impacts upon our everyday lives because of the ubiquity of security products that litter our cities and the constant stream of security announcements projected to the public. Notably, the permanent 'securityscapes' of bollards, gates, cameras and private security guards in the global hubs of London and New York, and more recently the states of emergency declared in Paris and Brussels after their terrorist atrocities, exemplify these trends.

But how did we get to the position where the risk of terrorism constantly evokes such a protective response in a quest for ever-greater levels of resilience? In the immediate aftermath of 9/11, defending the homeland and making it more resilient became the dominant rhetoric used by politicians in the Western world for how we should prepare for the next attack. In the years and decades following 9/11 a vast range of security strategies were subsequently deployed in the name of enhancing resilience and increasing the capacity to be able to adapt to the changing tactics and targeting preferences of would-be terrorists. As will be shown, such security approaches, driven from the top of government, have not proved universally popular, with growing resistance evident. Moreover, such strategies have often lacked the agility, flexibility and adaptability of approach that they purportedly represent. They are also seen by many as reactionary and governed by a 'command and control' structure that rides roughshod over community concerns and civil liberties. In many ways, approaches to contemporary security-driven resilience, to date, represent a particularly modernist way of thinking about uncertain and postmodern threats.

RISK, PROTECTIONIST REFLEXES AND RINGS OF STEEL

In June 2018, Paris unveiled its newly constructed but controversial defences against terror attacks: a 'ring of steel' for the iconic Eiffel Tower. Concrete and steel blockers that had encircled the tower since 2016 were replaced by a tall and apparently impregnable security belt at a cost of nearly €35 million. Quoted on the BBC, Bernard Gaudillère, president of the Société d'Exploitation de la Tour Eiffel that runs the monument, said the new walls were 'rock-solid for absolute security' and a more attractive option than hundreds of concrete blocks and armed police. More upgrades, planned ahead of the 2024 Olympics, will see the remaining temporary fences, which give the monument the look of a building site, replaced with something 'infinitely nicer and more romantic'.[8] For now, 6.3-centimetre-thick, bullet-proof glass walls form two sides of a security square, with the other two blocked off with 3.2-metre-high steel barriers formed from curved prongs in the form of the tower itself. The security ring stands exactly a hundredth of the height of the Tower. Given the increased fear of vehicle-as-weapon attacks that have plagued Western Europe over recent years, over 400 concrete blocks will for the time being remain in situ, and an armed security presence will still be in operation. When it was announced in February 2017 the Paris deputy mayor Jean-François Martins refused to use the term 'wall', calling the planned barrier an 'aesthetic perimeter'. He also noted that further security and armed soldiers in Paris would not scare tourists: 'What scares tourists is lack of security, not security.'[9]

As with many recent resilience-centred security interventions, not everyone agrees or approves. In Paris, locals have complained about the sheer cost as well as the lack of local consultation over plans that will mean restricted access to the site. They also allege that the city of Paris has used special measures and anti-terror laws introduced in 2017, and the ongoing state of emergency imposed in the wake of the deadly attacks of

November 2015 in which 130 people were killed at Paris nightspots, to initiate security changes without assessing their overall civic impact.

From a security perspective, the world before 9/11, at least, was far simpler than in modern-day Paris. Most risks were relatively well known and attack methods used by terrorists reasonably consistent, at least through the 1990s, with car bombings targeting financial districts or government offices the modus operandi of choice. Economic terrorism was the name of the game and the intention was to put pressure on governments to make concessions based on the threat of financial loss from attacks, or through valued international businesses packing up and leaving areas where bombings occurred. Such fears necessitated the adoption of 'fortress security', where security 'at all costs' trumped other aesthetic and civil concerns. This is not an unusual reaction to high levels of risk and threat, whatever the cause. During the 1990s, Ulrich Beck in his *World Risk Society* thesis argued that increasing levels of vulnerability evokes a 'protectionist reflex', necessitating withdrawal into safe havens.[10] Moreover, many commentators saw this progression as part of a historic social process by which security, at times of increased uncertainty, seeks to cleanse and order dangerous spaces.[11] As noted in chapter 1, such enclaving of a defined territory as a crude conflict resolution measure is as old as civilisation. But in recent decades, this has intensified as the rich and powerful insulate themselves in hermetically sealed and electronically surveilled zones, or gated areas, in an explicit display of defence and social control.

Some of the most explicit examples of such measures were seen in Northern Ireland in the early 1970s and 1980s, where fortification was used by the security forces to control designated areas at risk from terrorism. This was most notably around the central shopping area in the capital, Belfast, where access was barred, first by concrete blocks and razor wire, and later by a series of tall metal gates which became known as 'the ring of steel'. This was a term that was to gain new meaning, first in the 1990s in central London, and subsequently around the world in the new millennium, as a metaphor for high-profile in-your-face zonal security.

Despite a host of high-profile terror attacks against economic or iconic targets, and subsequent militaristic, security and crime prevention interventions in many Western cities during the 1990s, it is common for many to maintain that the inception of strategically organised counter-terrorism in contemporary society can be traced to the events of 9/11. While the events of that day were a major catalyst of this agenda, and brought the language of resilience to the fore, other earlier terrorist attacks are also important in helping us understand contemporary approaches. In the latter years of the twentieth century, in the United States, which had seemed immune to the acts of terrorism that had plagued other parts of the world, the 1993 World Trade Center attack horrified the US public and solicited a swift defensive response with both individual buildings and commercial districts increasingly attempting to 'design out terrorism'.[12] One journalist writing in the *New York Times* noted: 'Barricades and bollards have become the newest accessory on this country's psychic frontier . . . You might call it the architecture of paranoia.'[13] Two years later, in response to the Oklahoma City bombing, at the time the most devastating act of terrorism in the United States,[14] the US government further passed legislation[15] for structural robustness that increased security and for the bomb-proofing of federal buildings.[16] In the wake of these incidents, the practical responses initiated by statutory agencies to beating the bombers were rather reactionary, adopting crude but robust approaches to 'terror-proofing' cities,[17] as the American public became increasingly aware of the threat of home-grown terrorism.[18]

LONDON CALLING

In the latter years of the twentieth century, such target hardening as a form of defence was not without critique. Architectural critic Martin Pawley, in *Terminal Architecture*, argued that in light of an upsurge in terrorism, urban areas could well be punctuated by what he termed an 'architecture of terror', dominated by the need for increased security and preparing for the worst.[19] This was most notable in London where such high-profile security was most readily established in situ.

Throughout much of the twentieth century London was threatened by terrorist groups, most often linked to the Irish Republican cause,[20] but it was during the late 1980s and early 1990s that attempts to design out terrorism were first initiated at specific locations. The spectre of fortress Belfast was notably brought to London in 1989 when wrought-iron security gates were installed at the entrance to Downing Street on the orders of then Prime Minister Margaret Thatcher, to provide an effective means of controlling public access to this iconic location.[21]

By the early 1990s the targeting of global cities, and in particular their economic infrastructure, by terrorist organisations in order to attract global media publicity and cause severe insurance losses and significant disruptions in trade, meant enhanced security was considered in many vulnerable locations. In London, the Provisional IRA successfully attacked a number of key economic targets in the 1990s with large bombs targeting its financial hubs – the City of London (the Square Mile) and London Docklands, containing the famous Canary Wharf Tower. Notably, large bombs exploded in the City of London in April 1992 and April 1993,[22] and the subsequent reaction of civic authorities and the police served to highlight the use made of both territorial and technological approaches in counter-terrorism, which foregrounded 'resilience' responses to terrorism that became far more widespread a decade later.

On the evening of 10 April 1992, on the day of the UK general election, a bomb exploded at St Mary Axe in the heart of the City of London. This was the first major bomb in the City, and it was felt that an increased police presence, with officers carrying out spot checks on vehicles, was going to be the best operational response. Not all agreed. Leading City figures cited in *The Times* newspaper felt that a Belfast-style scheme should be implemented and that 'the City should be turned into a medieval-style walled enclave to prevent terrorist attacks.'[23] Others further disagreed, arguing, 'We wouldn't want the City turned into a castle with a moat around the outside.'[24] At this time though, such draconian defensive measures were dismissed as a propaganda gift to the terrorists, as well as being difficult to implement legally. However, because of the 1992 attack a parallel predicament was brewing that required defending – not from bomb damage but from a crisis of insurance where the private insurance industry would not cover terrorism risk, potentially making many areas of the financial district uninsurable. This forced the UK government to set up a new scheme to offer coverage to those wishing to purchase terror insurance, but at a much higher cost.[25]

A year after the St Mary Axe attack, the decision of reinsurers to withdraw from the terrorism insurance market was vindicated by a further bomb attack in the City of London on Bishopsgate in July 1993, which, it was initially claimed, would cost around £1 billion to put right. Those who had decided to take out terror insurance saw premiums skyrocket, in some cases by over 200 per cent. As the Provisional IRA noted in their own newspaper, *An Phoblacht*, 'As well as the huge cost of structural damage, the loss of buildings and the knock on effects of insurance costs, the City of London is assessing the damage to its prestige as a world financial centre.'[26] While financial security through insurance was at least being offered, albeit at high cost, physical security was also dramatically ramped up.

Only three months after the Bishopsgate bombing, what was referred to in the media as a Belfast-style 'ring of steel' was activated in the City, securing all vehicle entrances into the Square Mile. Essentially, the entrance points into the City were reduced from over 30 to just seven, and road checks manned by armed police were established.[27] The City's ring of steel represented a far more symbolic and technologically advanced approach to security, which tried to avoid the 'barrier mentality' of Belfast in favour of less overt security measures. It did, however, provide a highly visible demonstration that the City was taking the terrorist threat seriously, even if many entering the City did not realise its anti-terrorist purpose.[28] At the entrances of the ring of steel, the most technologically advanced automatic number plate recognition (ANPR) CCTV cameras available were installed as the City of London was transformed into the most surveilled space in the UK at the time, and perhaps the world.[29] A similar security scheme – the Iron Collar – was established in the London Docklands after the 1996 bombing at South Quay station, amidst fears that high-profile businesses might be tempted to relocate away from the area. Prior to 9/11, the counter-terrorism measures focused on London's financial zones were, first and foremost, protective devices, but they were also 'rings of confidence', providing reassurance to local business that some level of security was being delivered almost exclusively by the police and security forces.

PREPARING FOR THE WORST: 9/11 AND THE RISE OF RESILIENCE

During the twentieth century resilience was a term seldom heard within security circles, but the devastating events of 9/11 destabilised the whole notion of security – who does it, how it is carried out and, in particular, how it is framed. The unprecedented events of 9/11 brought to the fore wider concerns about different types of 'postmodern' terrorism and a society based on living with an acceptable degree of risk and danger.[30] This required a rethinking of existing security practices. While prior to 9/11 terrorist targeting tended, on the whole, to focus on attacking economic or military targets and the use of vehicle bombs, after 9/11 new attack trajectories came to the fore that were more indiscriminate and novel, including methods where attackers were prepared to kill themselves in pursuit of their goals. New targets of terrorism subsequently emerged with major concerns over protecting less well-defended 'soft targets' and most notably crowded places where people gather, such as shopping areas, markets, transport systems and sports and conference arenas.

In the post-9/11 world, not only were new and adaptable solutions to contemporary forms of terrorist risk sought, but new ways of managing this process were also initiated. This is not implying that 9/11 altered existing security approaches in the dramatic ways that many have claimed. Rather, a re-thinking and re-evaluation of risks, hazards and threats, and how to counter them, emerged and spawned new ways of thinking, or at least new ways of utilising traditional understandings.

Responding to new terrorist threats also got a new vocabulary as the concept of resilience became ever more central to the discussion of national security and attempts to convey a response which was *proactive* and which had inbuilt adaptability to deal with the fluid nature of the security challenges faced by many nations. In the context of security threats, resilience was more often than not seen as the ability of a society to absorb shocks and reorganise while retaining its essential structure and identity. At first glance, this type of approach appears to favour a business-as-usual, or status quo, approach to handling disruption. But look more deeply and the resilience-centred approach to counter-terrorism that began to emerge was radically different from pre-9/11 approaches and the reactive type of interventions seen in the immediate wake of these attacks.

The assumptions underpinning the new resilience philosophy saw terrorist attacks as impossible to predict and prevent given the limitless array of targets and the ease by which a handful of people could plan a strike. Preventing all forms of terrorism was likened to a fool's errand with the odds of success almost zero. So the emphasis shifted to 'preparing' for and bouncing forwards from an attack and learning to live with, and adapt to, persistent risk and danger, rather than the immediate pre- and post-9/11 rhetoric of 'defeating' terrorism.

The operation of security approaches undoubtedly adapted in the post-9/11 world, framed through the lens of resilience. What emerged, most notably in the UK and United States, was a shift away from dealing with security risks through ideas of civil defence and civil protection as an outdated overhang of Cold War systems of emergency management. Even before 9/11, the collapse of the USSR and a series of high-profile domestic disasters had stimulated calls to develop more contemporary ways of planning for civil emergencies that were less focused on wartime approaches and the involvement of the military. After 9/11, the concern that key sites would be targeted by terrorists accelerated this process, and made reform of emergency preparedness a key political priority. This 'upping the ante' in disaster management, catalysed by 9/11, was felt around the globe. In the UK, the term 'resilience' came to the fore to represent this shift in approach, and was eventually formalised through the 2004 Civil Contingencies Act that attempted to provide a central strategic direction for developing resilience based on a cycle of anticipation, prevention, preparation, response and recovery.

In the United States, too, in the wake of 9/11, there had been ongoing and heated debate about the ability of the American state, and its population, to respond to subsequent acts of large-scale terrorism. This moved away from the 1990s emphasis on physical security to focus on more holistic strategies for protecting high-risk areas. This led Stephen Flynn in *The Edge of Disaster* to paint a picture of an American nation still unprepared for dealing with major catastrophe and to argue that resilience should become the 'national motto' as Americans seek to embed security into nation organisations and the collective psyche: 'A resilient society is one that won't fall apart in the face of adversity. Protecting property and successfully evacuating populations that are potentially in harm's way lessen a . . . disaster's destructive impact . . . And preparing for the worst makes the worst less likely to happen.'[31]

The US undoubtedly took the global lead in the legislative reform around the counter-terrorist response, throwing the agenda of balancing civil liberties and state security centre stage with the swift passing of the Uniting and Strengthening America by Providing Appropriate Tools Required to Intercept and Obstruct Terrorism (Patriot) Act 2001, supported with the establishment of the Department of Homeland Security (DHS) in 2002. The DHS, however, also acted as a focus for a critical appraisal by the civil rights movement in the US which questioned how democracies can fight terrorism and still remain democratic.[32] Similar post-9/11 legal powers were rolled out in many other countries, and, often under the guise of enrolling communities in the fight against terrorism. For example, the Australian government's counter-terrorism white paper, 'Securing Australia, Protecting Our Community', released in 2010, listed resilience as one of the four key elements of the government's counter-terrorism strategy and a way of 'building a strong and resilient Australian community to resist the development of any form of violent extremism and terrorism on the home front'.[33]

Over time, there has clearly been a series of step changes in a range of contexts relating to the emergence of resilience policy linked to the threat of terrorism. In many Western countries, the emphasis has been placed on the need to be prepared in the increasingly risky world of the unknown and versatile aggressor, but also to build bridges and collaborative relationships in order to foster a more integrated management of emergencies.[34] However, many different commentators have expressed concern over the prioritisation of resilience to terrorist-related threats which continued to consume our collective thinking, and budgets allocated to hazard management, despite both their lower frequency and overall impact compared to other forms of risk.

SECURITY AS RESILIENCE

While national idiosyncrasies defined the structure, means and method of security-driven resilience policy directions, consistency is more apparent in the rhetoric and direction underpinning emerging policies. Historically, security and terrorism concerns have generally been referenced to national, trans-national or global scales, yet more recently local responses that require analysis through different frames of reference have emerged as the key focus. This places the needs and resilience of the individuals, communities and places, not states, at the centre of security policy. National security has therefore increasingly played out in the local realm under the rubric of resilience that has placed a particular emphasis upon *preparedness* and *anticipation*.

In this scenario, resilience was seen as a collective concern where multiple stakeholders, rather than just the security services, were given responsibility for ensuring security. Security policy, therefore, became increasingly focused on developing pre-emptive solutions to perceived security threats that narrowed formerly diverse concerns towards very specific forms of homeland security and sought to draw in a range of institutional stakeholders in counter-terrorism: government at central, regional and local levels, emergency planners, the police and private security professionals, a range of private-sector partners and, importantly, local communities.

In many countries, therefore, security became a potent driver and shaper of contemporary resilience practices, while at the same time security policy adopted the softer language of resilience. This is particularly the case when it comes to counter-terrorism strategies at national or pan-national (for example the European Union or United Nations) level, which provided further strategic direction for developing resilience through security and advancing counter-terrorism policies that aimed to reduce the risk of terrorism, so that people can go about their daily lives freely and with confidence.[35]

While such developments have progressed in a variety of ways, two strands stand out as worthy of particular attention: the evolution of physical protective security and resilient design; and the capacity for local communities to contribute to the counter-terrorism effort through heightened levels of community resilience. Both these strands of work have been catalysed by post-9/11 terrorist incidents with significant signal value. These include high-profile attacks in Madrid, London, Mumbai and Norway from 2004 to 2011,[36] as well as the more recent spate of vehicle-as-weapon attacks and gun and knife rampages in Europe, North America and Australia (2015–18). Both the advance of resilient designs and community resilience demonstrate attempts at adapting long-held security practices and advancing more innovative and agile ways of working. More negatively, these measures also illuminate how resilience can be used as a form of control or self-regulation. This has highlighted how a long-held tension between security and freedom is currently playing out and where resilience is not necessarily viewed as a positive development.

BUNKERING DOWN: RESILIENCE AS RESISTANCE

Initially, in the immediate aftermath of 9/11, there was substantial pressure for key buildings, places and iconic landmarks to be protected from terrorist attack by hardened security features in the name of increasing resilience. Here the objective of such resilience interventions was to change the fundamental nature of terrorist targets by reducing their physical vulnerability to terrorist threats and restricting opportunities for terrorists to penetrate target areas. In essence, such approaches amounted to engineering or designing in resilience through robustness and resistance.

Practically speaking, many highly visible security features – notably concrete 'planters' or steel bollards – were placed around key sites to stop car bombings, but they also cluttered the public realm. For instance, many argued that the US-wide effort to secure key buildings after 9/11 in a rather haphazard and makeshift way prioritised safety of building occupants over regard for social, economic or aesthetic considerations. Others described how the 'guns, guards, gates' posture adopted at this time was inappropriate, as such measures 'actually intensify and reinforce public perceptions of siege or vulnerability and thus heighten the sense of imminent danger and anticipation of attack'.[37] In Washington DC, for example, the erection of Jersey barriers and chain-link fences was unpopular with visitors: 'The nation's capital has become a fortress city peppered with bollards, bunkers, and barriers' due to both a lack of funding for 'anything nicer' and a lack of strategic coordination between policy-makers.[38] This pattern of reactive and retrofitted fortification was repeated in many countries. For example, in central London high-profile targets such as the Houses of Parliament and the US Embassy were protected by rings of concrete barriers and mesh fencing. The security cordons around London's financial zones were also reactivated, with heavily armed guards patrolling the streets.[39]

However, in time, such traditional 'bunker' approaches to security appeared largely inadequate as counter-terrorist strategies were rethought given the increased appreciation of the multiple and fluid threats faced from international terrorism against a range of easily accessible public spaces. The threat posed by no-warning, and often suicidal, attacks in a multitude of crowded public places began to set significant new challenges for the security agencies. The methods and tactics adopted by terror groups became increasingly novel, innovative and focused on mass casualty strikes or multiple coordinated assaults. Such attacks were tactically aimed at crowded areas with features in common – most notably their easy accessibility – that cannot be altered without radically changing citizen experience of such largely public places.[40]

As such, in the last decade the initial swathe of security bollards and defensive barriers that littered the landscape of many cities after 9/11 has slowly given way to more adaptive and flexible approaches, although in many cases bollard-type solutions still prevail or have been retained. The predominant view that has emerged is that security features, where possible, should be as unobtrusive as possible. This, in some cases, has led to built-in security features being camouflaged and subtly embedded within the cityscape. Examples of such features include concealed barriers in the forms of balustrades along the Government Security Zone in London, artwork or 'hardened' benches, lampposts and other street furniture that are erected as part of 'streetscape' improvements. These security features still provide a significant resistance – a 'hostile vehicle mitigation' functionality – with designs capable of stopping a seven-tonne truck travelling at 50 miles per hour.[41] This, as one commentator has noted, potentially 'represents the future of the hardening of public buildings and public space – soft on the outside, hard within, the iron hand inside the civic velvet glove'.[42]

With this key 'visibility' principle in mind, the design of the new US Embassy in southwest London has sought to incorporate a number of innovative and largely 'stealthy' security features into its design. Many of these features are reminiscent of medieval times, notably the blueprint for a stronghold castle – a protected keep surrounded by moats or ditches, which could be crossed using ramparts. Architects from Pennsylvanian firm Kieran Timberlake acknowledged that their designs had been stimulated by European castle architecture and that, in addition to the use of a blast-proof glass façade, they had sought to use landscape features imaginatively as security devices to avoid giving a 'fortress feel' to the site. A moat, ponds and multi-level gardens have also been incorporated to provide a 30-metre protective 'blast zone' around the site.

Although widely condemned by some for its architectural qualities, and most recently by President Trump for its semi-peripheral location, the embassy design highlighted a number of key features of contemporary counter-terrorism philosophy as applied to resilient design: the need to integrate effective protective security into the design of sites in ways that are proportionate to the level of risk faced; the increased importance of built environment professionals such as planners, architects and urban designers in security planning; and the need to consider the visible impact of security measures and, where appropriate, make these as unobtrusive as possible. These questions of proportionality, collective responsibility, visibility and public acceptability of protective counter-terrorism security have become important questions in light of more recent terrorist attacks across the globe that have used vehicles as weapons and reopened long-standing debates about the appropriate use of security bollards as a technique of enhancing physical resilience.

BEYOND BOLLARDS

In 2016 vehicular attacks accounted for the largest number of terrorism casualties in the West, resulting in over 600 deaths. The recent instances of vehicle-based terror attacks hitting Western cities in Berlin, Nice, Stockholm, London, New York and elsewhere have once again seen attempts to enhance resilience by putting in place measures that reduce vehicular access to public spaces through the widespread use of crash-rated security barriers, steel bollards or simple temporary concrete or wooden blocks.

However, such an approach to securing the public realm is seen by many as 'disproportionate' as it affects the vibrancy and accessibility of public spaces. For some, such hyper-security risks create 'sterile' public spaces where the public fear to tread. This has subsequently led to innovative alternatives to bollards being contemplated as part of a desire to maintain an open city and reduce the appearance of security. The need for 'resilient' security design of such types also highlights that counter-terrorism is a task that requires the input of a range of stakeholders who design, manage, secure and use public places and that work together, in an integrated fashion, to protect 'at risk' locations. A number of examples from New York, Melbourne and a range of Italian cities exemplify contemporary attempts to move beyond visible barrier methods of security and adapt security design to new risks and opportunities; in short to make them more resilient *and* liveable.

Times Square in New York, one of the densest and most visited public areas in the US, has, through the work of the Times Square Alliance, sought to embed 'belts of steel and granite'[43] in its recent public realm makeover to protect the users of the space from vehicles used either accidentally or intentionally against them,[44] and in so doing replacing the existing NYPD-inscribed blocks of concrete as protective measures. For Snøhetta, designers of the new public plaza, security was to be integrated as far as possible into the overall design so as not to engulf the civic experience:

> We wanted to be sure safety measures did not define the public space while also creating highly effective protective features in the most populated areas. [This design] focused on reducing visual and physical clutter and confusion in the Square, creating a simplified surface that allows people to move comfortably and naturally through the space.[45]

The 200-plus removable bollards installed have also been designed to blend in with other stainless-steel elements in the wider landscaping plan that includes ten 15-metre-long granite benches that act as security barriers and which have been orientated to define the area's public plazas. The overall master plan for the Square sought to balance reasonable protection with keeping the city's most symbolic and visible public space both open and appealing. While costly, the overall scheme has provided assurance to businesses and those frequenting the Square that safety and security are being taken seriously. In a 2017 survey, over 80 per cent of visitors agreed that the pedestrian plaza makes Times Square feel safer. Pedestrian injuries have decreased by 40 per cent, vehicular accidents have decreased by 15 per cent and overall crime in the area has decreased 20 per cent. Moreover, with the removal of vehicles, air pollution in the area has fallen by as much as 60 per cent, making the space healthier for everyone. In addition to the benefits to public health and safety, the survey shows that New York residents, Times Square employees and tourists all feel that the pedestrian plaza improves the Times Square experience, making it a more pleasant place to be.[46]

Total security cannot, however, be guaranteed. Following a (non-terrorist related) car crash in Times Square in April 2017 that killed one person and injured dozens of others before the vehicle was stopped by newly installed security bollards, a reappraisal of security was undertaken to further enhance pedestrian safety measures. This review was further catalysed by the vehicle attack in New York in October 2017, in which a rental truck was driven down a bikeway, killing eight people and injuring eleven others. Because of this attack, hundreds of concrete blockers were placed along the length of the entire bike path as well as in other city locations. In early 2018, New York Mayor Bill de Blasio, symbolically standing in Times Square, announced plans for over 1,500 permanent security bollards to be installed across the five boroughs to protect popular public spaces, at a cost of over $150 million, but noted that the city has taken steps to make sure that the bollards 'integrate into the life of the city'.[47]

This latter approach to integrating security into the everyday functioning of an area is similar to the philosophy being deployed in many other cities, where dedicated 'rings of steel' are encircling key locations through the use of physical interventions and surveillance measures, but where the speed of installation has been understandably prioritised over aesthetic and design appearance. For example, in Melbourne, such security has been installed since 2017, despite very visible protests by groups of residents and the artistic community and national government advice on the protection of crowded places that seeks to make these places more resilient to terrorism.[48] This follows on from specific 'hostile vehicle mitigation' guidance which argued that: 'No longer must we equate effective physical protective security with cold, sterile measures of austerity [concrete blockers]. Creative innovation [should pave] the way for seamlessly integrated protection measures that complement and enhance current needs and desires within public and private spaces.'[49]

Such creative innovation was the hallmark of discussions in London following the 2017 bridge attacks where a campaign was launched on Facebook to encourage the installation of 'safety gardens' instead of security barriers, and which could also serve as a memorial for victims of the attacks. In essence, what was proposed was the installation of large bulletproof plant pots creating a 'less intimidating' alternative to the existing security products and which could be planted with flowers 'to show the world that love and understanding will always triumph over hate and fear'.[50]

Similar discussions also took place in Milan and in other Italian cities, where plans for counter-terror flowerpots have taken root as a reaction to concrete barriers being thrown around famous landmarks across Italy during 2016 and 2017.[51] Proactive security was notably enhanced following a vehicle-as-weapon attack in Barcelona, Spain in August 2017. In Rome, concrete blockers were put in place around its main shopping streets and tourist areas including the Colosseum. In Milan, more concrete barriers appeared in the streets leading up to the city's main piazza that houses its famous cathedral, the Duomo di Milano. Security professionals in Genoa, Bologna, Naples, Palermo, Pisa and Turin also put protective barriers in place to separate vehicles and pedestrians.

The nationwide public reaction to the imposition of concrete blockers, however, stimulated a national conversation about the balancing of security with the look, feel and accessibility of public places. Notably in Milan, local artists sought to ensure that the overt military look of the installed concrete barriers was softened through creative intervention. A street art initiative, starting from the Duomo, spread throughout the city, aiming at transforming anti-terrorism barriers into open-air works of art. Similarly, in Palermo, Sicily, the city authorities called on painters, sculptors and designers to produce artworks on the concrete blockers to reduce their disturbing appearance.

Across Italy, this no-bollard philosophy attracted a lot of attention following world-renowned architect Stefano Boeri's call for a different approach. Boeri, best known previously for his vertical forest buildings, argued that in light of the recent rise of vehicle-led terror attacks, it was crucial to rethink traditional approaches to protective security to ensure a better integration of security in picturesque plazas, monuments and architecture, complementing instead of 'ruining our extraordinary historic and cultural heritage of urban collective places':

> We cannot afford to see the thousands of squares and public spaces present in the hundreds of European cities transformed into war check-points . . . A big pot full of soil has the same resistance to a Jersey [modular concrete barrier], but it can host a tree – a living being that offers shadow; absorbs the dust, subtle pollutants and the CO2; produces oxygen; homes birds.[52]

This approach is slowly being adopted across a range of Italian cities and has seen 40 large pots containing oleander flowers being placed around the perimeter of Piazza del Quirinale in Rome, an official residence of the Italian president.

SCANNING FOR RISK THROUGH COMMUNITY RESILIENCE

Following 9/11, new ways of governing risk became a cornerstone of resilience and required a shift from traditional ways of working, with fresh approaches needing enhanced levels of engagement in decision-making with different networks of formal and informal institutions and with citizens. Specifically, greater attention was focused on the search for collective resilience and greater levels of social responsibility.

This resulted in the shift towards the goal of greater preparedness for terrorist attack and enhancing resilience through collective vigilance. Such 'resilience' activities became increasingly focused on how the general public can assist security processes by being better prepared to cope in the event of an attack, and in so doing contribute to a further intensification of civic surveillance. The stated aim here was to develop better 'community resilience' that works in tandem with national security strategies but this has raised critical questions regarding how citizens are being mobilised in pursuit of state-driven counter-terrorist goals. Many see such approaches as the passing of responsibility for security away from government to a greater array of individuals and community groups, and seeking to create 'active' citizens or, more cynically, 'citizen spies' who contribute to strategic resilience efforts.

However, despite all the talk of how resilience will transform governance and engage with local communities, resilience approaches in the realm of security are still mostly premised on a conventional command and control approach steered from central government, with an expressed aim of developing a better adaptive capacity to adverse events. Notably, in the UK enhancing community resilience was illogically driven from the top of government through a Strategic National Framework on Community Resilience that was released in 2011.[53] Here, community resilience was projected through the lens of emergency planning with 'communities and individuals harnessing local resources and expertise to help themselves in an emergency, in a way that complements the response of the emergency services'.[54] This was also seen in terms of a 'commitment to reduce the barriers which prevent people from being able to help themselves and to become more resilient to shocks'.[55] Such attempts to enhance community resilience by the sharing of advice and guidance with the public about emergency response, and increasingly about preventing radicalisation and violent extremism in certain communities, were seen as measures that can reduce vulnerability to the occurrence and impact of terrorist attack. This gave a more cultural and social focus to resilience planning for terrorism as opposed to the highly technical focus of the majority of counter-terrorist work in the early to mid-2000s.

As strands of community resilience work have evolved since the mid-2000s, they have often focused on the notion that 'communities defeat terrorism' and the subsequent rolling out of communication and public awareness campaigns about the risk of terrorism. These efforts to enhance the resilience of the population have sought to draw local citizens into the counter-terrorist effort through encouraging them to pass on information and intelligence to the security services, raising the spectre of citizens 'spying' on fellow citizens.

Such a request to citizens from the state is not unique. In the US context, as Joshua Reeves argues in *Citizen Spies*, the post-9/11 surveillance systems established depended largely on habits that were inculcated for a long time, in particular through the Cold War 'red threat'. This meant that after 9/11, the mantra of 'If you see something, say something' came to be seen as part of an American's duty, potentially turning neighbour against neighbour.[56]

Under the banner of enhancing community resilience through reporting suspicious activity, this scenario played out in communities across a range of Western countries, but perhaps most visibly in the UK. In 2007, a concerted media campaign sought to ensure that all citizens understood the threats faced from international terrorism and encouraged the reporting of any suspicious activity to an anti-terrorism 'tip-off hotline' (with the slogan, 'You don't have to be sure. If you suspect it report it') and, more broadly, to work with the police to help them understand the radicalisation process.[57] From the outset, there was significant concern expressed at the announcements that the public were to be enrolled in the fight against terrorism; a message that was reinforced by a series of high-profile advertisements in the media and billboard displays in public places. For example, a Security Service press release in February 2008 claimed that 'terrorists will not succeed if suspicious activity is reported to the police':

> We want people to look out for the unusual – some activity or behaviour which strikes them as not quite right and out of place in their

> normal day-to-day lives. Terrorists live within our communities, making their plans while doing everything they can to blend in, and trying not to raise suspicions about their activities.[58]

One of the initial posters utilised the backdrop of a front door, saying, 'You see hundreds of houses every day. What if one has unusual activity and seems suspicious?' It continued, 'Terrorists live within our communities, planning attacks and storing chemicals, if you're suspicious of a property where there's unusual activity that doesn't fit normal day-to-day life, we need to know.'

Fast-forward a decade. In March 2018 the UK government launched a reworked public awareness campaign, Communities Defeat Terrorism, once again explicitly aimed at encouraging citizens to report suspicious activity that could indicate terrorism was being planned, and in so doing enhance the resilience of communities to the terror threat: 'We depend on information from the public. They can be our eyes and ears and help keep themselves, their neighbours, and communities safe by looking out for suspicious activity and reporting it to us.'[59]

In the context of the terrorist threat, this strategic development of 'community resilience' can be seen, first and foremost, as passing on the responsibility of responding to threats to communities and individuals as a supplement to more detailed institutional strategies. Yet, resilience here appears to be part of a complex process of self-regulation that seeks to prepare people to act in prescribed ways in an age of uncertainty where citizens, in the face of increased fear, anxiety and insecurity are being moulded into pliant subjects who do the state's work in local areas.[60] This pervasive process that seeks to pass responsibly to citizens is not explicitly promoted as 'doing the work of the security services' but is cloaked in the softer and more palatable language of resilience. It is a clever confidence trick and nudges people towards particular modes of behaviour where everybody has a moral responsibility in developing resilience and being an active and responsible citizen. Not doing so risks being labelled as immoral, irresponsible or abnormal.

In extreme cases, such 'responsible' citizenship can morph into citizen spying.[61] Informers and spies of course have a long history as a tool for social control; however, in most cases such spies have been agents of the state. These contemporary campaigns are different and are aimed at *everyone* as part of their supposed duty as a citizen.[62] In the current climate of fear, the way in which the state communicates risk to citizens has significant implications for harnessing or allaying fears about the current level of perceived risk from terrorist attack as well as inviting us to be involved in managing terrorist risk so as to ensure our own safety.

We are all counter-terrorists now! However, responsible citizenship is only taken so far. There is at the same time a deliberate curtailing of the role of the citizen to the *duty* of reporting suspicious activity without further judgement. Such a duty is now being increasingly rolled out to public-sector workers, who are encouraged to report 'radicalising' concerns they have about people they come into contact with.[63] This further raises serious concerns about pre-emption and prediction of future terrorist behaviour akin to the storyline in the Hollywood blockbuster *Minority Report* where a new 'PreCrime' police force could see into the future and stop crime before it was committed. Controversially, as one scholar noted, this 'has invoked a nationalised imagination of pre-criminal space [and] applied preventative surveillance to *all citizens*, for their own protection'.[64]

The danger from modern-day counter-terrorism communication campaigns is that they produce citizen spies with only very limited understanding of the problem. The significance of what has been reported is to be determined by the expert in terrorist risk. At the moment of judgement the citizen is removed from the equation. However, such a drive towards community resilience linked to state security might well have broader and more sinister intentions. It might encourage a general climate of what has been termed 'categorical suspicion' – the lumping together of groups of citizens as would-be terrorists.[65] It might also generate a habit of self-surveillance that creates a new kind of capacity, in which the surveillance work is undertaken as much by the watched as by the watcher.[66] In this mode of operation, individuals, communities and institutions are encouraged to adopt detective practices to gain information about community members in ways that emulate and amplify top-down monitoring, and in so doing actively supporting governmental security strategies. Here we are in danger of creating a climate where everybody is under suspicion and everyone is enrolled in enhancing community resilience for countering terrorism.[67]

IS SECURITY RESILIENT?

Security, and the countering of the terrorist threat, has increasingly adopted the language of resilience in the wake of 9/11. However, in many ways this is only a partial adoption of a broader resilience narrative that seeks to prepare populations for future risk and danger and, in particular, the next imminent catastrophe. For all the talk of preparing for, and anticipating, the next attack, how resilience has been drawn into the counter-terrorist effort is largely through command and control strategies that seek to prescribe one-size-fits-all solutions for resilient design (bollards) and encourage a particular mode of individual and community resilience through self-regulation. Within this, resilience planning embeds a range of assumptions about how 'everyday resilience' should be seen as the norm. More practically, this has meant looking at designing it into the city's fabric as well as moralising about how everyone, not just the emergency and civic services, should see security and resilience as *their* responsibility.

While the threats we face from terrorism today are increasingly novel, innovative and unpredictable, requiring increasingly complex and coordinated responses – hallmarks of the postmodern condition – what we can discern from many existing counter-terrorism strategies is that a modern approach still prevails based on top-down and blueprint approaches that do not necessarily account adequately for context. Here, given economic pressures and ingrained custom and practice, it is resilience as bouncing back or business-as-usual that currently predominates as the overarching philosophy.

Nevertheless, how we react to the risk of terrorism has had an impact on our public realm and civic sense for many years. The threat from terrorism can be seen to come as much from our policy responses to such risks as the actual act of terrorism. Both have the potential to harm the freedom of movement and expression that define a vibrant city, a humane and accessible public realm and a genuinely open society. Within this context, resilience-centred security must evolve and seek to balance effectiveness with community acceptability. How our public places are designed and monitored tells us a lot about the type of society we are and the type of society we would like to be. Likewise, citizens need to be increasingly active participants in, as opposed to passive recipients of, resilience strategies. This is of course a huge challenge and its difficulty should not be underestimated. As with mainstream community engagement, the public cannot be engaged homogenously and many conflicting viewpoints will emerge as to what is acceptable, and what is not, with regard to countering the terrorist threat. For the time being, the prominence of providing counter-terrorism strategies that meet local concerns, for many, can still be seen as a form of social control. Here the central state retains its 'whip-hand' status, potentially overriding local concerns, liberties and rights in areas it defines as being in the higher national interest. These processes further illuminate the particularly important two-part question, long established in critical security studies but only recently gaining prominence in counterpart critiques of resilience: 'What is being made resilient, and for whom?'[68]

6

STRESS-TESTING ECONOMIC RESILIENCE

The British people have taken for themselves this motto – Business carried on as usual during alterations on the map of Europe.

Winston Churchill, 1914

A resilient financial system is one that can absorb shocks rather than contribute to them.

The Bank of England, 2018

There is a popular view that the bursting of the housing bubble that triggered the global financial crisis of 2008 and led to the Great Recession was the fault of the poor who were sold mortgages on the cheap by lenders who knew they could not afford them. The massive availability of cut-rate mortgages allowed almost universal access to the housing market, drove up prices and created a housing bubble as banks bundled up 'poor' mortgages and sold them to investors. According to this version of history, as the *Washington Post* noted: 'When poor borrowers were not able to pay their bills, banks stopped issuing new mortgages. The number of buyers dwindled, prices plummeted, and the bust began. Homeowners were underwater across the country, and major banks were left with foreclosed houses that were essentially worthless as collateral.'[1] In short, the glut of cheap mortgages exposed vulnerable people to greater potential risk, distorted the market, making it unstable, and detonated the global economy.

As the opening credits of this story were unfolding in 2007, with predictions that US government-sponsored enterprises Fannie Mae and Freddie Mac, who bought mortgages from banks, needed bailing out, media commentators were lining up to blame the impending crisis on the large-scale defaulting on mortgages among those with limited financial means. The dream of cheap mortgages and universal home ownership was quickly turning into the nightmare of the subprime mortgage crisis. The majority of politicians and economists portrayed this as part of a broader narrative that 'we have been living beyond our means' for far too long. In essence, this was an attempt to take the heat off the financial markets as a central cause of the spiralling public debt, triggering a range of state-led austerity politics as a stabilisation mechanism. This could be viewed as a way for governments to win back the trust of the market, but is also an overly simplistic and disingenuous reporting of complex and intertwined events.

A more realistic picture is painted by Michael Lewis in his best-selling book *The Big Short: Inside the Doomsday Machine*, which put the blame for the origins and impacts of the housing and financial crises elsewhere entirely.[2] It was the 'greedy and heedless bankers' and governments whose risky behaviour and deregulatory zeal had, over time, created 'a crazy, man-made money machine, built on flawed mathematical models that most financial executives did not really understand themselves' who were to blame.[3] Under such a system subprime mortgages – exorbitant loans to people with little or no credit-worthiness – were given out like candy on Halloween and turned into toxic financial products called mortgage derivatives that were resold for massive profit in the global marketplace. Such selling continued apace as it became increasingly clear that the practice was being propped up by an uncertain set of loans. The opaqueness of what was occurring, clouded by years of deregulation and the establishment of murky practices (according to Lewis, Wall Street firms were able 'to hide the risk by complicating it') meant that when the house of cards collapsed it was unforeseen by almost everyone. The whole 'doomsday machine' in Lewis's view was being gamed by those who set up the system and who used conventional and misleading models that predicted long-term house price growth. In essence they used 'the foreshortened, statistically meaningless past to predict the future' to hoodwink themselves based on the promise of perpetual profit.

*

The worldwide financial crisis triggered by the bursting of the housing bubble in 2007 and 2008 cascaded like a tsunami through global marketplaces and led to a range of impacts to individuals, firms, cities, regions and national governments. This crisis marked the end of the consensus that for many decades had favoured economic and financial liberalisation and illuminated the hugely complex, interlinked and obscure financial system that had been created in a neoliberal image. The financial system was clearly out of control, with not even those who had been running it being aware of the huge risks it was storing up. Orthodox commentators were quick to blame the crisis on anything but the market. First it was the poor, and then the failures of government whose interest rates policy had fuelled high levels of cheap mortgages. But almost everyone else saw the crisis as a consequence of the liberalisation of the market that had gone too far and reached its tipping point, and been allowed to do so as a result of an irresponsible and poorly regulated system. As Columbia economic historian Adam Tooze recently depicted in *Crashed*, his landmark book on the cause and effect of the financial crisis, right-wing politicians, especially in the US and UK, successfully reframed the crisis as a result not of a rogue financial sector hell-bent on money-making, but of government fiscal policy that was too focused on welfare.[4]

Accordingly, the free market was *not* to blame; rather it was people and politicians who were not focused enough on the importance of markets. What arose from this state of affairs over the next decade, Tooze points out, was a spiralling and out of control 'doom loop' that has reshaped not just the global economy but international geopolitics. Ironically, it has led to recent calls to ease up on regulation and to the rise of authoritarian politics around the globe. As the foreword in his book succinctly notes, the Wall Street crash had major global ramifications:

> In September 2008 President George Bush could still describe the financial crisis as an incident local to Wall Street. In fact, it was a dramatic caesura of global significance that spiralled around the world, from the financial markets of the UK and Europe to the factories and dockyards of Asia, the Middle East, and Latin America, forcing a re-arrangement of global governance. In the United States and Europe, it caused a fundamental reconsideration of capitalist democracy, eventually leading to the war in the Ukraine, the chaos of Greece, Brexit, and Trump.[5]

Whatever the cause and effect of the crisis, in its immediate wake it placed the control and practices of financial markets centre stage within public debate. This subsequently catalysed discussion about how to build economic or financial resilience that to this point had been largely deployed to describe the economic impacts of environmental disasters or recovery from acts of terrorism. In the last decade, talk of financial and economic resilience is everywhere and 'has filtered into media and policy reporting on finance, with everything from housing markets and the high street to regions, cities, and communities being measured in terms of their resilience to the uncertain post-financial crisis world'.[6]

The financial crisis set in train a process whereby ideas of resilience became increasingly important across a range of economic governance fields and have come to occupy a central place within global discussions about the reform of the financial sector. In time this has also led to new adaptable approaches to modelling and assessing risk within the global economic system being advanced.

Drawing on a series of vignettes from a range of private- and public-sector organisations, this chapter will illuminate how the practices underpinning economic and financial resilience have progressed since the crash. This will chart a journey from a conservative approach, which sought continuity and promoted 'business as usual' following the crisis, to a situation where complexity is increasingly embraced to cope with an unknown future. Here, while the fundamental aim of incorporating complexity is to be better able to predict the future in order to generate stable conditions in which to better manage risk, there is also a sense that things have changed and that we can never return to the headless days of the early 2000s.

The journey of economic resilience reflects the broader evolution of resilience as a universally applied idea. Economic resilience had conventionally been viewed as simply the maintenance of continuity amidst economic volatility, with risk shielded by the buffer of insurance. After the financial crash economic resilience further embraced ideas of what were called non-linear systems, with terms such as financial and operational resilience becoming central to the logic underpinning the management of future economic risks. This has brought about change in the ways the financial sector has sought to embrace an unpredictable future and do things differently. Resilience in this new context was seen as a process by which economic risks are assessed against the capability to respond to those risks. It has meant not only putting a process in place by which external risk can be quelled by better understanding the complexity of the global finance system (financial resilience) but also an internal introspection about how individuals and organisations can reflect upon their vulnerabilities and deficiencies and promote resilience-building and self-regulation within their organisations (operational resilience).

The volatility and unpredictability of the twenty-first century has had many implications for economies at all scales, and for the workings of the finance industry. As with many other ways in which we can view resilience, from an economic perspective we can identify a shift in the ways in which risk is assessed, managed and accepted as the systems and processes underpinning the economic and financial system have modified. This has been spurred on by the perpetual need for markets to cushion themselves against economic peaks and troughs through developing new and increasingly adaptable ways of modelling future risk and building longer-term resilience.

RESILIENCE AS CONTINUITY

After a crisis, disruption or disaster, it is not unusual to hear politicians and business leaders proclaim that in the short term we should seek 'business as usual'. It is a phase that has been in common usage since the eighteenth century, when shops reopening after a fire or flood would put up a notice saying 'Open for business as usual'. In popular parlance, the saying has often been attributed to famed British wartime leader Winston Churchill who, in 1914 as the then first lord of the Admiralty (a top position in the Royal Navy), used the phrase to refer to a government policy of non-interference in business affairs, given the expectation of a quick victory in the First World War. This use of the term was repurposed during the Second World War, when Churchill served as prime minister. It became a symbol of defiance and hope as bombed stores placed makeshift 'Business as Usual' signs outside their premises.

Over time, the idea of keeping the economy going *at all costs* when shocked and of promoting economic growth became central to both neoliberalism and early ideas of economic resilience. In this context, privatisation of the public sector, deregulation of the finance sector and lower corporate tax paid for by public spending cuts has paved the way for not only a perpetual state of inequality where the rich get richer and the poor stay poor,[7] but also a situation where collective responses to crisis have become difficult to muster. Here, resilience has emerged either to frame such a collective stabilising response to disruption by the financial sector in combination with government assistance, or to illuminate how global markets and financial practices might be adapted to help deal with an uncertain future where disruption is anticipated.

Before the financial crisis, the concept and measurement of 'economic resilience' initially aligned with conventional resilience models that emphasised stability and equilibrium, and the extent to which they could resist disruption or 'bounce back' following external disturbance. Early work focused on the extent to which small nation states were able to survive and thrive in the face of fluctuating global economic conditions. Work by economist Lino Briguglio and colleagues at the University of Malta saw economic resilience as the 'nurtured' ability of an economy to recover from, or adjust to, the effects of adverse shocks to which it may be inherently exposed.[8] Here such a 'bounce-back' framing referred to three different types of capabilities required to recover quickly from, withstand, or avoid shocks. Economic resilience was associated with *shock counter-action* such as policy tools that might counter-balance negative shock effects, for example through tax cuts. Another capability was the capacity to resist or withstand shocks and reduce or negate their effects – *shock absorption.* This might be seen to come through internal measures (what economists term endogenous) such as a flexible labour force and a diverse economy by which resources can be shifted between sectors. The ability of an economy to *avoid shocks* altogether is viewed as an inherent resilience trait and the opposite of economic vulnerability. This of course assumes a good deal of knowledge about how any given risk might propagate, and an ability to predict risks that might be faced.[9]

This idea of economic resilience – as promoting stable, business-as-usual conditions – was used as a way of explaining the economic success of a number of vulnerable countries in terms of high levels of income and their ability to recover from, or adjust to, the negative impacts of *external* economic shocks. Notably, in what was termed the 'Singapore Paradox', it was demonstrated how Singapore, an economy highly exposed to external shocks, has managed to consistently achieve high rates of economic growth through building its economic resilience. In short, what was demonstrated was that those countries that are inherently vulnerable tend to put a lot of time and effort into resilience measures to help negate the weaknesses presented by external vulnerability. As history tells us, such proactive responses to vulnerability are an inherent hallmark of social progress. They are also a resilience trait.

In the early 2000s, the idea of economic resilience as ensuring continuity was further applied to areas suffering disaster. In this context, American economic geographer Adam Rose saw economic resilience as 'the ability of an entity or system to maintain function (e.g. continue producing) when shocked'.[10] This approach moves firmly into the context of emergency management, and draws on both ecological and engineering resilience as the basis for organising the resilience process. Economic resilience in this sense became the ability of nation states and government agencies to embed a disaster mitigation process into the practices of governing, ensuring the ability to continue operating within the global economy at a regular capacity. This type of approach further grounded the understanding of disaster events as disruptions to the flow of capital. Economic resilience therefore became measurable through the assessment of economic disruption in the affected location *after* the event.

For example, Howard Chernick in *Resilient City* shows how the initial fear that the competitive economic primacy of New York would deteriorate as firms fled the city after 9/11 proved groundless. This was despite the destruction of billions of dollars' worth of property and infrastructure that led to a massive reduction in rentable office space, job losses of over 125,000 in the three years that followed the attacks and the massive price hikes in insurance coverage for acts of terror.[11] Longer-term analysis has shown that despite being thrown off track by 9/11, the city's economy subsequently rebounded strongly, especially in terms of stock market performance and jobs growth, illustrating just how resilient disaster-stricken economies can be.[12] Indeed, despite the high impact and cost of major terrorist attacks, stock markets have proved very resilient and often recover within days or weeks. This can be demonstrated by 9/11 as well as subsequent attacks in Madrid in 2004, London in 2005 and Mumbai in 2008. Famously at the London Stock Exchange on the morning of 7 July 2005, the FTSE 100 (the top 100 companies listed on the London Stock Exchange) tumbled as much as 3.5 per cent in 90 minutes, wiping more than £44 billion off the value of the stocks in London. However, by that afternoon it had bounced back to close just 1.4 per cent lower than at the start of the day. The economic impact of the London attacks was merely a short-term blip caused by market uncertainty.

THE NECESSITY OF INSURANCE

In the quest to maintain continuity and return markets to stable conditions with 'business as usual' after a disaster or disruption, the availability of insurance is central. Insurance is one possible method of reducing financial uncertainty, transferring risk and helping to stabilise markets. Insurance contracts can make the incalculable calculable by using statistics to objectively assess the potential and put a projected financial value on anticipated loss. This helps steady the market by providing certainty of coverage against losses and hence reduces vulnerability. Conversely, as we highlighted in earlier chapters, where insurance is not available for certain risks or is too costly, financial protection diminishes and vulnerability is enhanced.

Uninsurability has a long backstory. During the late 1980s and early 1990s there was growing concern that the solvency of insurance companies could be threatened as a result of future predicted disasters and old financial liabilities which were increasingly coming to the fore and being concentrated in certain companies and particular geographical locations. In essence many risks were becoming uninsurable – the very definition of entering *Risk Society*. A series of catastrophes at this time posed a major challenge to the insurance industry. Notably, in the US, the estimated losses caused by both Hurricane Hugo hitting Charleston ($4 billion) and the Loma Prieta earthquake in California ($6 billion) in 1989, together with the unforeseen losses resulting from Hurricane Andrew hitting Florida in in 1992, illuminated the limitations in the traditional approach to quantifying the costs of catastrophe risk. At this time, there was particular concern emerging about the potential for climate change to drive changes in the likelihood and impact of extreme weather events. This was a long-standing concern, yet one that was crystallised by the release of the First Assessment Report of the Intergovernmental Panel on Climate Change (IPCC) in 1990. At this time, it was generally accepted that the conventional methods of predicting the future were too rudimentary and that traditional techniques were not appropriate to estimate future catastrophe losses. Notably, the lack of accurate historical data, both in terms of quantity and quality for 'black swan' – low frequency high impact – events threatened the solvency of many insurers as risk acceptance could not be accurately calculated for either particular risks or localities.[13] This chain of events led to international concerns over how the limits of insurance would affect the stability of the market, or what we might today term economic resilience.

Because of concerns about incalculable risks that might threaten their solvency, insurers increasingly fell back on old techniques of risk pooling by which risk and potential losses could be distributed evenly among a large number of contributors. Risk pooling provided a safety net that helped businesses and households acquire insurance. At the same time, it protected the insurance industry from economic catastrophe by transferring their risks to an insurance pool to cover unforeseen and infrequent risks. The concept at the heart of risk pooling is that large numbers of those with an exposure to particular risks can be grouped together to minimise the cost impact of those with the highest risk. Those with the highest risk will still pay more but at least coverage remains commercially available in most instances. When it doesn't, and insurance is not commercially available, national governments will often have to step in and provide the backstop facility. In essence, pooling risk becomes the tried and tested way in which the insurance industry forces governments to provide a de facto insurance facility and take the burden of risk in order to maintain market strength.

Such a scenario played out in the early 1990s in the City of London – the Square Mile, the birthplace of private insurance and one of the hubs of the global economy. Here, losses experienced by the insurance market in the late 1980s as a result of a string of disasters – including the fire on the Piper Alpha oil platform, the oil spillage from the *Exxon Valdez* and a series of earthquakes and hurricanes in the US – meant a number of large insurance claims were sought against City-based insurance companies.[14] Most notably the periodic terrorist bombing of London at this time by the Provisional IRA proved to be a tipping point and meant the insurance industry was hence unable to predict the likelihood and potential costs of such attacks and would not cover terrorist risk.[15] Here the nature of terrorist attack defied most of the normal 'laws of insurance'. Insurers could not quantify the risk as they didn't have accurate financial risk profiles in place for areas such as the City, and so adequate information about potential liability could not be accurately calculated.

The exclusion of terrorism from standard insurance policies took effect from 1 January 1993, forcing the UK government to provide a backstop to terrorism insurance coverage. In December 1992 the UK government became the so-called 'insurer of last resort', behind a pool of insurers who had agreed to set up a mutual company, Pool Reinsurance (Pool Re), to provide cover in the traditional way. Under this scheme, the insurance industry was effectively passing on all the collected premiums in return for the transfer of the terrorist risk to the government, which was in essence reinsuring the scheme. Simply put, properties that wished to be insured against terrorism would pay a (much-increased) premium to Pool Re that would go into a collective pot. If in the event of a terrorist attack the pot of premiums collected was not big enough to cover losses, the government would meet the vast majority of further claims. To date, this mutual pool has never been exhausted and premiums collected have been sufficient to pay out against losses suffered. The broader effect of this pooling arrangement was that businesses were at least able to purchase insurance and market confidence was maintained. Without such a mechanism being in place many financial businesses would have relocated from London and the UK at this time.

In the post-9/11 world, the partnership between insurers and government played a critical role in managing risk and ensuring short-term economic stability.[16] In the US, the risk of terrorism was not thought to be high and before 9/11 insurance against losses sustained from terrorism was essentially free and bundled up with other types of hazard insurance. After 9/11, as economists Jonathan Schwabish and Joshua Chang have illustrated, 'the insurance industry spiralled into a disequilibrium that left business without affordable insurance to guard against terrorist strikes'.[17] As in London a decade earlier, the insurance industry bore the brunt of multi-billion-dollar losses from the damage and disruption in Manhattan, and immediately reacted by excluding terrorism from standard coverage. This left many businesses in 'high risk' areas with either no coverage or coverage that was exorbitantly priced.

Such private market 'failure' meant a government-backed scheme was urgently required and the UK Pool Re model was put forward as a starting point for any US model. Time was of the essence as it was feared that excluding terrorism from standard polices would have a negative impact on the broader economy. As the chairman of the American Insurance

Association noted at the time: 'It's not an issue of profitability for the industry; it's an issue of economic stability to the entire economy. Without insurance protection from terrorists, banks will hesitate to approve loans for real estate, construction and manufacturing', adding, 'No one can price this risk.'[18]

A government-backed pooled scheme was eventually agreed in November 2002 with the signing of the Terrorism Risk Insurance Act, which provided a federal backup to a privately orchestrated scheme until the market stabilised and regained its footing. The act was designed to facilitate the development of a robust market for terrorism insurance and provide a backstop solution to insurers. As such, for a transitional period the federal government would pay 90 per cent of all losses until the end of 2005, when the scheme would be looked at again.[19] In the absence of private market innovations and solutions, sustaining a viable private market for terrorism insurance has continued, to date, to depend on this federal buffer.

ADAPTING TO CATASTROPHE AND COMPLEXITY

While quick rebounding from a disruptive event, or insurance backstops, can highlight a particular type of economic resilience based on ensuring market stability and confidence, the multifaceted cause and effect of the financial crisis that engulfed large parts of the global economy in 2008 drew attention to the overall brittleness of the financial sector. Here resilience became an increasingly heard term linked to ways of responding to, and futureproofing, post-crisis economies. In particular, the bursting of the housing bubble, and the subsequent financial crash, illuminated the complexity of the global financial system and emerging concerns over unknown risks. This served to focus attention on new ways of modelling such intricacy and interconnectedness in order to enhance the accuracy of future forecasting. Resilience in the post-crash world can therefore be characterised as the ability to avoid 'tipping points' and to adopt appropriate anticipatory and preparedness policies to reduce risk and vulnerability.

Unlike conventional bounce-back or equilibrium approaches to economic resilience that are concerned with the performance of the entire system, the focus of attention for newer models of economic, or financial, resilience is both on external factors that cause a shock *and* internal factors that contribute to the impact of the shock through a systemic weakness or vulnerability. Here, a lack of resilience capacity is seen as something that can be enhanced through policy intervention, training and a process of learning. In this way, the call for greater resilience is seen as both a proactive and positive response to crisis that allows for bouncing back *and* adapting after disruption. Resilience is further viewed as a capacity, or quality, that can be enhanced or added to individuals, organisations or governments so that they can cope better with future disruption. This positions resilience-thinking as a key agent of change, where learning from repeated experiences of adaptation and challenging the way things are traditionally done allows for the thinking through of new future approaches that are forced to work with increasing levels of complexity.

Such complexity approaches, as has been previously noted, have emerged in various guises since the 1960s as a reaction to the limitations of modern forecasting methods that were not nuanced enough to detect tipping points or unplanned shifts in the trajectory of a system. While initially complexity science talked of chaos theory and butterfly effects, the superior computing power that has advanced apace since the 1990s has enabled ever more sophisticated complexity models to emerge and be put to work in predicting the stability of markets. In the 1990s and early 2000s, emerging ideas of complexity were also regularly used as a metaphor to describe existing patterns of market behaviour within a fluid financial system. These were termed variously complex adaptive systems or non-linear systems within the growing field of 'econophysics'.[20] As a result, statistical modelling approaches became the dominant application of complexity science into economics and finance as greater predictive knowledge was sought through specialist algorithms, complex mathematical equations and ever more realistic computer simulations.

One significant application of such approaches in the new millennium was in catastrophe modelling (often referred to as 'cat' models), which was upgraded as a way to help insurance companies, governments and other financial organisations anticipate the likelihood and severity of potential future catastrophes *before* they occur. This further allowed effective planning for their financial impact. Catastrophe modelling essentially uses bespoke computer software in order to quantify probability and size of potential loss for specific clients in view of particular hazards faced in a location, and vulnerability of insured property.[21]

Cat models are a more sophisticated way of utilising historical data trends as a basis for offering insurance coverage. They do however, simplify a very complex reality intrinsic in interactions between a hazard and its impact. While cat models cannot capture the full spectrum of risks that exist in the real world, or the full range of factors that affect their impact, what they can do is reduce the degree of uncertainty (although this is higher with more extreme events where there is less empirical data available). Over time, the use of cat models has grown in importance and allowed insurers and risk managers to better assess risk, set premiums, purchase reinsurance or catastrophe bonds,[22] *or* to withdraw from a market if it is seen as too risky.

Through embracing emerging ideas in complexity science and technological developments in computing, first-generation catastrophe models helped provide tools to better understand uncertainty and enhance economic resilience to extreme events. In the aftermath of the financial crash, an increasing array of more sophisticated complexity modelling has been utilised in the financial sector to better comprehend how markets might be understood, reimagined and made more resilient. For example, in their work on how financial resilience has performed in response to the credit crisis, political economists James Brassett and Christopher Holmes have illuminated how resilience-thinking has expanded and been attached to finance in the United Kingdom.[23] This turn towards resilience was especially noteworthy at the Bank of England where particular divisions dedicated to financial resilience were established to feed into the bank's periodic financial stability reports as well as to drive post-crisis regulatory innovation. The bank's adoption of resilience has been mirrored across advanced economies in the post-crash period to ask questions of financial regulation and broader economic policy.

While in the post-crash environment talk of financial resilience has largely been concerned with the restoration of stable market conditions, such conversations now explicitly acknowledge the inherent complexity within financial systems and the need to think of them as non-linear and adaptive. This has had a series of significant ramifications. Notably, it has served to draw attention to the importance of *market discipline* as a key aspect of emerging approaches to financial resilience. At the same time that many of the shady practices that facilitated the credit crisis were becoming known, the turn towards greater self-control or self-regulation has forced the financial institutions and other major stakeholders in the financial industry to act more transparently and consider risks to their shareholders when conducting business.

In a free market economy, market discipline had historically provided both internal and external governance mechanisms in the absence of direct government intervention within the financial industry. However, the ineffectiveness of such self-regulation was exposed by the market crash of 2008. Since the late 1970s government policy and a liberalisation process in many advanced economies encouraged the deregulation of the financial sector to explicitly stimulate business growth. In the UK for example, the 1986 Financial Services Act was passed by the Thatcher government to make the financial services sector in London more competitive. At this time, the market was seen as overregulated and required freeing up. The day the London Stock Exchange's rules changed on 27 October 1986 was christened the 'Big Bang' because of the increase in market activity expected from a combination of measures designed to alter the structure of the financial market.[24] In hindsight, such a move to encourage business also resulted in less oversight of activities and less disclosure of information about new activities undertaken by financial institutions. This widespread liberalisation process culminated with the financial crisis in 2007/8. Most explicitly, the collapse of Lehman Brothers, fourth largest investment bank in the US, due to its exposure to the subprime mortgage crisis, laid bare the risk banks were running in search of higher profits. These risks were going unchecked by the regulators up until the point it was too late.

As has been made abundantly clear by a series of government commissions and inquiries into the financial crash, markets operating under deregulated 'free market' conditions couldn't be trusted. In April 2011, as part of the Financial Crisis Inquiry Commission, the US Senate released a 639-page report written by two senators – Carl Levin and Tom Coburn – entitled 'Wall Street and the Financial Crisis: Anatomy of a Financial Collapse' which tellingly noted that 'the crisis was not a natural disaster, but the result of high risk, complex financial products, undisclosed conflicts of interest; and the failure of regulators, the credit rating agencies, and the market itself to rein in the excesses of Wall Street'.[25]

Responses to the financial crisis not only called on enhanced and more transparent market discipline but a reining back in of deregulation.

Therefore, a combination of discipline and regulation was brought to bear to increase the safety and soundness – the resilience – of the market. While former readings of economic resilience focused almost exclusively on what markets could do to help stabilise themselves, in a post-crash world financial resilience was cast as something that engages more with state regulators in partnership with the market. It is a more holistic view of the financial system intended to insulate it against prospective crises. According to one of the key architects of financial resilience at the Bank of England, such crises are likely to be propagated by complex adaptive networks under stress: '*Complex* because these networks were a cat's-cradle of interconnections, financial and non-financial. *Adaptive* because behaviour in these *networks* was driven by interactions between optimizing, but confused, agents.'[26]

Here the financial system is cast as an integral element within a wider 'system of systems' (both governmental and market driven) and where developing the capacity to cope with any disruptive event is given the highest priority. In essence, what is being proposed is that financial resilience is some sort of quality, or capacity, that agents acquire to help them, individually or collectively, to cope with uncertainly in an optimal way. This acknowledges that a 'distributed preparedness for resilience' is optimally required rather than the conventionally fragmented and discordant system of firm-by-firm contingency planning and risk management.[27]

Such optimisation had a number of key elements, chief among them working out the right sort of regulatory interventions and the better forecasting of future risks. In the aftermath of the financial crisis, the leaders of the largest economies concluded that future disruptions could only be prevented, or their impacts reduced, if the overarching liberalisation process was reined in. Politically this was also sending a powerful message to the general public who wanted much greater supervision of a financial sector (particularly the banks) that was running low on trust.

Regulations were rethought after the financial crisis, seeking to encourage firms to keep their books in check, ultimately helping them to become healthier institutions. However, in terms of attitudes towards regulation from the financial sector, little of significance changed. The need for, and cost of, heavy regulations was constantly questioned as the global economy began to stabilise in what has been described as a 'cat and mouse dynamic' between ongoing processes of responsive regulations and financial innovation.[28]

While the adoption of regulations is often difficult and time-consuming, if we then take the innovation side of this equation, we can see many measures and technologies being introduced that attempt to provide better prediction and forecasting and to stop a single failing financial institution cascading through the global economy with devastating effect. Notably, new financial technologies – so-called fintech – are emerging, such as machine learning, artificial intelligence or predictive behavioural analytics, which will assist the financial industry in making better and more streamlined decisions across the board.[29] These will aid financial resilience and, additionally, improve forecasting and cybersecurity capabilities.

A FOCUS ON OPERATIONS

In recent years the focus on enhancing financial resilience in order to cope with complex and interconnected disruptive crises has shapeshifted into additional concerns for operational resilience. This was defined by one financial risk specialist in a 2017 speech at the Bank of England as 'the ability to adapt operations to continue functioning, when – not if – circumstances change'.[30] While the quests for both financial and operational resilience within the business sector have broadly similar objectives – to absorb and bounce back from shocks – operational resilience is focused more on the day-to-day governance activities that are being designed into financial institutions. The aim here is to allow them to adapt to disruption and to stress test this capability in a variety of scenarios covering both known *and* unknown risks. Operational resilience also differs from financial resilience through its focus on people, culture and technologies adopted to thwart, and learn from, disruption. Operational resilience takes a macro-level view of the financial system and how this might produce risk that could affect an individual firm, but also focuses on response capabilities being developed at the level of the firm. However, it also focuses on identifying vulnerabilities and building resilience through new practices, assessment tools and coordination with other firms. The argument here is that focusing on particular systems and processes in isolation will give an incomplete view of risks faced and resilience required.

In moving forward with seeking a step change to improve operational resilience within the UK financial sector, in July 2018 the Bank of England

and the Financial Conduct Authority released a consultation paper entitled 'Building the UK Financial Sector's Operational Resilience'. This noted that 'operational disruption can impact financial stability, threaten the viability of individual firms' and that 'firms . . . need to consider all of these risks when assessing the appropriate levels of resilience within their respective businesses'. In short, the financial sector needed an approach to operational risk management that included preventative measures and the capabilities – in terms of people, processes and organisational culture – to adapt and recover when things go wrong.[31]

Ensuring that financial businesses are resilient to disruption is both a necessity and a challenge. It requires understanding of the system complexity within the firm, as well as connections and dependencies in the external environment. It further entails a deep appreciation of the current operating environment that is full of threats, cyber vulnerabilities and cost pressures. At the organisational level, increased resilience stresses identifying skill gaps, barriers to change and upskilling staff, and awareness of how fintech, such as AI, and distributed ledgers using Blockchain technology,[32] can assist in building a resilient and secure financial ecosystem. The push for operational resilience also seeks to extend existing operational risk management approaches through the introduction of what have been termed 'impact tolerances', which can be focused on the most important business services. Such approaches are seen as better informed and more robust than conventional 'risk appetite' approaches. Conventionally, a firm's risk appetite is the amount and type of risk a firm is willing to accept, or avoid, in achieving its business objectives. By contrast, impact tolerances describe a firm's tolerance for disruption, under the assumption that disruption to a particular business service *will* occur.[33]

The approach taken at the current time by financial bodies to prepare for inevitable disruption is to seek to combine impact tolerances and scenario testing to establish a proportionate, or desired, level of operational resilience. Such testing through plausible scenarios – a key staple of resilience work – allows firms to map severity of stress produced against impact, such as system downtime, to see if operational resilience is sufficient or needs to be improved. One of the most popular ways to model this is through stress-testing scenarios. In essence, this approach seeks to predict the market impact of a potential future scenario but allows human experience to be inserted into technical risk analysis. As we cannot accurately predict the impact of some future event, it is important to test a range of possible scenarios to gain an understanding of potential future outcomes that can then be planned for.

If the financial crisis taught us one thing it was that the failure of single institutions can damage the entire financial system and economy. If we then conceive of operational resilience in the financial sector as the ability of firms and the system *as a whole* to prevent, adapt and respond to, recover *and learn from* operational disruption, then rigorous and repeated stress testing becomes paramount. Now, armed with algorithms and models derived from bigger and better data which, it is claimed, present better forecasting, more realistic stress testing run by regulators such as the Bank of England, the European Central Bank or the US Federal Reserve can better monitor how financial institutions are doing in their quest for greater resilience.[34]

For example, since 2014 the Bank of England's periodic health check on the financial sector has included tests to assess the longer-term resilience of lenders. This has involved advancing hypothetical scenarios that put the sector under severe stress to see how they will cope in conditions of uncertainty. The initial scenarios used focused on economic conditions such as large falls in GDP, the value of the pound or house prices, or steeply rising interest rates. Over time, the complexity of the scenarios has become greater in an attempt to better mimic the real world. For example, as reported in the *Guardian*, in the 2017 tests the banks, for the first time

> have been tested not only on their ability to withstand economic shocks. They have also been tested on an exploratory scenario that will examine banks' resilience over seven years of weak global growth, low interest rates and high legal costs and fines for misconduct. It will also look at the viability of their business models.[35]

In 2018, amidst ongoing fear of cyber-attacks,[36] the Bank of England further announced that financial organisations would have to undergo cyber stress tests to establish a reasonable recovery time following a significant cyber-attack. Such (cyber) stress testing has now been written front and centre into the Bank's overall strategy for enhancing operational resilience. This is about both identifying vulnerabilities in the defences and operational procedures of individual firms, as well as mitigating the systemic risk within the overall financial ecosystem. Similarly, since 2009 the US Federal Reserve has, under the Dodd–Frank Act, conducted annual stress tests on banks. This is to both help measure the sufficiency of capital available to support a financial company's operations throughout periods of stress and to better understand the range of a financial company's potential risk exposures.[37]

In essence, key financial authorities on both sides of the Atlantic are demanding that firms can demonstrate that they, singly and collectively, have concrete measures in place to deliver resilient services, regardless of the type of disruption. As a senior Bank of England official remarked in June 2018 in the wake of disruption caused by financial meltdowns at TSB and VISA, and the release of the bank's operational resilience discussion paper, 'I would like our firms to be on a WAR footing: withstand, absorb and recover.'[38]

Such a stance was very evident during 2018 in the UK as it prepared to exit the European Union in 2019, and in the US as trade disagreements with other countries caused fears of market disruption. In the immediate aftermath of the 2016 referendum result that indicated the UK wished to leave the EU – so-called Brexit – senior politicians in Europe were lining up to warn of the uncertainty ahead that would impact, in unknown ways, on markets. Since then, many stress tests have been carried out by the finance industry and governments who have played out a variety of scenarios to try and ascertain how resilient the economy would be in these different pictures of the future. Official tests carried out in 2017 saw all the UK's biggest lenders pass the bank's stress tests, indicating that they could cope in the event of a 'disorderly' Brexit process and continue to lend money to support the UK economy. The worst-case scenario the bank imagined in the stress tests included a 33 per cent fall in house prices, a rise in interest rates from 0.5 per cent to 4 per cent within two years, and the unemployment rate rising from its current rate of 4.3 per cent to 9.5 per cent. Further stress testing carried out by the Bank of England was reported in late 2018 and highlighted that while the UK's financial system could cope with the sort of 'severe economic shock' predicted by a disruptive Brexit, it would still have significant ramifications. Specifically, it could push the UK towards the biggest economic slump in modern memory with the economy shrinking by nearly 8 per cent – more than the effect of the financial crisis – as a result of a lack of new trade deals, severe disruption at borders and uncertain economic conditions. Similar to 2017 tests, such economic disruption could result in house prices falling by 30 per cent, unemployment doubling and inflation and interest rates rocketing. Just as worrying as these worst-case stress-test scenarios was that over 50 per cent of businesses were reported to have made no contingency plans for a no-deal Brexit. As the governor of the Bank of England noted:

> The level of preparedness of businesses and infrastructure, infrastructure such as ports, customs systems and transportation operations, will be important determinants of how well the economy adjusts to new trade barriers. Evidence from surveys and other UK authorities suggests that the country is not yet fully prepared for a cliff-edge Brexit.[39]

Echoing the Bank of England tests, in 2018 the European Central Bank and the European Banking Authority also scenario-played how banks could cope with, and prepare for, a general economic downturn, increased market volatility and political uncertainty that could theoretically occur as Britain plans to leave the European trading bloc in March 2019. Such testing was explicitly about resilience, with the European Banking Authority noting, 'The stress test is designed to provide supervisors, banks and other market participants with a common analytical framework to consistently compare and assess the resilience of EU banks to economic shocks.'[40]

Brexit-linked stress testing and scenarios were further used by financial consultants who are attempting to model the possible impact of the 2018 trade dispute between the US and China that saw large-scale tariffs placed on each other's goods. In running a series of different scenarios, analytics group FactSet have come up with a worst-case scenario depicting a trade war. This vision used the market's Brexit reaction as a template, with results signposting the global stock market dropping by between 8 and 17 per cent. The testing also took account of knock-on effects of impacts in the US and China with the data run indicating that countries most closely aligned to the US and China would fare worst.[41]

FINANCIAL RESILIENCE IN THE SHADOW OF INFLEXIBLE NEOLIBERALISM

While the ideas of resilience have permeated economics for many decades, it was in the aftermath of the financial crisis that ideas of building a more resilient financial system became mainstreamed within the national and international finance sector. Since 2007/8 ideas of resilience have become progressively more important across a number of economic domains and are now central in discussions of global financial reform. The World Economic Forum, the World Bank, the International Monetary Fund and the G20, among others, have all advanced agendas focused on building resilience, in either companies or the wider financial system. The stated intention is to create a more resilient financial sector and a global economy less prone to the impact of shock events.[42] The underpinning objective has been to reduce systemic risks and to put in place a programme of work to ensure the financial sector had the flexibility to respond to crisis and disruption at pace.

The financial crash revealed the inherent complexity and interconnected nature of the financial system. This is a structure that had been established in the mirror image of neoliberalism with its profit, deregulatory and privatisation impulses. The post-crisis response, when it came, sought a more stable and less risky financial system while acknowledging the need to better understand the complexity of global markets and to prepare for both known and unknown risks. Here the aim of resilience strategies – both financial and operational – was to advance adaptation and change that could better allow the economy and markets to future-proof themselves in the long term against uncertainty and disruption.

The financial crisis gave an unprecedented opportunity to redraw economic globalisation with the embedding of resilience-thinking in the financial sector, and to change convention and think afresh. Resilience-thinking in this area is different from the traditional and dominant neoliberalism of the 1980s to the 2010s,[43] which endeavoured to govern complexity and uncertainty by balancing the levers of the market and the state in order to advance policy goals that would create stable and efficient markets. The use of resilience ideas has notably enabled new ways of understanding complexity, how the future might be better predicted and who should be responsible for, and involved in, formulating future scenarios.

The assimilation of resilience into financial and economic risk management views systemic risk in financial market activity in different ways to traditional markets which took a much more limited view. In this depiction, as economist Kate Raworth has pointed out in her ground-breaking book *Doughnut Economics*, the finance industry was based on the myth of banks turning people's savings into investments with the market being smoothed out by financial trading. The financial crash busted these myths and illuminated how markets actually create not stability but flux.[44] This is why a more complicated view of markets has been developed by the financial sector. This is an observation that resembles the dynamics of complex adaptive systems and 'non-linearity' in the physical world. In rejecting simple ideas of complexity inherent in former economic approaches, resilience-thinking embraces complex and interdependent policy-understandings of what interventions might be required.

In a resilient financial world, the skills, capacities and capabilities required to cope with uncertainty, and to govern effectively, are also different. They are more focused on learning, flexibility, adaptability and responsiveness than those seen in classical work on stabilising markets. Resilience-thinking is not against government intervention or regulation per se as it seeks new ways of delivering and operating policy. Market failures can be understood to be as much about the limits to forecasting under conditions of complexity (which is seen as a key risk element) as about the degree of regulation in place that may, or may not, create barriers to effective adaptation in the event of crisis. Indeed, failure through the lens of resilience is viewed as both a disruption as well as a learning opportunity. Both illuminate the intricacies of the system as well as how stakeholders or agents act within the system during disruption.

As has been shown, such experiences of market failure, or scenarios that exemplify failure, can be used by operators or regulators to model how events may play out in practice – their predictability – and illuminate which type of resilience intervention might be best deployed. This has been facilitated by increasingly complicated risk modelling and fintech and scenario planning that stress test the ability to respond to crisis. Such testing is also about being proactive and anticipating an uncertain future and therefore places such endeavours well and truly in the resilience-thinking camp.

REFRAMING ECONOMIC RESILIENCE

In the last decade, economic and financial resilience, as ideas and practices, have undergone fundamental change. They have transitioned from approaches that were fixated on creating stable market conditions as quickly as possible and were concerned largely with known risks to one that is embracing system and governance complexity as it attempts to adapt and transform. The question here is: to what extent does this represent a bounce-back or bounce-forward version of resilience? Is it about the survival of markets or thriving in conditions of uncertainty?

The incorporation of resilience into the economic and financial world has led some to question 'the conceptual stretching of "crisis management", which at least in principle serves to naturalise financial market activity and those state interventions made in its name'.[45] In other words, if the neoliberal market is the natural order of things then its fundamental premises should remain unquestioned with reform the responsibility of the bankers themselves. They should clean up their own mess. No help, or scrutiny, is required.

In practice, and despite small-scale changes, this ingrained ethos of self-responsibility has meant that shifting the balance between the market and the state in regulating the system has proved a difficult – some say an impossible – task given the obdurate and conservative nature of the global economic system. The nature and extent of the financial crisis meant a wide-scale state-backed response was inevitable as a short-term political response, with regulations brought in to rein in the worst excesses of the financial system and to appease an angry public. Subsequently we have seen stress tests adopted as a key element of operational resilience. We have also witnessed an accelerated use of big data and AI models to improve understanding, forecasting and the prediction of risk. Cumulatively we might see such change processes as progressive but whether they are sufficient to fix and adapt the 'broken' financial system is another matter. The actions of state intervention and the market since the crisis in fact support the view that the focus has been on enhancing predictive power – a defensive position that seeks to mitigate risk – rather than actually transforming the existing customs and practices within the financial sector. These still largely operate on theories based on achieving stability, equilibrium and reproducing the status quo. If it ain't broke, don't fix it.

A fixation with equilibrium economics has previously blinded us to the vulnerabilities it can store up as system efficiencies are optimised, and signposts us towards alternative structures that are adaptable to changing conditions. If we think of resilience as an adaptive impulse then, as Kate Raworth has argued, 'Building diversity and redundancy into economic structures enhances the economy's resilience, making it far more effective in adapting to future shocks and pressures.'[46] This should not just mean ad hoc and short-term modification that, when the crisis is over, reverts to a default conservative position. It should demand active adaptability that can bring about a longer-term transformation.

There is a truism when dealing with catastrophic risk of all kinds, including financial, that there is a window of opportunity for post-event interventions to be implemented until powerful stakeholders seek to return to 'normal' operating and the status quo. Indeed, a decade on from the financial crisis, and with the global economy and financial institutions far more stable, there has been an ongoing debate as to whether or not post-crisis regulations should be replaced – marking a return to a more liberal approach. As author of *Crashed* Adam Tooze affirmed, change was needed but not too much change: 'Not surprisingly, in the wake of the crisis, it was time for a rethink. Not that the basic principles of financial globalization were questioned.'[47] Instead for some the time for excessive regulations – seen by some to be reducing profits, killing business and posing a threat to the stability of the financial institutions in general – has now passed.

Indeed, the perceived success of resiliency measures, such as stress tests for banks that have been introduced as part of a long-term strategy to ensure financial crashes can be resisted and will not cascade through the whole system, are now seen by some, including US President Donald Trump, to reinforce the idea that the time for excessive regulations is over. Regulatory compliance is seen as excessively expensive and, so some argue, now that better resilience is being achieved, bankers should return to prior practices. This is a myopic view. It is important to understand, especially now as the debate is shifting to whether or not the current regulations are still required, that the present frameworks in place might not be enough to prevent another crisis.

Economic and financial resilience should be seen as a never-ending journey. You cannot say with certainty that crisis will not occur again but through new and adaptable approaches you can make it less systemic and limit its impacts. Financial resilience rules and regulations should, of course, be reviewed and adapted over time as context changes and forecasting becomes increasingly nuanced. But it would be damaging and short-sighted to simply abandon the emerging resilience frameworks that have been established. The trick now is to ensure they are fit for purpose, and that means baking in flexibility and adaptability in a way that means they not only can bounce back but also bounce forwards when disruption hits.

7

THE SEARCH FOR ORGANISATIONAL AGILITY

I am the future of the world, I am the hope of my nation.
I am tomorrow's people, I am the new inspiration.
Coca-Cola, 'Tomorrow's People' advertising campaign, 1986

If an organisation is disorganised, disaster is likely – just ask the residents of New Orleans.
Frank Landy and Jeffery Conte, *Work in the 21st Century*[1]

In July 2018, the UK government warned that they were undertaking preparation for expected increases in civil disorder, to manage risk to food supplies and to stockpile medicines, medical devices and blood plasma products because of fear for a no-deal Brexit when the UK was expected to leave the European Union in March 2019. Simultaneously, local councils in the southeast of England who were concerned by plans being drawn up by the government to cope with potential traffic chaos released reports on new customs checks that will be imposed after Brexit. Under a scheme named Operation Brock, it was proposed that four lanes of the M20 motorway in Kent be converted into a temporary 20km-long lorry park, as any permanent customs-check solution would be years in the making. Reports highlighted how the fear of large-scale tailbacks could become a reality given growing concerns that government preparedness plans would not be delivered on time. There does not appear to be a Plan B. This was reinforced by a further announcement in October 2018 that a second motorway in Kent is also being prepared as a post-Brexit lorry park. Highways England, who are responsible for drawing up the plans, noted that this was just a part of wider 'resilience planning' should further capacity be required in the future.

Such a potential crisis brings to mind incidents at the turn of the millennium in the UK, which also saw the motorway network brought to a halt and culminated in a significant reorganisation of the UK response to civil disturbance or crisis. In September 2000, British farmers and truck drivers launched a dramatic campaign of direct action to protest about increased fuel tax duties that led to inflated petrol prices. This campaign of strategically targeted protests on the national transport system included the blockading of oil refineries and their distribution networks together with go-slow convoys on motorways. This subsequently created a fuel crisis that paralysed a number of critical infrastructure sectors and brought the country to a virtual halt. The week-long fuel drought cost the UK economy approximately £1 billion. Post-event analysis revealed that the impact had been greater than anticipated due to the vulnerability of the oil distribution network, which had been organised along just-in-time delivery principles. This was further magnified by the chain reaction it set off among other interconnected sectors such as such as transportation (including the panic buying of fuel), health care, food distribution and financial and government services. Politically, these protests led to critical questions being asked regarding 'who was in charge' of coordinating the response within the petrochemical industry and emergency services. Recent rounds of privatisation and reorganisation had left a disorganised chain of command without authoritative leadership and had forced the UK government to design emergency solutions on the hoof to safeguard the country's fuel supplies.

Ultimately, the fuel protests, combined with the impacts of an ongoing outbreak of foot and mouth disease and a series of major flooding incidents, led to the reorganisation of the UK crisis response. It was in the summer of 2001 that the ideas and language of resilience came to the fore in framing the requirements for a new way of managing crisis through greater preparedness and the encouragement of joined-up responses. This ethic emphasised more holistic solutions to risk management required of governments, service sectors and other emergency managers in order to create strong and transparent institutional arrangements to protect increasingly complex infrastructure and aligned social systems. Just a few months after such discussions had started about how best to implement this approach, the events of 9/11 and the concern that key sites would be targeted by terrorists significantly sped up this process and led to swift and wholesale reform of response procedures for all types of crisis and disruption under the banner of UK Resilience.

*

We are told we are living in a VUCA world – where *volatility*, *uncertainty*, *complexity* and *ambiguity* have been combined into a trendy management catchphrase to give a sense of our unpredictable existence. First used in the late 1980s in theories of strategic leadership, the acronym was popularised when used extensively by the US military to describe the sense of chaos brought about by the end of the Cold War in the early 1990s, and later in the wake of 9/11. The concepts underpinning VUCA have subsequently taken root in emerging ideas that apply in a wide range of organisations to look at the factors that cause organisational failure, and to sharpen the capacity to look ahead, plan ahead and move ahead. This poses a number of important questions: Why are some organisations better than others at coping with, preparing for and responding to unknown disruption in their current operating environment? Why do some organisations when facing disruption and challenge focus on defending their existing 'status quo' position, while others see opportunity in adversity, and can successfully grasp the chance to adapt and change? In short, why are some organisations more agile and resilient than others?

In 2007 *Transform: The Resilient Economy: Integrating Competitiveness and Security* was released by the US Council on Competitiveness (USCC), which argued that 'enterprise resilience' was one cornerstone of economic competitiveness and new value creation required in the post-9/11 world. Resilience was seen as a transformational idea that if done correctly could turn new security requirements into 'a productivity-driver, not just a sunk cost' for business. In short, enhanced resilience was good for homeland security and could produce clear competiveness benefits for private companies and the public sector. Managing the rapidly changing risk landscape as an emerging 'competitiveness challenge' demanded resilience. This was seen by the USCC as 'the capacity for complex systems to survive, adapt, evolve, and grow in the face of turbulent change'. In more practical terms a resilient organisation was seen as 'risk intelligent, flexible and agile'.[2]

In this scenario, resilience was required for organisations both to respond to disruptions by sustaining performance and, if possible, leverage opportunities that allow positive adaptation. Simply put, resilience of either kind can provide assurance against bad events occurring, seek to facilitate change and improve the capacity to adapt before the next disruption. Here, resilience is often viewed as the governing of growing complexity and uncertainty, and of thinking through how best to organise a response to crisis. Traditionally this has been done by developing and maintaining an appropriate range of systems and processes that allows an institution or firm to minimise the impact of disruption and to 'bounce back'.

In the twenty-first century much of the discussion on what makes for good organisational governance and improved resiliency increasingly draws attention to approaches that are adaptable, flexible and learning-based, and which foster 'adaptive capacity'. This, in theory, allows for new forms of innovative practice to be integrated in governing rapidly changing, complex and interlinked systems where adversity can be used as an opportunity to slingshot an organisation forwards. Resilience, in many contexts, is therefore emerging as the outcome from undertaking many challenging activities in an organisation and learning how to survive and thrive in conditions of uncertainty *before* disruption hits.

New organisational arrangements that adopt resilience-thinking require decision-making to be concerned with more holistic approaches to problems and to be carried out by a wider network of stakeholders. While on the surface, this might look straightforward, this is not an easy task, and as has been illustrated previously in this book, governing a public- or private-sector institution increasingly requires a shift away from conventional practices that emphasise technical, bureaucratic and incremental ways of working. The problem here is that, in many contexts, institutions are trapped in traditional patterns of operation and outdated ways of working where existing custom and practice shapes future possibilities of change. As will be demonstrated, the ability of institutions to develop resilient attributes that allow them to adapt to emerging challenges from both known and unknown risks is a major undertaking.

Nearly all organisational structures can be visualised as a pyramid with the leader, the general, the CEO, or the city major at the apex. However, such a centralised and hierarchical organisation does not work so well when confronted with a fast-moving disruption, as it lacks agility. By contrast, a more decentralised, or flatter, organisational structure is usually more agile and better able to see the big picture when crisis hits, and can accept and utilise alternative opinions to aid its adjustment. Flatter operating environments also increasingly enable trial and error learning that runs against the grain of how most organisations traditionally function. Conventionally, decisions made in most organisations are premised on a fail-safe world rather than one in which it is safe-to-fail. Encouraging experimentation and doing things differently, without penalty if things go wrong, is seen as one of the ways of building an agile or resilient organisation.

The incorporation of such principles into organisational futureproofing as a fully fledged commercial strategy was first evident in the years preceding 9/11 as private-sector companies sought to build 'enterprise resilience' to resist shock and make themselves more competitive. As will be demonstrated through examples from a number of companies, notably including Intel, Coca-Cola and NASA, the emphasis placed on organisational agility as a key pillar of corporate resilience has grown rapidly in recent years. Simultaneously, resilience-thinking also found application within public administrations, culminating in international standards for organisational resilience being developed. Within the public sector, we can look most notably to cities and their complex networks of interconnected infrastructural, social and economic systems as an exemplar of where resilience principles have been taken to the max. In the urban realm, global programmes of urban resilience-building have been rolled out by organisations such as the United Nations and the Rockefeller Foundation, who have put a premium on long-term plans for developing joined-up solutions for joined-up problems.

By drawing together learning points and key principles from private- and public-sector attempts to embed flexibility, agility and adaptability into the everyday practices of organisations, it is possible to illuminate a set of key attributes required for putting organisational resilience into future practice effectively.

RESILIENCE AS COMPETITIVE ADVANTAGE

The complex vulnerabilities and associated disruptions of today shine a light on the importance of developing corporate resilience to survive and thrive through enhancing both business continuity and competitive advantage. In the wake of 9/11, emergency or 'resilience' planning became a highly influential area of strategic policy in many areas of government and business. There was growing importance placed on developing robust processes and procedures for managing risk as a way to sustain key functions and improve the ability of an organisation to perform under conditions of disruption and stress. Greater importance was placed on business continuity planning as well as more nuanced forms of risk assessment and 'horizon scanning' that could better detect and plan responses to expected threats and possible crises.

In the private sector, developing such responsive capabilities was also an important way to assure stakeholders, or investors, that all was 'under control' and that a given company had the ability to bounce back from disruption speedily and return to normal performance levels. As a result of the shock of 9/11 and the terrorist attacks in London in July 2005, MIT academic Yossi Sheffi, in *The Resilient Enterprise*,[3] explored how the response to disruptions that occur in private-sector companies was changing. This illuminated that the focus of such action was not solely on the security measures that might be deployed by institutions, but had shifted towards broader notions of 'corporate resilience' and specifically on how investments made to embed such resilience might in turn be beneficial in terms of 'competitive advantage'.[4] Particular emphasis was placed on threats of disruption to the supply chains, both because of their increasing complexity and in terms of the plethora of threats that can undermine a supplier's ability to deliver. In this complicated and intricate network, the range of potential disruptions was infinite and each would need to be handled differently. Some were seen as easier to prepare for than others. For example, much data and many insurance statistics exist for disruptions from 'known' risks that can be used by firms as proxy measures for risks faced and the responses required. However, unknown types of high impact disruption were more difficult to plan for due to limited data availability. This uncertainty is magnified if we consider the myriad vulnerabilities that exist in the complex supply chain ecosystem. As a result, resilience in supply chain management, together with a focus on adaptability, has become increasingly important for business continuity. As Sheffi highlighted, supply chain resilience was not just about the ability to manage risk, but crucially to do so in terms of dealing with disruption effectively in ways that position you advantageously from your competitors. This means not only understanding the risks to your own company but also all the vulnerabilities across all your suppliers and subcontractors.

A decade after releasing *The Resilient Enterprise*, Sheffi returned to the theme of supply chain vulnerability in *The Power of Resilience*.[5] Extending his analysis through examples of how companies more recently have coped in light of mega-disruption, he reinforced the message that companies need to think beyond conventional risk management at the level of the firm and focus on resilience and continuity planning across their entire global supply network. A recent example of the need for corporate resilience comes from the automotive industry where in 2011 Japanese car makers Toyota and Nissan were both forced to abandon operations because of a lack of parts from suppliers following flooding in Thailand. It took many weeks for normal business to resume and resulted in a combined financial loss of over US$1 billion.[6] The impact of this flooding event and other disruptive incidents subsequently created a powerful trend for car makers towards consolidating purchases with larger global suppliers in order to create a more resilient supply chain.

A further example, this time of effective corporate resiliency, comes from the actions of software firm Intel after the 2011 Japanese earthquake, tsunami and nuclear crisis. In the aftermath of the triple disaster, Intel, who are recognised as having one of the world's most complex, technologically advanced supply chains,[7] were able to continue trading in Japan amidst the chaos of the disaster recovery operation. That they were able to stay operational was because of long-standing business continuity planning that had been embedded across the product lifecycle – from factory design to testing – and which allowed the supply chain to recover quickly. As Intel themselves proclaimed, 'Global manufacturing operations are organised with flexibility and continuity in mind, with redundancy and expansion capacity built into our factories wherever possible.'[8] Over many decades, Intel had advanced generic rather than specific plans to cope with *any* type of disaster and disruption to safeguard keeping the business going with little or no impact on customers. The plans they drew up focused on relocating operations, deploying redundant processing capacity, maintaining communications throughout the organisation and periodically auditing the business continuity plans across their supply chain to ensure everybody was fully prepared. Especially commendable was the establishment of Intel's Corporate Emergency Operation Center (CEOC) to coordinate multi-site emergency responses, with worldwide on-site emergency operation centres. This system of organisational resilience was activated when the earthquake and tsunami struck. After making sure employees at two Intel facilities in the country were safe, the CEOC focused on supply chain continuity. Some suppliers were asked to provide more parts and materials, and ways were explored to make the chip-manufacturing process more efficient. This was a very successful and coordinated strategy and, according to the company, they were able to prevent production delays throughout the crisis 'as a result of our structured processes, ability to react appropriately, and strong supplier relationships'.[9] It is an exemplar of business continuity in the face of major disruption and how a crisis was turned into an opportunity to innovate and refresh patterns of working.

Intel are not alone in placing a premium on corporate resilience. In 1986 Coca-Cola might well have seen its young customers as the future of the world, the hope of the nation, but in the new millennium, as its CEO Muhtar Kent remarked, 'A global business like Coca-Cola has no choice but to be resilient [as] in some corner of the world there is always an external disruption that can have bearing on our business.'[10] This was likened to doing business in a 'reset world' where a company has to be fully attuned to changes in the external environment that included not only disaster events, but also changes in consumer attitudes and political and economic shifts. Tuning into what is happening around you requires great strategic dexterity and foresight and, as Muhtar Kent proclaimed: 'The world's most resilient organisations are those that do more than just prepare for change and turbulence. Instead, they see – and seize – opportunity in the eye of the storm.'[11] Grabbing this opportunity and meeting corporate expectations to double the size of the business over the course of this decade has led Coca-Cola to build resilience into the whole organisation, from top to bottom, from 'the suppliers, retailers, technologies, people and infrastructure' that bring the beverages to market.[12] To do this Coca-Cola has established a range of company-wide risk management and resilience procedures to help it to continue to thrive amidst disturbance. Such business resilience is defined at Coca-Cola as the requirement 'to strengthen our business, supporting our growth strategies by identifying risks and opportunities and enhancing our ability to respond to disruptive events'.[13] Operationally, the company has also advanced an award-winning business resilience framework that covers seven areas of work that aim to prevent, transfer and respond adequately to risk by better understanding its intricacies and impacts, and to be better able to adapt, based on experience and changing circumstances[14].

Resilience within the context of complex organisations like Intel and Coca-Cola means understanding that long-standing internal processes can be a block on resiliency. In this regard, one of the most studied organisations has been the National Aeronautics and Space Administration – NASA – which suffered two space shuttle disasters in 1986 and in 2003. Both these incidents have been blamed on conventional risk management procedures that in hindsight failed to cope with out of the ordinary conditions. The *Challenger* disaster of 1986 was caused by the failure of the now infamous rubber O-rings on the booster rockets, which cracked in the cold weather, causing the space shuttle to explode as their failure cascaded through its intricate engineered structure. This disaster, which saw seven astronauts lose their lives, cast a shadow over how institutionalised risk procedures that had proved their worth over many decades were found wanting in unusual conditions.[15] Moreover, these failed procedures were repeated in 2003 when protective foam tiles that had fallen off the *Columbia*'s external fuel tank during the launch struck the left wing of the shuttle when it re-entered the Earth's atmosphere, causing damage that ultimately led to the space shuttle disintegrating.

Public management experts Arjen Boin and Michel van Eeten have noted that at NASA there was a deep commitment to astronaut safety and robust processes in place to detect emerging problems based on innovative engineering knowledge, but things still went wrong. Here, 'time-proven safety mechanisms had become institutionalized in its organizational culture' that ultimately proved maladaptive. In this case, the risks to the shuttle were deemed acceptable from an engineering point of view. However, in thinking through the way in which risk decisions were made a host of official evaluation reports concluded that the crucial vulnerability in NASA safety systems was *the inability to deal with surprises* that could not be dealt with by existing protocols. In essence, 'NASA had no proper procedures that would allow the organisation to identify signals of doubts, coming from respected engineers, which were not substantiated by engineering data.'[16] NASA's inflexibility meant it was unable to shift out of its existing procedures when it mattered. In addition, when engineers were shouting about concerns, they were unable to rethink what to do, nor adapt, in accordance with the changing context. Institutional obduracy, and a tension between existing structures and how to cope in conditions of uncertainty had closed off options. This ultimately meant that NASA's ability to adapt in the moment was restricted by the very procedures that for decades had been key elements of a universally respected culture of safety.

ADAPTING PUBLIC BUREAUCRACIES

The private sector was quick to adopt principles of resilience to aid risk management and enhance competitive advantage. Nevertheless, until recently, public organisations and administrations have paid only limited attention to issues of growing risk within ever more complex systems and bureaucracies. Where work was undertaken in the public sector, it has tended to focus on crisis management organisations and how different agencies network and collaborate across organisational boundaries amid disruption. What has become clear here is that public-sector organisations are more constrained in the actions they can take to enhance resilience compared to their private counterparts as a result of additional obligations such as ensuring equality of provision for all, and recent rounds of budget cutting as a result of downsizing or austerity policies.[17]

This is not to say that ideas of resilience have been completely absent from ideas in public administration. In the early 1990s, Christopher Hood, Oxford Professor of Government and Public Administration, identified resilience as one of the key group of ideas becoming influential within the ideas of so-called New Public Management (NPM). NPM ideas developed during the 1980s as part of an effort to make the public service more enterprising and to improve its efficiency by using private-sector approaches. Within this style, resilience was seen in terms of improving endurance, robustness, survival and adaptability, and defined as 'the capacity to withstand and learn from the blows of fate, to avoid "competency traps" in adaptation processes, to keep operating even in adverse "worst case" conditions and to adapt rapidly in a crisis'.[18] In the NPM world, resilience and 'success' were measured in terms of security and reliability and the avoidance of 'down time' in the face of disruption. Additionally, the focus of attention in thinking was placed largely on administrative design rather than the failings of individuals. Such an approach asked questions about the establishment of backup systems that can help maintain normal capacity – redundancy – and the extent to which interdependent parts of the system are integrated or are separated in order to insulate themselves against the spreading of disruption. Similarly, NPM also questioned the ability of an administration to foster diversity. This viewed the maintenance of self-contained units as beneficial in stopping failure from spreading. The argument here is that without a variety of viewpoints 'groupthink' pervades, whereby too many similar opinions about options can lead to decision-making paralysis.

Since their initial introduction into public administration through NPM, resilience ideas have been progressively advanced during the twenty-first century as a way to better understand the effectiveness and efficiency of systems that are increasingly complex, interconnected and at risk from a wide range of disruption and uncertainty. This further extends prior work on accidents and why organisations fail,[19] to focus on how public administrations can thrive in conditions of complexity, bounce back and learn from disruptive challenges. Like many other stories of resilience across different fields of study, the focus of attention has been simultaneously both on how to deal with known risks via tried and tested measures, as well as cultivating a capacity to cope with a variety of unknown future challenges.

The growth in attention to resilience in the public sector is the identified need to be flexible and adaptable in the face of crisis. It is also intended to foster the capability to build a set of 'institutional capacities' that allow the organisation to cope with a wide array of risks and disruptions in order to return to normal as swiftly as possible. Ideas from work on 'learning organisations' that facilitates the development of its members and continuously transforms itself have been influential here. This body of knowledge highlights how organisations can enhance their ability to learn from incidents of disruption or failure, by allowing knowledge exchanges across, and between, organisations. Such observations of learning are central for embedding the agility to deal with known and unknown disruptions, to continuously transform and innovate processes, and to generate the capacities required for resilience. This ever-changing and feedback-rich culture sits in contrast to institutional inertia – the 'stickiness' of institutions – where they tend to move slowly, resist change and perpetuate existing embedded practices. Viewed in this way, resilience represents a complicated challenge, often referred to in the public administration literature as a 'wicked' problem that is difficult or impossible to solve because of imperfect, ambiguous and changing requirements that are often difficult to identify. In this sense 'wicked' has come to imply difficulty overcoming resistance to change.

Work on learning organisations tells us that swapping embedded organisational habits and behaviours for new forms of innovative practice that are more varied and agile, and which sit within organisational structures that are less hierarchical, flatter and more responsive, will enhance resilience. This is about designing institutional routines and developing capacities in normal conditions to be used in extreme conditions, and simply implies the promotion of collaborative decision-making. In essence, the implementation of resilience challenges traditional public administration values and processes in seeking change and transformation towards more integrated and holistic working, rather than command and control leadership models. Enhancing the connectivity of the array of individuals and organisations working in different sectors and silos within strategic resilience efforts is also crucial. But in practice the ceding of power and control to new stakeholders and governance configurations from other public, private and non-profit organisations, as well as the broader public, has proved challenging. This is because resilience implementation in public administrations is, in most cases, in conflict with bureaucratic values such as efficiency, which are difficult to balance with adaptability, redundancy and innovation.

IMPLEMENTING RESILIENCE IN PUBLIC PRACTICE

One example that demonstrates the enhancing of organisational resilience in action comes from the UK, where in mid-2000 legislation mandated local governments to develop Local Resilience Forums (LRFs) to improve responses to a range of emergencies. The aim here was to break out of conventional and remote 'emergency planning' practices and develop a multi-agency partnership across a defined geographical area. This was to ensure that preparing for emergencies was done in a more coordinated and effective way, with all local responders working together. The LRFs were tasked with developing strategic emergency plans detailing how public authorities, emergency services, utility providers, business and civic communities and others would cope with, and respond to, disruptive incidents. The focus here was on both developing a generic plan based on capabilities required to cope with all types of conceivable disruption, as well as detailed plans for particular priority risks faced.

In practice, piecing together such partnership teams and devising plans from stakeholders who had previously often operated in relative isolation was not easy. In reality, this often initially meant not a wholesale change in the operation of local emergency planning networks as desired by government, but a formalisation and expansion of pre-existing arrangements. The new resilience governance system also sought to broaden the scope of the risks to be focused on, with priorities emerging from more detailed risk assessment and horizon-scanning activities. So-called capability reviews were also central in identifying gaps in organisational ability, informing the planning process regarding the scale of response required and using operational exercises to test new procedures and to learn from the experiences.

This example and further empirical studies show that despite the popularity of resilience, its implementation sometimes leads to small incremental changes and the maintenance of existing approaches rather than more radical change. The push for organisational resilience confronts the normal functioning of public administrations by highlighting the need to replace silos with horizontal management, take interdependent linkages with external partners and communities into account and encourage flexible and adaptive processes rather than preserve existing routines that maintain the status quo. The development of organisational resilience further requires managing *both* short-term responsive capacities *and* longer-term transformational ones, represented by the close relationship between different organisations required in responding to crises and disruption.

THE RESILIENT AND SMART CITY

Improving organisational resilience in the public sector is a multifaceted solution to a complex set of problems. It represents a significant challenge because it requires coordination of the efforts of numerous parts of an administration or administrations, adopting flexible and adaptive processes to accommodate changing circumstances. It further means allocating resources to preventative measures in anticipation of uncertain future threats. Nowhere has this been more challenging than in the intricate networks of infrastructure, people and economies that make up contemporary cities.

The twenty-first century more than any other is the century of the city, where rapid growth and greater global connectedness concentrate risk in urban areas and make them increasingly vulnerable to an array of shocks and stresses. The political prioritisation of the safety and security of organisations and communities and the need to enhance preparedness against an array of perceived hazards and threats (including terrorism, earthquakes, disease pandemic, global warming-related flooding, economic crisis and social breakdown) have been focused predominantly on cities because of their particular vulnerability as densely populated political, economic and cultural centres.[20]

Under such circumstances, city managers and administrations are increasingly seeking to enhance *urban resilience* by addressing underlying risk factors and by reducing the exposure and vulnerability of people and assets to a range of current and future threats. Here urban resilience functions as an operational framework for reducing the multiple risks faced by cities, ensuring there are appropriate levels of resources and capacities to mitigate, prepare, respond and recover from a range of disruptions. Urban resilience is ultimately, then, seen as positive change required to avert disaster or keep city services functioning as best they can during disruption.

The adoption of resilience principles at the city level is also reframing and transforming conservative and often rigid organisational practices and structures. Until recently approaches to risk challenges were seen as short-term issues, based on pre-defined technologies and on siloed governance structures or approaches, and have tended to be reactive to particular 'locked in' prior decisions and predicted scenarios based on the simple extrapolation of current trends. By contrast, practices of urban resilience have sought to question these pre-existing assumptions and strived to proactively embed 'foresight', robustness, inclusivity, cost-effectiveness and long-term adaptability into a variety of city-building activities. Increasingly, cities are becoming better at identifying the challenges for which we need to adapt and suggesting a range of alternative scenarios for futureproofing, and when these might need to be implemented.

Technical and 'smart' solutions tend to be at the forefront of such approaches. As urban studies scholar Simon Marvin and colleagues have noted in *Smart Urbanism*, 'All over the world, an emerging form of smart urbanism is increasingly presented as a vital response to meeting the future challenges of the urban condition.'[21] Such a push towards high-tech solutions to current problems and challenges, together with the complexity of the urban condition, are increasingly blending the narratives of resilient and smart cities as urban managers seek ways of envisioning the future metropolis.

The idea of a smart city was centred on combining ubiquitous computing and urban management and it remains characterised by pervasive wireless networks and distributed sensor platforms, which can provide a wealth of real-time information to aid city operations. Both resilience and smart narratives are increasingly concerned with providing the *adaptive capacity* that will allow future cities to cope with an increasingly complex and uncertain future and in monitoring urban areas in order to proactively anticipate risks. Both narratives also seek to take a more strategic and holistic view of the city, trying to knit together, integrate different urban subsystems and better understand their interlinkages. The city is therefore conceived as a 'system of systems', or complex interwoven network of functions and services that cannot be managed effectively in traditional organisational silos.

The parallel development of urban resilience and smart city narratives see technological innovation as a part of, if not the major component in, solutions for coping with current and future urban challenges. This is increasingly being combined in practice through the advance of so-called smart urban resilience.[22] This viewpoint presents a vision of the digitally enhanced and optimally functioning city, where urban managers can deploy predictive technologies to alert them to possible dangers, hazards and service disruption. Adopting such an approach, it is assumed, will subsequently allow the city to bounce back to normal as soon as possible after disruption. For example, multinational computer company IBM brought together ideas of technological functioning and localised pre-emptive resilience in their vision for a smarter city: 'Smarter cities drive sustainable economic growth and prosperity for their citizens. Their leaders have the tools to analyse data for better decisions, anticipate problems to resolve them proactively and coordinate resources to operate effectively.'[23]

Today it is increasingly common for smart cities to be run through operations centres that have emerged to provide insight to city leaders and assist them in advancing a smarter, safer and more efficient city. These futuristic multi-purpose control rooms, more akin to NASA's Mission Control at the Kennedy Space Center in Florida with its ubiquitous banks of computer screens and high-tech gadgetry than to a city government boardroom, have proliferated in dozens of global cities. Operationally, we are increasingly living in the age of dashboard governance,[24] where the key information required to achieve a number of objectives can be visualised and simultaneously viewed on a single screen, extending beyond just the simple monitoring of current information trends, and allowing the operator to see into the future and intervene in real time.[25]

Opened in 2010, the much-celebrated IBM-built 'Intelligent Operations Centre' in Rio de Janeiro, Brazil, now integrates the vast majority of the city's management functions, including transport data from the subways and roads, vehicle accidents, weather patterns, crime statistics, grid updates.[26] It also provides its citizens with real-time social media updates, in what many have hailed as the model for 'smarter city' development. The need identified was generated by a history of fragmented government operations and the need to bring together diverse information held by different government departments in one amalgamated data set that could be utilised in one central place. As an IBM press release noted of the Rio Operations Centre, it 'integrates over 20 city departments to improve emergency response management and collaboration across the city. Predictive analytics capabilities use information to decide how to best react to current events and how to best plan for what is likely to happen in the future in order to minimise impact on citizens.'[27]

Another emblematic example of tech-driven smart urban resilience comes from Mexico City, where a state-of-the-art surveillance centre was built in 2011 by the Mexican telecoms giant Telex and the French military supplier Thales. Here the control centre amalgamates the data feeds from up to 47 municipal agencies and provides an array of advanced tools for surveillance, crisis response and day-to-day city operations. Thales, whose self-proclaimed objective for the project was to 'simplify complexity', argued that this centre served to empower strategic decision-makers by 'delivering clear, timely and operationally relevant information about their environment'.[28] Most notably, the military-inspired and cryptically named C4I4 control centre[29] has been hailed as the centrepiece of *Ciudad Segura*, the world's most ambitious urban security programme, established to help the city cope with spiralling crime rates and improve security across the metropolis.[30] The centre has the capability to monitor the city's thousands of surveillance cameras to assess crowd density and movements, as well track vehicles in the city's main streets thanks to its automatic number plate recognition technology. Additionally, the operations room can monitor and activate the city's system of panic buttons, loudspeakers and a range of environmental sensors that are able to capture and analyse weather systems and seismic sensors, all in real time.[31]

In the smart and resilient city, big data monitoring via dashboard-enabled control rooms, fed by an array of sensors, field devices, new technologies and social media analytics, provide 'new mediating points through which knowledge about the urban context is coordinated, produced and enacted'.[32] This has created opportunities to utilise a greater amount of information to aid resilience-focused practices and to better understand the changing nature of city life. However, such a vision of the future city is not unproblematic and raises a number of key questions in relation to whose resilience is being enhanced and by whom. Often, concerns over a lack of transparency come to the fore, raising questions about how, in search of greater resilience, we had better balance social and political acceptability with technological and economic concerns. While social factors have often been overlooked in the smart cities drive, concerns over data privacy and bulk data surveillance are necessitating that ethical and legal questions are increasingly at the forefront of technological advancement in the smart urban resilience field.

As smart cities have evolved, social life has become increasingly networked and interconnected, with the digital realm aided particularly through algorithms – computer codes embedded into technology to solve problems by auto-generating solutions – and with artificial intelligence occupying an increasingly central role in city decision-making. Such 'algorithmic urbanism' uses code to predict what will happen in an urban environment, not only making predictions about individual data flows but, by mashing everything together, to model an entire city, and predicting how citizens will interact with urban infrastructure. The attempts of such operation centres to understand, declutter and simplify the disordered complexity of urban systems inevitably mean that what is represented on urban dashboards is 'sanitized, decontextualized, and necessarily partial'.

This in turn necessitates that we need to pay particular attention to the political and ethical biases that could be fed into how this smart system is configured, and what this means for public administration, values of transparency and maximising citizen participation.[33]

More fundamentally, the drive for smart urban resilience raises questions about inbuilt risk. Put simply, do smart city systems enhance resiliency or do they increase vulnerability? On one hand smart systems can aid urban managers' awareness regarding risks faced and desired amelioration measures. However, on the other hand the economic modelling of smart cities based on the optimisation of services is, by design, driving out redundancy, or slack, from urban systems, as networked infrastructures are ever more tightly coupled. This has the side effect of enhancing vulnerability through a reduced capacity to adapt, transform and innovate within an increasingly interdependent urban system. Such networked and cyber-driven assemblages have been shown to be particularly predisposed to systemic failure, or overloading, increasing susceptibility to 'cascade failure' within and between a range of critical urban infrastructural systems and vulnerability to being hacked. As smart city experts Rob Kitchin and Martin Dodge have noted, 'Smart city technologies are promoted as an effective way to counter and manage uncertainty and urban risks through the effective and efficient delivery of services, yet paradoxically they create new vulnerabilities and threats, including making city infrastructure and services insecure, brittle and open to extended forms of criminal activity.'[34] For example, a cyber-attack targeting city services in Atlanta, Georgia in March 2018 created a serious impact on the city's ability to deliver basic services, taking months to resolve and costing millions of dollars to rectify. This ransomware hack, at the time the worst cyber-incursion into any US city, disabled 30 per cent of the software programs used by the city, and affected a number of central city services, including online services for citizens to pay bills and request utility services.

INTERNATIONALISING CITY RESILIENCE-BUILDING

During the twenty-first century, the quest for greater urban resilience has gone global, being adopted internationally by a range of global governance networks. Notably, the United Nations Office for Disaster

Risk Reduction (UNISDR) 'How to Make Cities More Resilient' campaign launched in 2012 aims to increase the resilience of cities to disasters and climate change impacts by utilising a risk-based approach to steer decision-making. This campaign now has nearly 3,500 city members, mainly in the global south.

From a more Western-centred viewpoint, more than 100 major cities throughout the world have joined the 100 Resilient Cities (100RC) programme, pioneered by the Rockefeller Foundation, to develop resilience strategies to face down disruptive events and address vulnerabilities that amplify crises and erode coping abilities. Launched in 2013, the 100RC campaign is 'dedicated to helping cities around the world become more resilient to the physical, social and economic challenges that are a growing part of the 21st century'.[35] In mapping out these challenges, urban resilience was seen as 'the capacity of individuals, communities, institutions, businesses, and systems within a city to survive, adapt, and grow no matter what kinds of chronic stresses and acute shocks they experience'. While this approach has many of the hallmarks of emerging approaches to organisational resilience in both the public and private sector, it differs in the explicit focus it gives to the leadership required to facilitate joined-up thinking. Thus, key within the 100RC campaign is the funded appointment of a chief resilience officer (CRO), who works directly with the chief executive, or mayor, of a city, pursuing collaborations across government, private and non-profit sectors. As Michael Berkowitz, the then CEO of the initiative noted, an effective CRO is a person able to 'work across the sectors and siloes to coordinate, to connect the dots, to advocate, to keep the resilience issues and resilience perspective in all the decisions that the city is making'.[36] In practice, the CROs and their coordinating units are becoming like dealers in trading zones where they are expected to maintain the network and negotiate agreements to embed resilience principles throughout the DNA of all city operations.[37]

BUILDING BACK BETTER

One of the most 'at risk' cities in the Rockefeller network of cities is New Orleans, whose struggles with post-Hurricane Katrina recovery display organisational change in action in pursuit of greater resiliency. When

Hurricane Katrina struck in August 2005, its devastating impact was, at the time, the costliest and most devastating environmental disaster in US history. The hurricane and subsequent floods cost nearly 2,000 lives and caused property damage along the Gulf coast from central Florida to Texas estimated at the time at $108 billion, much of this due to a storm surge. The most significant death and destruction occurred in New Orleans, where the levee system flooded, leaving 80 per cent of the city under water. The subsequent recovery and rebuilding programme has illustrated the maladaptive nature of historical flood defences, and facilitated a larger discussion about how best to enhance future urban resilience in innovative, adaptive and equitable ways.

The impact of Katrina on the city in 2005 highlighted a string of failures around a lack of preparedness and coordination by and between local, state and national government stakeholders, requiring a significant overhaul. In their forensic account *Clear as Mud*,[38] planners Robert Olshansky and Laurie Johnson shone a light on the complex and contested politics of post-disaster recovery in the city as it sought to embed resilience principles into future development activities. This has been a far from easy process and was beset by complex administrative issues played out across multiple scales and involving multiple agencies and funding arrangements. *Clear as Mud* is also a tale of failure and maladaptation, especially of the levee system that broke, and the negligent decisions to site large swathes of housing for the poor in flood-prone areas.

While Katrina was a catastrophic event it was, as Olshansky and Johnson noted, 'decades in the making' and exacerbated by significant and underestimated vulnerabilities. This local institutional context is worth detailing, as it highlights how decisions made years before can be 'locked in' to current and future decisions, severely compromising attempts to increase urban resilience in the present. In this case, there was a systematic recycling of mitigation and design failure in relation to the levee system that was to provide flood protection. A succession of levee-building programmes – notably after the Great Mississippi Flood of 1927[39] and Hurricane Betsy in 1965 – served to encourage new development in low-lying areas, instead of being seen as a warning of high flood risk, increasing the exposure of thousands of households. The city lived with a false sense of security, reinforced by national risk management policies, which had allowed thousands of dwellings to be built in vulnerable areas with only minimal protection (yet which were still eligible for flood insurance).[40] By 2005, this engineering-focused protective system was still incomplete, having been delayed by political wrangling, tax cuts, reductions in design standards and construction quality, as well as ongoing maintenance problems, all of which contributed to the systems failure when Katrina hit.

Katrina further represented a failure of anticipation and good governance. Resilience is increasingly premised upon accurate risk assessment and the prediction of future danger. In the case of Hurricane Katrina, the risks and vulnerabilities were apparent and well known.[41] However, they were not dealt with adequately because of tensions between national and local government, and fear of overreacting and spending limited resources in a disproportionate way. Notably, the restructuring of the Federal Emergency Management Agency (FEMA) – an outcome of the post-9/11 reorganisation of emergency management with the creation of the Department of Homeland Security and the establishment of a new, all-hazards national response system – gave the agency less power and responsibility for integrating various emergency functions and federal response plans. Significantly, this had shifted some of their function away from 'natural' disasters and towards counter-terrorism. Combined with a reduced federal budget for new levee construction, this left many fearful that a large-scale hurricane would devastate New Orleans. In the late 1990s and again in early 2000s, the US Army Corps of Engineers and the Environmental Protection Agency unsuccessfully sought significant federal funds for wetland restoration to act as a hurricane impact buffer. Consequently, one senator prophetically noted in 2005, just before Hurricane Katrina hit: 'It's not a question of if; it's a question of when. Instead of spending millions now, we are going to spend billions later.'[42]

If pre-disaster preparedness was chaotic then the planning of the city's recovery and rebuilding was equally fraught and disjointed. In the wake of Katrina, up to 49 neighbourhoods advanced their own recovery plans, with very little integration between them as consensus could not initially be reached. Over time, these myriad local plans were replaced by a legally binding master plan where transparency and citizen participation has significantly improved within neighbourhood planning projects.

Public administrators have further sought to reduce vulnerabilities and enhance resiliency in New Orleans. Interventions have been focused not only on the technical and engineering efforts previously used in attempts to mitigate the impact of hurricanes, but increasingly on adaptation and nature-driven responses. Attempts to 'build back better' in New Orleans played out as a series of tensions between rapid restoration and longer-term sustainable and equitable change, most notably in the pressures to abandon large swathes of the city to water, providing a buffer against future hurricane impact. This culminated in the 2013 Greater New Orleans Urban Water Plan; a long-term vision for urban water management and the first regional urban water plan in the United States. The plan sought to meet the challenges of the city's precarious coastal location, and the growing risk of climate change-induced storms and flooding, through a more holistic approach. The central aim of this plan was to use the landscape as protective infrastructure and to repurpose wasted water assets to provide better spaces for residents to enjoy. As opposed to the overly technical and 'single purpose' designs of the past, the approach was formulated through a series of local workshops as part of a collaborative design process inspired by the Dutch adaptive delta management approach (see chapter 4). The Urban Water Plan is essentially a resiliency planning study that aims to develop sustainable strategies for managing the water resources and provide a roadmap for mitigating flood risk, and improving the quality of water for all.[43]

Ten years after Hurricane Katrina, in 2015, city authorities further launched their long-term vision for overall urban resilience up until 2050 – Resilient New Orleans. This strategic policy was the centrepiece of the city's participation in the 100RC initiative and demonstrated the remarkable progress taken by the City of New Orleans to improve resiliency in the wake of catastrophe and the need to plan in the face of future uncertainty.[44] What resiliency efforts in New Orleans demonstrate is the need to embrace change. Open-ended processes of design have been used as a medium to interrogate different possibilities, utilising innovative methods to establish different adaptive pathways. By advancing resilient urbanism in this way, risk management has been enmeshed within urban development practices through an ongoing, collaborative process that seeks to eliminate maladaptation and enhance adaptive capacity within the built environment and local communities, as a means to survive in an increasingly volatile world with 'new normal' levels of urban risk.

A BLUEPRINT FOR ORGANISATIONAL RESILIENCE?

Not only has improving organisational decision-making in pursuit of resilience gone global, the need to enhance organisational agility is also increasingly an international best practice to which both the public and private sectors aspire. In 2017, the International Organization for Standardization (ISO), a worldwide federation of national standards bodies, produced a blueprint standard for organisational resilience of any size and type, industry or sector. This standard argued that organisational resilience should be a strategic organisational goal for effectively managing risk. Resilience, it noted, was key for any organisation wanting to thrive in an ever-changing world, with 'Organisational Resilience – Principles and Attributes' providing the context to better understand resilience and providing a 'framework to help organisations futureproof their business'.[45] Here organisational resilience was seen as 'the ability of an organisation to absorb and adapt in a changing environment to enable it to deliver its objectives and to survive and prosper'.[46] A commitment to enhanced organisational resilience was seen to contribute to better anticipation of risks and vulnerabilities, to improved coordination and integration of management disciplines, and to lead to a more nuanced understanding of external relationships that impinge on organisational goals.[47]

Importantly, there is a specific emphasis in the ISO guide on creating a culture that supports resilience throughout an organisation; a characteristic that has long been overlooked in technical and bureaucratic programmes for managing risk. As such the international standard supports a far more holistic notion of resilience than, for example, a focus on supply chains. It recommends not just building an understanding of external context but establishing the capability to influence it not only through coping with disruption but also through cultural change. In short, organisational resilience 'is influenced by the way in which uncertainty is addressed, decisions are made and enacted, and how people work together'.[48]

However, enhancing resilience at the level of the organisation, whatever type or form, is far from easy as it is predicated on transitioning from a less resilient set-up. The rolling out of this ISO standard or national equivalent across thousands of businesses has highlighted inherent tensions that organisations face when embracing the changes they need to better control risk. In looking at the take-up of the ISO equivalent British Standard, management expert David Denyer noted that leaders have had to consider what drives the need for organisational resilience and what the possibility of this being achieved is. He argued that in terms of drivers, leaders need to distinguish between those that are *defensive* (stopping bad or unwanted things happening and protecting results) and those that are *progressive* (making good or desired things happen and achieving results). In terms of thinking through how resilience can be achieved, is it *consistency* (standard routines) that is emphasised or should a focus be placed on delivering changes that improve *flexibility* (agility and adaptability)?[49]

These four traits, if placed in a quadrant, allow four perspectives on organisational resilience to be illuminated, often reflecting on the ability of organisations to change. First, preventative control – a combination of defensive and consistent behaviours – that often characterises technical organisations, such as critical infrastructure providers, who already have a strong safety culture and where the move towards resilience often involves tweaks in existing practice. Second, what Denyer refers to as 'mindful action' – a combination of defensive and flexible approaches – where the importance is placed on advancing a culture of resilience to improve the overall capability of an organisation to respond well to disruption. Here, in moving away from situations that might paralyse decision-making by groupthink, multiple perspectives for determining problems and solutions are sought to challenge evidence and embedded assumptions. Third, performance optimisation – an amalgamation of progressive and consistence approaches – where there is a focus on improving existing competencies to boost efficiency and enhance productivity. This is typically undertaken by refining existing approaches rather than fundamental transformation, and only intervening in radical adjustment if necessary. Here, progression in organisational resilience focuses on trying to create a situation of 'zero trauma' where change occurs steadily and is controlled and implemented in sequential steps. Fourth, adaptive innovation that combines progression and flexibility where improving organisational resilience is about proactively changing before it is too late and is focused on learning and innovation. Here, risk-free creative thinking is encouraged to view problems afresh and to serve as a catalyst to change underlying assumptions, customs and practices. Ultimately, decisions for transformative change should be arrived at by consensus and flow through the organisation from top to bottom.

TOWARDS ADAPTIVE INNOVATION FOR AGILE ORGANISATIONS

However, despite all the talk of organisational resilience, the majority of organisations are still ill prepared to deal with uncertainty and create adaptive response capabilities. In the new century, there is a greater urgency for organisations to embrace resilience-thinking when confronting a multitude of possible disruptions that can affect how they function and perform. Amidst the impact of extreme weather events induced by climate change, fear of terror attack, cyber-disruption, ongoing economic crises, erratic political behaviour and a host of other difficulties, organisations are increasingly seeking to ensure they are not only better able to anticipate and respond to potential risks, but that they can positively harness the opportunities which disruption brings.

Whether it is a multinational private corporation, utility company or city partnership, the need to consider how organisations function and adapt to changing circumstances is a key focus for resilience. Here, context, as in all good resilience approaches, is considered vital with all the standard documents clear that they do not 'promote uniformity in approach across all organisations' and that initiatives should be fit for purpose and 'tailored to suit an individual organisation's needs'.[50] Innovation should be especially encouraged. Doing things differently and ensuring that the future is not an extrapolation of the past requires a change in mindset and, in particular, an approach to failure and experimentation that sees it as a trial and error learning opportunity, rather than something that should be punished and never tried again if it does not work.

While acknowledging that different organisations will adapt in diverse ways from divergent start points, and follow differing pathways, we can draw out a number of umbrella principles or attributes that inform the enhancement of resilience across a wide range of organisational types and which can be utilised to plan resilience. This poses questions as to which organisational designs need to be created to match the complex landscape of risks and threats that are now confronting organisations. It also asks how adaptive behaviours can be promoted in an environment where existing institutional habits can be difficult to overcome.

First, organisations need better knowledge about the risks and dangers they face. Improving risk awareness and the development of sentinel capabilities, which enable anticipation and understanding of emerging threats to an organisation and their supply chain, is central to the avoidance of reaching tipping points. With an appreciation of the enhanced complexity, and the types of risk faced, organisations are increasingly focusing not only on known risks that have traditionally been the preserve of risk management, but also giving more attention to unknown risks, especially low-probability high-impact 'black swan' events. Often advanced forms of scenario planning are undertaken to identify risks, map these against organisational objectives and devise contingencies for coping and thinking through how disruption may become an opportunity to innovate and bounce back better.

Second, the ability to shape shift is paramount. Resilience is moving away from a focus on preserving the status quo, or defensive notions of achieving stability, and towards the need to improve agility and flexibility. This can be developed as a result of learning from experiences (an institution's own, or those of others, including failures) or simulated events or stress testing. For example, a firm might adopt standard processes and products that are interchangeable, giving it more agility to withstand and recover from significant disruptions, as well as better respond to fluctuations in product demand. Emergency planning networks might also run a mock exercise based on a cyber or terrorist attack scenario and report on how the multitude of involved stakeholders communicated with each other, followed protocol or successfully deployed equipment. It is only through such exercising that gaps in plans and procedures reveal themselves, presenting an opportunity to adapt operating approaches before a real-life disruption hits.

Third, do not put all your eggs in one basket: have a contingency strategy. Resilience is most effective when it allows several ideas to run in parallel. While this might run contrary to traditional ways of working that tend to prioritise a singular best option, in an uncertain world we need more than a Plan A. Organisations need to develop a Plan B, C, D and beyond, envisioning a range of adaptive pathways that can be put into practice in the face of future disruption. Creating alternative pathways also poses a question of how much spare capacity, redundancy or slack there should be within an organisation, or its supply chain, to give it breathing space following a disruption. This is often projected as a cost-benefit calculation, and frequently viewed as an expensive, suboptimal option that can lead to cost increases in products or procedures. There is clearly a delicate balancing act at play in how much slack should be planned for, as focusing on building redundancy that might assist in coping with a possible disruption can inhibit the efficiency of operations in normal conditions.

Fourth, change and doing things differently is a necessity. Resilience is all about adjusting patterns, innovating and being willing – and able – to change. Organisations need to consider what factors might be required to enable change and, conversely, what factors are currently blocking change possibilities. The resilience journey should help organisations arrive at a new terminus by disrupting custom and practice routines and opening minds to new possibilities. This poses a key question about how best to restructure the activities of organisations in order to break down the structures that protect traditional bureaucratic settings, such as command and control leadership, and risk averseness, while simultaneously moving towards proactively developing overall organisational resilience.

Fifth, you cannot function in isolation and build resilience. Organisations are not islands and therefore understanding the linkages and 'interdependencies' with other organisations in a vicinity, or within a complex network of suppliers, has been central to the current resilience surge. As US political scientist Stephen Flynn has pointed out: 'Companies also need to make sure that they look outside their gates and map their dependencies on the local community and regional systems. It is futile to become an island of resilience in a sea of fragility.'[51] The aim should be to spread resilience practice beyond the boundary of one organisation and to produce and sustain mutual relationships with other stakeholders and sectors that allow a collective response to responding to, or recovering from, crisis or disruption. This might come in the form of London producing a citywide emergency response plan with a large array of emergency responders, public authorities, private businesses and community and voluntary groups. It might also be demonstrated by Coca-Cola producing a business-wide contingency plan across its entire supply chain.

Sixth, there is no 'I' in team. Building resilience is a challenge requiring collective action. Nobody wants another NASA, where conventional decision-making removed alternative viewpoints. Good collaboration and teamwork, integrated working and the avoidance of organisational silos have been shown repeatedly to be key in seamless organisational resilience operations. While, conventionally, hierarchical arrangements tend to frame problems and provide solutions in terms of action plans, more recently new and increasingly plural governance approaches are extending traditional processes through dialogue and consensus building with a greater number of stakeholders. Ultimately, better decisions emerge from a diverse group.

Seventh, resilience-thinking, for many establishments, represents a new dawn and should be allowed to infiltrate through the entire organisation. Just as changing structures and processes is vital in transitioning towards organisational resilience, adapting culture, values and leadership is essential in 'mainstreaming' resilience-thinking through an organisation. This will help create an ethos with shared beliefs and values that enable devolved decision-making and problem solving. Building a culture of resilience and applying it not just within internal operations but upstream to suppliers and connected stakeholders further defines a resilient organisation. Here organisational resilience can be viewed as both a top-down activity in terms of values and direction setting and one that is delivered by others lower down the chain of command. Such shared cultural traits, depending on context, might include a well-informed and engaged workforce allowing better decisions in the face of the disruption; distributed leadership models rather than hierarchies; and a conditioning for coping with disruption because of learning from smaller, everyday disruptions that serves to streamline response and recovery processes.

Overall, resilience-thinking provides a management – or governance – framework for addressing such complexity and future disruptive challenges. It further advances institutional capabilities that improve the capacity to prepare for, and respond to, disruption and to advance a new culture that can aid organisational adaptation and development. Despite the availability of ample evidence of its utility and a range of standards about how to do it, the bold and innovative transformation called for by organisational resilience often falls foul of rational economics that suggest that change is costly but without a calculable payoff. This has meant that the benefits of building a resilient organisation are usually considered alongside long-term costs and the disruption to stable working practices.

Resilience is not a zero sum game and pivoting towards resilience will cost time and money. Potential savings from being better prepared to respond to disruption are always hypothetical and are not included in annual accounts. Making the business case for organisational resilience is not easy and cannot rely on cost-avoidance alone. However, facilitating change in organisational structure and processes, and growing a culture of resilience, can help focus an organisation and make it more flexible and responsive to external changes. Collaborative advantages accrued by the push towards resilience can thus infer competitive advantages in terms of the ability to react to unknown disruptions and market fluctuations with more agility. In short, organisations should invest time and effort in resilience to both reduce their vulnerability to disruptive events and improve their performance by enhancing the ability to capitalise on opportunities that disruption brings. There is no point in advocating resilience after a disruption has occurred just as it is pointless to close the barn door after the horse has bolted. Organisations must act on resilience now. To survive and thrive amidst turbulent times, where disruption is increasingly common, organisations must continuously adapt, or die.

8

DISASTER RESILIENCE: WHERE IT ALL COMES TOGETHER

Disaster comes only because of ignorance.

Judah the Prince

Disaster resilience is everyone's business and is a shared responsibility among citizens, the private sector, and government.

US National Academies, 2012

On 12 January 2010, just before 5 p.m. local time, a magnitude 7.0 earthquake hit Haiti, followed later by sizeable aftershocks. The quake lasted only 35 seconds but incredible destruction and chaos ensued. Between 100,000 and 300,000 people died and over 300,000 were injured, although reliable figures are unlikely ever to be produced. It was estimated that three million people were affected by the quake – nearly one-third of the country's total population. Of these, over one million were left homeless in the immediate aftermath. Eighty per cent of rural housing was destroyed. Poorly constructed buildings built over many previous decades collapsed. In 2017, nearly 40,000 people were still displaced from their homes with many areas remaining uninhabitable, and over 2.5 million citizens were still in need of humanitarian aid.

The collapsed buildings and destroyed infrastructure that defined the war-like landscape of the disaster zone came, in large part, because of Haiti's lack of building codes. Without adequate reinforcement, such structures disintegrated under the force of the quake, killing or trapping their occupants. Nearly 4,000 schools were damaged or destroyed. In the capital, Port-au-Prince, the main cathedral and the National Palace were both heavily damaged, as were the UN headquarters and many other government buildings. The city's already damaged and fragile critical infrastructures – a result of devastating tropical storms that tore through the country in the summer of 2008 – were ill-equipped to deal with a significant seismic shock. The quake also decimated the majority of the country's crops and irrigation canals, dealing a devastating blow to an agriculturally reliant society.

A large-scale humanitarian assistance operation immediately swung into action in order to provide medical assistance, food and water to survivors. Many countries around the world pledged funds and dispatched rescue and medical teams. Tent encampments sprang up everywhere but many remained in camps for a long time or returned to damaged structures. Relief efforts were significantly hampered by the lack of electric power, the loss of communication lines, limited supplies of gasoline and main roads being blocked with debris. After a week, little aid had reached beyond Port-au-Prince. Conditions on the ground were desperate, with crowded and unsanitary conditions giving way to looting, as things got progressively worse as a result of the breakdown in social order. Hospitals were largely unusable, a combination of destroyed buildings and a lack of power meaning survivors were forced to wait days for treatment. Morgues quickly filled up and corpses were stacked in the streets. Then in October, nine months after the quake, disease struck with cases of cholera surfacing. This was a result of raw sewage from the encampments of UN peacekeeping forces flowing into the main rivers. It created an epidemic that eventually affected nearly 1 million people and killed over 9,000.

Humanitarian recovery efforts were further hampered by confusion over who was in charge of the recovery effort. In the following months concern was expressed by the Haitian prime minister, who claimed that the numerous foreign non-governmental organisations (NGOs) were not monitoring their activities, making it almost impossible for the Haitian government to accurately work out where best to deploy its own resources. The one-size-fits-all model of relief adopted by the NGOs proved ineffective and lacked adaptability. Large areas of the capital remained without power for significant stretches during any given day because of stalled repairs on the electricity grid. A distrust of humanitarian organisations further grew due to the slow pace of rebuilding, despite vast quantities of pledged international aid. One relief organisation was accused of wasting half a billion dollars in donated funds by building only six homes while siphoning off millions of dollars on internal expenses. Similar claims were levelled against another well-known aid agency who were accused of using their position to help leverage reconstruction contracts for overseas firms.

The Haiti earthquake was dubbed the first social media disaster, as survivors took to social networking sites to search for information to help reunite them with their families. The Internet was also central for coordinating initial relief efforts. One project crowd-sourced feeds from Twitter and Facebook to assist aid organisations in constructing maps of the areas affected, and in determining where to best allocate resources. Fundraising was additionally facilitated through social media. The Red Cross, whose previous largest fundraising campaign had raised $190,000, successfully raised US$8 million within the first three days through their various social media profiles.

The remarkable resilience of the Haitian people shone through in the wake of the 2010 quake, with the population quickly coming together to help each other, collectively working with rudimentary tools to save people from the wreckage, to find enough food and to set up makeshift clinics to treat the injured. The years following the 2010 disaster have been peppered with further catastrophic events which have enhanced ongoing famine and poverty crises, but community resilience has remained strong as after each tragedy the rebuilding process begins once again.[1]

Over time, programmes of resilience building have been enacted as a priority to enable the community to be better prepared for disasters. Key to such efforts has been building strong bonds between community members that will be invaluable when disaster hits. Programmes have also been put in place to teach citizens to identify risks and vulnerabilities in the community and to prepare for potential disasters, as well as how to conduct evacuation effectively.

In contrast to community-centred recovery efforts, a different story unfolded when it came to post-disaster reconstruction. Instead of a collective community response, what was witnessed was a race to the bottom as firms competed for no-bid contracts to rebuild the island's infrastructure. In a modern-day gold rush, disaster capitalism ran wild.[2] Catastrophe represented an opportunity not only to build back but also to make money in the process. Only a small fraction of the estimated $14 billion in pledged aid found its way into the pockets of ordinary citizens, as predatory capitalism trumped the humanitarian mission. In an unprecedented money grab, companies actively competed for reconstruction contracts at a luxury Miami hotel a mere two months after the earthquake. Getting the Haitian economy back up and running as quickly as possible saw massive investment from Washington poured in to construct state-of-the-art business parks. In late 2011, standing alongside former US President Bill Clinton, the Haitian president proclaimed the island was 'open for business' with a focus on attracting multinational companies to purpose-built factories that were easily supplied with abundant and cheap labour.

While Haiti's pre-earthquake high levels of poverty, weak governance and poorly built and maintained infrastructure compounded disaster recovery, the post-quake situation in 2010 elucidates many lessons about the usefulness of enhancing disaster resilience. It showcases how politics, social needs, economic deals, infrastructure supply and organisational arrangements intersect in many and varied ways before, during and after disasters. The 2010 disaster was both a shock event of devastating power, but also a 'slow-burn' event, years in the making.

*

Recent major disasters and serious disruptions have put increased emphasis on how quickly somewhere can recover following a large-scale shock and have meant that disaster risk reduction or *disaster resilience* has grown in prominence. When we look at how to interpret the great transition from risk towards resilience in the early twenty-first century, then we can look to disasters for many explanations. Whether in terms of the relatively simple characterisation that sees risk viewed differently as the modern passes into the postmodern era, or how we get to grips with reframing disaster as a complex human-induced process rather than something that is 'natural' or divine, disasters illuminate many reasons why we need to invest in resilience as an urgent futureproofing strategy. Responses to disasters can also teach us lessons about a darker and more unethical side of resilience that needs to be surfaced.

A disaster is a large and complex jigsaw puzzle and much more than the sum of its parts. Like resilience, it can mean different things to different people, but generally it can be considered 'a serious disruption of the functioning of a society, causing widespread human, material or environmental losses which exceed the ability of the affected society to cope using its own resources'.[3] Understanding disasters and disaster resilience is to appreciate the interconnected nature of what causes vulnerability and what can be done to reduce risk. This asks some fundamental questions: how are natural or man-made hazards assessed and how much are they a consequence of poor decision-making and human intervention in natural systems? How have decades of neglect weakened critical infrastructure to the point of collapse when stress is applied? How well do we prepare for disaster, and is disaster response organised as a joined-up endeavour? How are local people involved in resilience efforts before, during and after a disaster? How does new technology and social media come to the rescue in a disaster zone? To what extent is the cause of disaster and rebuilding works entwined with capitalist markets and private security contractors where profits trump social concerns? And, ultimately, how can disaster resilience help us plan better for an uncertain future in ways that enhance resilience for all?

In exploring these questions, this chapter focuses on the shift from just coping with disaster to being resilient to a disastrous event. Unpacking this transition will illuminate a number of key trends in evidence before, during and after a disaster that connect to causes, vulnerabilities, preparation and recovery operations. First, it has become clear that disasters are *not natural* occurrences and viewing them in such a way blinds decision-makers to their own failures. Blaming nature for human-induced activity and decisions that enhance risk and increase vulnerability is a cop-out and needs to be challenged. Second, in untangling the threads of a disaster, we can see an explicit unfairness unfolding as the free market seeks opportunity in crisis while the socially and economically sidelined remain in desperate need. In thinking through the important two-part question of resilience for whom by whom we need to be very aware of the tendency for exploitative 'disaster capitalism' to take hold quickly. Third, and more positively, disasters have promoted a revaluation of our collective need to enhance resilience against an array of shocks and stresses and to try as far as possible to futureproof our world. Such collectivism is evident in unified strategies for disaster resilience at local, national and international levels. However, is there evidence that such approaches are succeeding as disaster events continue to become more frequent and impactful, with the year 2017 unprecedented for costly disaster events? This forces us to constantly re-evaluate if more could, and should, be done to give society the tools to bounce forward after a disaster and to keep us safe in the uncertain future.

THE DRIVE TO REDUCE RISKS

Until recently, the focus of disaster management activities had been on coping with events as they unfold. Now a renewed focus is being placed on reducing the risk and vulnerability faced, and the damage caused, by a full range of hazards. What has become known as disaster risk reduction is underpinned by an ethic of prevention and takes the view, much like a doctor treating a patient, that prevention is better than cure. This approach tries to reduce exposure to hazards, which will decrease the vulnerability of people and property, while at the same time improving preparedness and early warning for disruptive events. Disaster risk reduction is about making better choices and takes the view that there is no such thing as a 'natural' disaster, only natural hazards. Disasters are the manifestation of how much impact a hazard has on society and the environment, making us more vulnerable to – or more resilient against – them.

Discussions about the cause of disaster being supernatural, natural or man-made have been debated over many centuries. As we saw earlier, in the wake of the great Lisbon earthquake of 1755, philosophers of the day argued that patterns of building combined with geological causes had led to disaster. Ever since then it has become clear that disasters result from a combination of hazards and human decision-making that has enhanced vulnerability. While natural hazards occur and have impact, a disaster does not come out of nowhere. There is now a consensus that disasters occur when societies, and the locations where they live, have increased their risk and vulnerability. Despite such a consensus being reached, government, international organisations and especially the media continuously label such disasters as 'natural' or in some cases 'acts of god'. An act of nature does not cause a disaster; extreme vulnerability does. Natural disasters are a myth that we need to expose if we are to reduce disaster risk and build resilience. We need to reveal how disasters are related to, for example, maladaptive urban planning, human-induced climate change, decrepit infrastructure, rapid and unchecked urbanisation and environmental degradation which compound the effects of natural hazards, cause a disaster or enhance its impact. These are largely human acts. They are not acts of nature or god.

Calls to drop the 'natural disaster' tag are periodically mobilised in the wake of catastrophic disasters but it persists, fundamentally affecting how the public perceives risk. Eminent anthropologist and geographer Neil Smith, writing in the aftermath of Hurricane Katrina in 2005 argued that there's no such thing as a natural disaster, reasoning that 'in every phase and aspect of a disaster ... the contours of disaster and the difference between who lives and who dies is to a greater or lesser extent a social calculus'.[4] Like the Enlightenment philosopher Rousseau after the Lisbon earthquake, Smith argued that it was 'important in the heat of the moment to put social science to work as a counterweight to official attempts to relegate Katrina to the historical dustbin of inevitable "natural" disasters'.[5] When such an analysis was undertaken, it readily revealed a number of important features that turned a tropical storm into a large-scale disaster.

First, in terms of *causes*, we cannot separate out natural hazards from social processes, with Katrina being widely seen as evidence of increasingly extreme weather because of human-induced climatic change. While some still dispute the science underpinning climate change, it would be foolhardy to ignore the strong indication that rising seas and more frequent weather abnormalities are not random occurrences. However, politicians immediately declared the death and destruction of Katrina to be an act of nature. Here, as Smith argued, the supposed 'naturalness of disasters' become an 'ideological camouflage for the social (and therefore preventable) dimensions of such disasters, covering for quite specific social interests'.

Second, in terms of *vulnerability*, some residents of New Orleans were clearly more vulnerable than others as a result of centuries of class and racial bias in city decision-making. This left large concentrations of poor and largely black communities living in lower-lying flood-prone areas. As attempts to evacuate so tragically illustrated, the wealthy got out of the city in their cars and had adequate supplies and credit to support their departure. They could also rely on insurance to support rebuilding once the waters subsided. This was the polar opposite to many poor and vulnerable communities where evacuation under their own steam wasn't an option and where insurance was unobtainable or unaffordable.

Third, the poor level of *preparedness* crippled responses to the impending disaster. At all levels of government, the risks from such extreme weather events were well known and tested for. However, when Katrina hit Florida days before New Orleans, and began to pick up more and more energy, turning into an almost unprecedented storm, no out-of-the-ordinary preparations were in evidence. No FEMA personal were on the ground until New Orleans was submerged. The organisation was hamstrung by being overseen by an inexperienced political appointment and having its budgets cut to subsidise homeland security.

The devastation of Hurricane Katrina was *unnatural*, precipitated by decades of poor, ideologically or class-based decision-making that enhanced risk and vulnerability for the poorest and most in need. It is a terrible indictment in one of the world's wealthiest nations, but is far from an isolated occurrence. The same accusations emerge from many recent disasters that have brought destruction and misery to millions around the globe and which are sloppily labelled as natural disasters in the media and among a range of influential policy-makers. These, oddly, are often the same commentators who extol the virtues of resilience as a futureproofing strategy of choice.

Such contradictory logic has now spawned a counter-reaction in terms of an online movement – #disastersarenotnatural – which is seeking to ensure everyone acknowledges the true cause of disasters. In a corresponding 2017 op-ed on the openDemocracy website it was argued: 'Disasters such as hurricanes and earthquakes result from a combination of natural hazards and social and human vulnerability. Calling them "natural disasters" artificially naturalises the harms they cause.'[6] Written in the midst of the year that would later go on to be seen as unprecedented for worldwide disaster costs, the commentary was a call to arms for disaster and resilience professionals, and scholars, to stop using the term 'natural disaster'. Decades after it was demonstrated that natural disaster was a misnomer,[7] the practice was still going strong, with authorities 'continuously blaming "nature" and putting the responsibility for failures of development on "freak" natural phenomena or "acts of God".'[8] This is often used for blame avoidance and to shield attention from the economic opportunities that disaster recovery brings for those in a position to exploit them.

EXPLOITING DISASTERS

Nowhere does thinking through who gains and who loses out in resilience efforts have as much resonance as in the aftermath of disaster. What has become abundantly clear is that not only has poor, or negligent, human action been culpable for disasters, but that death and destruction are often viewed by others as an opportunity to exploit a crisis for profit. Both failure and opportunity are cloaked in the logic of neoliberalism. The triumvirate of competition, deregulation and privatisation has driven a mode of human progress that has cut corners in policy-making, leaving urban planning lacking sufficient regulation, environmental policy arguing for more, not less, resource exploitation, and economic policies that are driven by a quest for profitable opportunities for shareholders. Free market ideology does not consider the creation of risk and social vulnerability. Poverty and inequality, and the retention of existing class and power relations, are seen as the natural order of things, with death and destruction as collateral damage in the arena of disaster.

Such an exploitation of disastrous events – whether triggered by natural hazards or malicious threats linked to terrorism or war – is not a new phenomenon but has undoubtedly grown enormously in the twenty-first century, accelerated by existential security concerns following 9/11. However, the engagement of the private sector in security policy-making is by no means a new enterprise. In January 1961 the outgoing US president, Dwight D. Eisenhower, used his final broadcast to the nation to introduce the concept of the 'Military-Industrial Complex', cautioning against the 'unwarranted influence' of the private sector in the militarisation of the nation that might endanger civil liberties or democratic processes.

Catalysed by 9/11, through other terrorist attacks across the world, and through conflict in Iraq, Afghanistan and elsewhere, the idea that security-related corporations can reap financial and political benefits from the effects of hazards and conflict has gained prominence. The role of the private sector in US homeland security and the effective 'marketisation of fear' are reinforced by such events as military and security firms have rushed to exploit the nation's 'nervous breakdown'.[9] The events of 9/11 have been well documented as an opportunity not to be missed for the private sector. Lucrative rebuilding contracts were up for grabs and an opportunity to exploit fear by rolling out an array of sophisticated security technologies presented itself. The vast expenditure that was pumped into a sagging US economy after 9/11 to finance the war on terror – both across the homeland and further afield – was a classic example of what Naomi Klein has characterised in *The Shock Doctrine* as a 'disaster capitalism complex' to rival Eisenhower's warning.[10] Here, the neoliberal ethos of disaster capitalism operates by delivering massive shocks to the system and then using the ensuing period of chaos and confusion to reassemble the pieces of what has been broken into a new arrangement that facilitates predatory exploitation by the market.

After 9/11, security and military-related business had both a blank slate and blank cheque to do its worst. Facilitated by public anxiety and counter-terrorist legislation that prioritised security over civil liberties, 9/11 signalled a surge in ongoing trends towards an increasingly militarised Western society. While the trends of monitoring vast areas of life through ubiquitous electronic surveillance, the repression of protest and the barricading of high-income areas of cities with gates and bollards were not new, 9/11 legitimated such actions. This led to a rapid expansion and deepening of these trends and their penetration into everyday life.[11]

As the dust was settling around Ground Zero in New York, business interests were explicitly promoting a view that technological advancement would become all-important in the battle against global terrorism. In this worldview, only the private sector had the expertise and innovative potential to advance a complex security response. A short time afterwards, surveillance scholar David Lyon, in *Surveillance after September 11*, presented a meticulous account of how different aspects of surveillance had been advanced and integrated into society in the immediate aftermath of 9/11, which had provided an opportunity to give 'some already existing ideas, policies and technologies their chance'.[12] Surveillance became a key commodity alongside a technological drive to develop enhanced digital, automated and biometric systems for homeland protection.

Security overseas was also being outsourced as the military underwent dramatic restructuring that saw ever more complex supply chains established in line with *en vogue* corporate models. Everything that could be subcontracted was subcontracted. In a particularly vivid example, then US defence secretary Donald Rumsfeld sought to hollow out and downsize the US army. Full time troops were replaced with cheaper reserves or National Guardsmen, with war-zone contracts for various military tasks offered to companies like Haliburton, Lockheed Martin and Blackwater. Such transformational change was zealously carried out with the private sector becoming responsible for myriad commissions that gave material form to Eisenhower's warning of the coming of the military-industrial complex.[13] All of this was going on while the US and others were waging war in Iraq and Afghanistan and shifted disaster capitalism into a new 'self-referential' or 'postmodern' phase where the West was essentially 'creating' the disaster as well as being the first responder on the ground.[14] Destruction, however it was caused, was the stalking horse for reconstruction opportunities that would surely materialise, just as night follows day.

Similarly, the growth of the corporate security sector that specialises in disaster capitalism was made more visible in the aftermath of Hurricane Katrina and exposed decades of public asset stripping and the perpetual disrepair of flood defences. As the partially submerged city struggled to survive, with tens of thousands fleeing, being forcibly evacuated or sheltering in the Superdome without food or water, many disaster 'entrepreneurs' rushed in to exploit money-making opportunities. What was perhaps most startling about this exploitation was that the same private military contractors that had been working alongside troops in the far-flung war-zones in Iraq and Afghanistan were lining up for a slice of the domestic market.[15]

Reconstruction ideas that extolled the virtues of the free market and removed red tape were quickly devised in plush meeting rooms far removed from the chaos in New Orleans. While billions of dollars of no-bid contracts were handed out like confetti, many of the residents who had not been evacuated were quickly realising that the rights to their property had been appropriated. One infamous statement made by a congressional representative from Louisiana even professed divine providence as a social cleansing mechanism: 'We finally cleaned up public housing in New Orleans. We couldn't do it, but God did.'[16]

Blank-slate reconstruction plans were the order of the day, with many predicting that rebuilding would equate with gentrification on an unprecedented scale. Such top-down planning, lubricated with billions of dollars of public money, was seen as the expected response, so used were corporations to exploiting crisis and disaster. A universal blueprint for disaster capitalism was created in the aftermath of Katrina that is the polar opposite of shock-resistant resilience, deliberately ignoring the complex social and political dimensions of a disaster in terms of its context, causes and impact. As Neil Smith summarised, disaster reconstruction in New Orleans did not flatten social difference, but 'cuts deeper the ruts and grooves of social oppression and exploitation . . . There is no such thing as a natural disaster, and the supposed naturalness of the market is the last place to look for a solution to this disastrous havoc.'[17]

THE RISE OF DISASTER RESILIENCE

Framed by 9/11 and subsequent high-impact disaster events hitting New Orleans, London and a range of other populated areas, disaster resilience as a concept began to gain significant traction in the mid-2000s as a way of preparing for, and responding to, widespread disruption. While it is a repackaging of some accepted disaster risk reduction practices, disaster resilience has been described as both an outcome and a process.[18] Initially, the intended aim – or outcome – was to bounce back to normal in the short term, which tended to adopt a top-down and reactive approach favouring the preservation of the status quo. For many though, this band-aid solution took attention away from inequalities resulting from disaster and the social and economic practices that supported this. By contrast, more recent approaches have focused on the *process* of building longer-term disaster resilience. This involves supporting the capacity of individuals, communities and states to adapt in ways that are relevant to their context and to learn lessons from previous disaster events.

Disaster resilience can be seen as part of broader ideas of *resilience* that are about absorbing and recovering from shocks and disruption and also positively adapting, learning and transforming their structures to better prepare for long-term and persistent uncertainty. Disaster resilience is the capacity to respond to vulnerability and risk, and an outcome of better disaster risk management. A resilience perspective refocuses conventional disaster management towards disaster risk reduction and preparedness activities and pays attention to pre-disaster actions as much as recovery. Using resilience to frame disaster has a number of advantages, chief among them that as a concept it is understood by the majority of responders and communities affected. Resilience, if adopted effectively, can be a positive, forward-looking approach that engages with individuals, communities and systems, and emphasises how to adapt and change in an uncertain world.

Now widely adopted in disaster studies, resilience-thinking has been incorporated into United Nations framework documents for disaster reduction. Notably, at the time where ideas of resilience were strongly emerging on the international stage, the Hyogo Framework – *Building the Resilience of Nations and Communities to Disasters* – was the global blueprint for disaster risk-reduction efforts between 2005 and 2015.[19] According to the Hyogo Framework for Action, disaster resilience was linked to the degree to which individuals, communities and public and private organisations could effectively arrange themselves to *adapt* and importantly *learn* from past disasters and reduce their risks to future shocks and stresses.[20]

National frameworks for tackling disaster adopted similar approaches. In the UK, the Department for International Development (DFID) adopted a resilience model as their core approach to tackling disasters of all kinds.[21] This model is illustrative as it draws out core elements of disaster resilience that should be considered if long-term resilience building is to be effective on the ground.[22] In the DFID approach, context is seen as all-important and there is no resilience blueprint or one-size-fits-all approach. The first task in effective disaster resilience is to understand whose, or what type of, resilience is being built. Is resilience aimed at an institution, government and infrastructure system or a social group? Aligned with the resilience *of what* is the question of resilience *to what?* Is resilience needed to cope with a sudden shock such as an earthquake, or longer-term stress such as climate change or persistent poverty? Better understanding resilience requirements also shines a light on the importance of the capacity to respond, and the usefulness of existing social and institutional arrangements for coping with disruption and disturbance.

DFID here outline that a range of responses are possible that might be characterised as the good, the bad and the ugly. The 'good' revolves around the idea of bouncing back better. This is in essence a bounce-forward model of resilience, where capacities are enhanced, vulnerabilities and risks reduced, and systems better able to deal with future disruptive change. The 'bad' involves steadying the situation on the ground – a bounce-back resolution, or short-term fix, where pre-existing conditions prevail. This, while stabilising a crisis situation, doesn't cure the underlying problems, making it highly likely that shocks or stresses will occur again and again. For example, many government-backed insurance schemes or aid policies subsidise the cost of rebuilding in the path of danger. In the 'ugly' worst-case scenario, infrastructural, economic and social systems collapse, leading to a devastating reduction in capacity to cope with future disruption. This can create the conditions conducive for disaster capitalism to take root.

BOLSTERING US DISASTER RESILIENCE

Outside the international development context in which DFID operates, Western governments have advanced strategies to make the homeland more resilient to shocks, stresses and disruptive challenges of all kinds. Many national policies for embedding disaster resilience into vulnerable communities have tended to emphasise the coordination and response to disaster events and signal a need for multi-agency responses. In such instances the initial shock poses a threat to integrated systems, increasing susceptibility to 'cascade failure' within and between a range of social and technical infrastructures. Considering such a house of cards effect has become increasingly important, given the interconnectedness between different systems, ranging from the Internet and electrical transmission grids to social and economic networks.

We saw in chapter 7 how the doctrine of UK resilience emerged as a response to fear of terrorism and the concerns that the UK was ill prepared for a 9/11-scale attack. Resilience partnerships and forums therefore emerged in cities and regions to coordinate the actions of many different stakeholders, and to generate and test plans for an array of possible disruptive challenges. In the US, by contrast, a national approach emerged at a slower pace, driven by the very real risks associated with multiple hazards and potential disaster events. In the wake of Hurricane Katrina, issues of leadership and planning that plagued response efforts led to Congress passing the Post-Katrina Emergency Management Reform Act of 2006. This act clarified FEMA's roles and responsibilities as the primary federal agency responsible for disaster preparedness, response and recovery, and provided additional responsibilities to federal agencies to address the shortcomings from the response to Katrina. Five years later, in 2011, President Obama issued Presidential Policy Directive 8, which emphasised an 'all-of-nation', 'all-hazards' approach to disasters.[23] Organisationally, it effectively melded together the capabilities of federal, state and city authorities to respond to crises. In doing so, it refocused government resources on both mitigation – preventing disasters from getting worse – and resilience – how communities actively prepare for, respond to and recover from a major disaster. Specifically, a *National Response Framework* was initiated to manage *any* type of disaster or emergency response, regardless of scale, scope or complexity.

The development of this new disaster response governance system was driven by ongoing research. In 2012, after many months of hard work, the US National Academies published *Disaster Resilience: A National Imperative*.[24] This was a response to the increasingly frequent and destructive human-induced and natural hazards, which were killing thousands of Americans each year, injuring scores more and disrupting and destroying a vast number of buildings, businesses, homes and infrastructure services.[25] *Disaster Resilience* sought to set out on a new path that focused on the value of building a culture of resilience across individuals, households, communities and the nation overall, as a way of lessening the impact of disasters and their impacts *before* they occur.

The driving force behind this framework was not only to enhance preparedness for impending disaster, but also to reduce disaster cost. The report noted that in 2011 multiple disasters had caused over $55 billion in economic damages that were borne by the taxpayer, very little of which was covered by insurance. Noting that such federal expenditure in disasters had been growing steadily for the past 60 years, it argued: 'If we continue on our present course, data suggest that the cost of disasters will continue to rise, both in dollar amounts and in social, cultural, and environmental losses to communities.' Resilient communities, it was hoped, would plan ways to reduce disaster losses, rather than waiting for a disaster to occur and paying for it afterwards. Understanding the economic benefits of resilience measures was central to this new disaster resilience ethos, with estimates given in the report arguing that every dollar spent beforehand on disaster mitigation saved $4 in damages when a disaster struck.[26]

Disaster Resilience envisioned a more resistant and adaptable America projected to 2030, where resilience was seen as something that can be done before, during and after a disaster, and was defined as 'the ability to prepare and plan for, absorb, recover from, and more successfully adapt to adverse events'. Enhancing such abilities was seen as a function of proactive, rather than reactive, planning, investment and shared policy decisions. Working collectively meant each individual, all businesses and every community, alongside all levels of government, should take responsibility for resilience to disasters.

As individuals and communities were seen as the 'first line of defence against disasters', there was particular emphasis on advancing community capacities to cope with adversity. Inspirational stories of community resilience that emerged in the wake of Hurricane Katrina, perhaps most notably from the Vietnamese community, were used in the *Disaster Resilience* report to illuminate how even disadvantaged groups cut off from mainstream society can sustain strong internal ties that protect against some disaster impacts. It highlighted the importance of understanding culture and of working together to improve disaster resilience. Before Katrina struck, some 40,000 Vietnamese lived in relative isolation in New Orleans and saw the storm as an opportunity to rebuild their community to be even stronger. Before the storm, they had established community evacuation plans, coordinated through the local Catholic church, and after the storm the community worked together, drawing on collective skills to rebuild the area. This was in contrast to surrounding areas that struggled to cope.[27]

GLOBAL DISASTER RESILIENCE REDUX

On 11 March 2011, large areas of the city of Sendai in the Tohoku region north of Tokyo, Japan, suffered catastrophic damage from an offshore earthquake and subsequent tsunami. Thousands were killed, and countless others were injured and made homeless. The city, founded in 1600 and nicknamed the City of Trees, lay in ruins. Four years later the global disaster community congregated in the city for the World Conference on Disaster Risk Reduction in order to update the Hyogo Framework for Action. Since the original agreement was signed in 2005, disasters across the globe had continued to bring untold death, destruction and human misery: over 700,000 people had lost their lives, over 1.4 million had been injured and approximately 23 million had been made homeless because of disasters. Overall, more than 1.5 billion people had been affected by disasters in various ways, with women, children and people in vulnerable situations disproportionately affected. The total economic loss was estimated at more than US$1.3 trillion.[28]

On 18 March 2015, the revised international framework for risk reduction from disasters was adopted by UN member states. The Sendai Framework for Disaster Risk Reduction, drawing on the lessons learned from implementation of the Hyogo Framework, focused on the need for improved understanding of disaster risk as a whole.[29] This was articulated in the four priority areas of understanding disaster risk, strengthening disaster risk governance, investing in disaster risk reduction for resilience and enhancing disaster preparedness for effective response and to 'build back better'. The new framework emphasised a renewed commitment to promoting the local assessment of risk to disasters in order to enhance implementation of disaster resilience. There was to be a concerted effort to foster 'collaboration and partnership across mechanisms and institutions' for implementation. The Sendai Framework also highlighted the importance of anticipation and preparedness, observing that it is urgent and critical to anticipate, plan for and reduce disaster risk in order to 'more effectively protect persons, communities and countries, their livelihoods, health, cultural heritage, socioeconomic assets and ecosystems, and thus strengthen their resilience'.[30]

Also recognised in the Sendai agreement was the importance of new technologies, including social media, big data and mobile phone networks, for warning and informing local communities about risk. Since 2005 new forms of social media (Twitter, Facebook, YouTube, Instagram and others) had emerged as open, distributed, digital communication platforms enabling people and social networks to create and share information and ideas worldwide. In times of disaster, social media has become vital, enabling people to communicate and share resources and information at pace. The emergence of such two-way communication channels signified a chance to broaden warnings to diverse community groups in times of crisis. These technologies were seen to have the potential to limit the breakdown of communication through over-reliance on a single platform and thereby to ensure warning messages are received. However, the use of social media in disasters was not unproblematic and presented policy-makers with new challenges, notably the creation of rumours and misinformation that can deflect valuable time and resources away from areas in need.[31] As well as sending out real-time warnings, social media can also be used as an emergency management tool to receive requests for assistance, for monitoring response activities and to establish situational awareness in a disaster zone. As in Haiti, uploaded images and information can help assess damage estimates and where response activities should be prioritised.

The Sendai approach, like the Hyogo framework before it, also focused attention on the important role of not just physical, but also social infrastructure. Social networks matter considerably when a crisis actually arrives. Evidence from a large number of disaster events is now unequivocal that the strength of social ties between individuals has proven to be a way to mitigate shocks and reduce deaths during disaster. Living in a community where people know and trust one another is among the most important factors in surviving disaster. Work over many years by Daniel Aldrich, a professor in political science and public policy at Northeastern University in Boston, has demonstrated that strong social ties allow for easier sharing of information and the overcoming of barriers to collective action. Better-connected communities show better recoveries after major crises,[32] and, because social networks can be strengthened and deepened, local communities and organisers can invest in programmes which build resilience to future shocks. These are exactly the types of programmes being encouraged by the Sendai Framework and which have proved invaluable in response and recovery operations in more recent disaster incidents.

THE YEAR OF THE DISASTER

The impact and cost of disasters in 2017 set records around the world. Many of these destructive events occurred as a combination of extreme weather, which saw higher than usual temperatures and rainfall, and poor human decision-making. Raging wildfires engulfed large tracts of parched land in California, Chile, Brazil and Portugal. Super-storms crashed into coastal areas as far apart as the Caribbean and Ireland, and over 1,400 people were killed in monsoon rains that hit India, Nepal and Bangladesh in South East Asia in September. The strongest storms since 1968 were recorded in China in August as Typhoon Hato rammed 99-mile-per-hour winds into the mainland. Massive landslides induced by record rainfalls and deforestation activities caused chaos in many countries. In Sierra Leone, more than 1,000 were killed in August as rivers of mud cascaded onto unregulated settlements. Immense earthquakes killed nearly 400 people in Mexico City in September as buildings collapsed, despite state-of-the-art alert systems and early warning apps in operation. Two months later over 600 people were killed and 80,000 injured in a massive quake on the Iran–Iraq border. Globally, figures released in 2017 estimated that only around 30 per cent of losses from major disasters over the last decade were insured, leaving a gap of trillions of dollars in uninsured damages.

In the US there were multiple mega-disasters recorded in 2017. According to the Federal Emergency Management Agency (FEMA), the major hurricanes and wildfires alone collectively affected 47 million people, or nearly 15 per cent of the population. The hurricane season notably produced seventeen named tropical storms. Ten of these were upgraded to hurricanes, with six being ranked as major hurricanes. These included Harvey and Irma, the first major hurricanes to hit the continental US since Hurricane Wilma in 2005. In most reporting, they were immediately labelled as 'natural' disasters. The combined cost of these disaster events in the US set a record of $306 billion in losses from damage.[33] Markedly, among this total there were sixteen 'billion dollar' disasters in 2017, tying with the single-year record set in 2011.[34]

The insurance industry had perhaps its busiest year on record, with the National Flood Insurance Program paying out over $8 billion in flood insurance by the end of 2017. This figure masked the vast uplift in insurance costs for flood-protection policies from private providers that are often very expensive, largely because of the difficulty of accurately assessing a home's flood risk. Many less wealthy homeowners therefore took a chance and did not take out coverage. According to the Insurance Information Institute, only 14 per cent of Americans living in the southern states had flood insurance as of 2016. In the wake of Hurricane Florence, which bore down on the Carolinas in September 2018, some were further reporting that only around 5 per cent of properties in those states had flood insurance offered by FEMA, leaving more than a million homes without coverage.[35] Only those living in federally declared flood zones are compelled to purchase insurance.[36]

Coping with such a massive scale of disruption was beginning to worry big businesses, who were seeing their bottom line hit, supply chains disrupted and market volatility increase, all of which called for greater organisational resilience. In September 2018, the US Government Accountability Office (GAO) in a report to Congress further laid bare the pressure that federal government responders were under in the previous year.[37] The report indicated that requests for federal disaster aid had increased tenfold in 2017 when compared with 2016, putting strain on already stretched budgets. Valuable insights were provided in the GAO report into how federal responders coped with the 'unprecedented challenges' during 2017 and how a recent focus on joining up and testing disaster-relief procedures helped to resolve many of these operational challenges. In particular, federal and state-wide coordination efforts that were boosted by post-Katrina legislation and the development of the *National Response Framework* undoubtedly smoothed preparedness and response activities before, during and after the events of 2017.[38]

Nevertheless, other responders were reported to have found such agreed response and recovery processes challenging and overly complicated. This was seen as both a function of having to learn new arrangements and 'the sequential and overlapping timing' of the major disaster events of 2017 that caused shortages of qualified staff in the right place at the right time. This meant that the recovery workforce often felt overwhelmed by what was expected of them and their organisation. In one instance, over half of FEMA workforce deployments were serving in a capacity in which they were not necessary qualified, with many uncertified workers being brought in to backfill key roles.

HARVEY AND HOUSTON

In 2017, four near-sequential disasters – hurricanes Harvey, Irma and Maria, and the California wildfires – created an unprecedented demand for federal disaster response and recovery resources. Hurricane Harvey was particularly devastating, with nearly 130cm of rain causing record-breaking floods that inundated vast parts of the city of Houston and Southeast Texas. Harvey was the wettest tropical cyclone on record in the US and the first major hurricane in twelve years to make landfall in the US.

Ahead of the impending storm there was an important question raised in the media as to the role self-reliance, as opposed to centralised federal responses, would play in governing the response to the disaster. When Harvey hit the response was chaotic. FEMA was estimated to be 30 per cent understaffed due to being overwhelmed by ongoing disaster events across the nation. Staff on the ground were underprepared as a result of budget cuts that had hampered FEMA's ability to meet basic training needs. In a further example of poorly coordinated response, the Texas National Guard was not called out until several days after the disaster began.

The confusion about who was in charge of responding meant that many residents and communities were forced to rely on themselves and their social networks for help and disaster relief. Thousands sprang into action in a spontaneous display of community resilience as the poor rescued the poor. It was all hands on deck as the whole community responded, highlighting a change of direction since the haphazard and overly centralised response to Katrina in 2005. In Houston, community volunteerism was seen as a positive addition to the response effort rather than a hindrance. Such do-it-yourself community responses can be exemplified by the 'Cajun Navy' – ad hoc volunteer groups comprising a flotilla of private boats – who quickly descended on southeast Texas and joined the official rescue mission and subsequent clean-up and recovery efforts.[39] The Cajun Navy illuminated the importance of social networks that has become an increasingly vital part of local and national response to disaster.[40]

Citizens of Houston also had help from social media. For many the Hurricane Harvey disaster was the first 'social media storm' that unfolded in real time on social media, underscoring the central role those platforms play in spreading and consuming information. Survivors used social media to summon rescue or appeal for aid. Harvey was the first disaster where calls for help were greater on social media than on overwhelmed 911 systems. Those further away also used updates on Twitter to keep in touch with developments. The Facebook 'Safety Check' was activated and groups were established to provide a hub of vital information. Disaster relief organisations and dedicated social media managers turned to the platforms to coordinate aid, spread information and make requests. Incredible crowdsourced rescue maps were produced based on social media feeds that significantly assisted with prioritising the rescue effort. Having previously asked residents to use their dedicated phone line rather than social media to summon help, Houston police were forced to use Twitter to ask anybody who could volunteer with a boat to get in touch. Emergency managers issued further warnings over social media for residents to evacuate immediately.[41] In one, now infamous, Facebook post, an official in Tyler Country urged residents to leave or face death: 'Anyone who chooses to not [evacuate] cannot expect to be rescued and should write their social security numbers in permanent marker on their arm so their bodies can be identified. The loss of life and property is certain. GET OUT OR DIE!'[42]

A SCENE OF DEVASTATION

In the state of Texas, nearly 50,000 homes were affected by Hurricane Harvey, with over 1,000 completely destroyed.[43] Nearly 700 businesses were put out of action. An estimated 300,000 structures and 500,000 vehicles were damaged or destroyed and over 100 people died because of storm-related incidents.[44] Over a four-day period, the resulting floods displaced more than 30,000 people. Throughout Texas, approximately 336,000 people were left without electricity and 17,000 required rescuing. The enforced closure of oil refineries and heavy industry ahead of Hurricane Harvey's arrival further created a fuel shortage and long lines of cars formed at gas stations. The damage caused in one of the nation's most industrial regions further led to the release of a stream of toxic pollutants from chemical plants and oil refineries.

Overall, the cost of disaster relief and recovery is currently estimated at around $125 billion, tying Harvey with Hurricane Katrina in 2005 as the costliest tropical cyclone on record. But only a proportion of this damage – around $20 billion – was covered by the National Flood Insurance Program and was dwarfed by uninsured losses. This was a case of insurance for the few but damage for the majority, as most residents had forgone insurance due to its exorbitant cost. Even where insurance had provided a compensatory mechanism against risk, it was not necessarily a panacea that will see building back better. With policy coverage often stipulating that a like-for-like replacement is required this, paradoxically, encouraged rebuilding in vulnerable areas. In the wake of Harvey, the media reported on one alarming case where a house valued at $115,000 had been rebuilt eighteen times in sixteen years at a cost to the National Flood Insurance scheme of over $800,000.[45] Insurance against floods also relied on flood hazard maps produced by FEMA that demarcated where homeowners are required to purchase flood insurance. However, such maps were based on risk assessments that look backwards rather than forwards and were thoroughly inadequate and outdated. In any case, they were largely ignored by developers.

In Houston, the metro area was devastated as all-time record daily rainfall accumulations on both 26 and 27 August led to widespread flash flooding. There was more than a year's rain in less than a week. The month of August was the wettest in Houston since records began in 1892, more than doubling the previous highest monthly total. As the storm approached questions were already being asked about the causes, embedded vulnerabilities, and preparation for what was seen by many as an inevitable and predictable disaster. A commentary in the respected *National Geographic* captured the mood, asking, 'After Harvey, Are Epic Rains the New Normal?' How can cities prepare for extreme weather that is no longer so rare?[46] The urgent need for future-looking resilience was further raised because of Houston's third 500-year flood in three years.[47] Global warming had changed the odds considerably. As the storm peaked, a mandatory evacuation was issued for large parts of the city with fears of flooding, and up to 3 metres of water predicted.

While there is little doubt that climate change made the impact of Harvey worse, past decisions about how the city should be planned can, in the cold light of day, be seen as severely maladaptive and a primary cause of the disaster. As one commentator noted, 'Fuelled by the oil economy, the city expanded without much thought to the consequences.'[48] The 40 per cent expansion in the city's population since the 1990s had put development land at a premium and led to flood-prone land being recklessly developed. However, buyers were not aware of the risk. As the *Texas Tribune* reported: 'It was well known Houston's reservoirs would flood. The only people who didn't know were those who bought homes inside them.'[49] If they had known the risk they are highly unlikely to have purchased the property, and if they had, would at least have obtained insurance. Legally speaking, Texas law only required that those selling homes disclose whether a property is in a 100-year floodplain.[50] It did not require disclosure of whether a property is within a 500-year floodplain, or a reservoir basin.[51]

Built in the 1940s, Houston's flood control system was no match for Harvey. Comprising two enormous reservoirs that functioned as floodpools and stored stormwater run-off in periods of high rainfall, the defences were powerless to stop the water rising. Previous decades had seen an unprecedented amount of concrete poured as a city that prided itself in having minimal zoning regulation had allowed massive unchecked urban sprawl, sometimes overlapping or abutting the floodplain. That flood control system worked well when the reservoirs were surrounded by prairie and wetlands that provided the capacity to absorb water like a sponge. But encroaching development had ripped up much of the natural defences, and had not set aside open spaces or improved drainage. This stored up huge vulnerability for residents as Houston's growth created perfect flood conditions which could, and should, have been avoided. Shockingly, an analysis of development permits in 2015 found that over 50 per cent of developers had failed to heed guidance issued by the US Army Corps on mitigating the destruction of wetlands.[52] When Harvey struck there were 14,000 homes on or near the floodplain, over 5,000 of which flooded when the dams overtopped. In short, there was nowhere left for the vast volumes of water to go as hard surfaces increased the rain-water run-off and accelerated its speed as it bore down on inappropriately planned neighbourhoods. This brought with it not just water but raw sewage from overwhelmed sewers.

Urban planning in Houston, while an extreme example of building blind and ignoring the consequences, is not an uncommon practice and has led insurers to refuse to cover stored-up risks as part of standard polices. As an executive at the global reinsurers Swiss Re noted in the wake of Hurricane Harvey, extra costs mean that developers fail to take these risks into account, with an ethos of 'a dollar today is worth more than a dollar saved tomorrow'. National politics is also central to encouraging a culture within planning that prioritises resilience. The Obama administration had moved in this direction when they established a Federal Standard for Flood Risk Management that required builders to consider climate change and sea level rise in development decisions. This standard was repealed by President Trump ten days before Harvey hit.

REBUILDING FOR ALL?

In the wake of Hurricane Harvey, calls were made to put local residents, not officials, in charge of the rebuilding effort, such was the fear that prior mistakes would be repeated. The *Houston Chronicle* argued that Houstonians should be the significant voice in charting *their* city's future towards resilience, and not an elite task force of disaster 'experts'.[53] In what was labelled a 'shock doctrine – the exploitation of a crisis to radically transform a city's physical and social landscape',[54] there was an immediate concern that reconstruction funds would be shunted from poor neighbourhoods and towards wealthy districts. There was also a real fear that a knee-jerk reaction would lead to calls for grand projects akin to New York's 'Rebuild by Design' competition that would prioritise technical solutions and exclude many residents from the supposedly democratic process of planning. Others also expressed immediate concern about the rolling back of environmental and worker protections as the disaster capitalism playbook was enacted that would make future disasters worse, as public institutions were undermined by free-market motives.

As Houston was drying out and entered 2018, various reconstruction efforts were ongoing, but these were invariably slow. Federal assistance had largely run out. Many remained homeless (the so-called Harvey Homeless) or living in unacceptable conditions. In many lower-income neighbourhoods, where only a fraction had insurance, the expense of repair was too high for much progress to be made. To promote this forgotten Houston, community groups established a series of social networks and used the hashtag #NothingIsNormal to promote their cause to the world, and particularly the richer parts of the city, that many areas are still struggling to cope.

Where reconstruction and rebuilding has progressed, to date it has tended to focus on the downtown core where the ability to cope with future disasters has been boosted by technology. In March 2018 a $9.4 million federal grant was made available to install a multi-site flood warning system which Mayor Sylvester Turner called 'another significant step in making us more resilient' to major flooding.[55] New building codes for the city were suggested that would require new buildings outside of Houston's floodplain to be constructed 60cm above the ground, and would require developers to retrofit flood-retention ponds in previously paved areas.

Perhaps the most important development that will affect Houston's future disaster resilience occurred in August 2018, when the city joined the Rockefeller 100 Resilient Cities Network to create a long-term vision to build resilience to the shocks and stresses. In developing a comprehensive, and hopefully inclusive, resilience strategy, Houston will join communities across the globe who are already investigating what it would mean to be resilient in the face of increasing risks and uncertainty.[56] The aim is to embed emergency preparedness, sustainability and community cohesion into every aspect of their social and physical infrastructure planning and governance so all parts of the city are made more resilient and less vulnerable to future disasters. In announcing Houston's elevation into this network, the president of 100 Resilient Cities noted:

> With the experience of Hurricane Harvey still fresh on the minds of many in and around Houston, we see ample opportunity to work with the city in creating a long-term vision to address risks, build new opportunities, and ultimately build a more resilient Houston by leveraging the experiences of the 100RC Network and by fostering an inclusive, comprehensive resilience planning process.[57]

The expectation that weather extremes will become more frequent and devastating has become a stark reality in locations such as Houston. This was not an abnormality but a harbinger of an uncertain and volatile future where existential threats abound and greater resilience and adaptive capacity are being urgently sought.

DISASTER RESILIENCE 2.0

Whether it's thinking through the causes, the exposed vulnerabilities and the preparedness actions, or how response and recovery is carried out, nothing concentrates the mind like a disaster. Whether attributed to natural hazards, human decisions or malicious threats, disasters are going to shape our world for the near future. More and more time is being spent preparing for 'extreme' future scenarios as a way of reducing risk and vulnerability and enhancing resilience. Communities, organisations and states are taking greater steps to protect themselves against the next 'big' one.

Financial losses from disaster events are also rising fast, as is the massive toll on human suffering, especially among the less wealthy. Disasters are indiscriminate, but their effects are not. In many hazard-prone areas, a form of resilience apartheid is in operation where misguided choices have enhanced vulnerability among those least able to protect themselves. Human decision-making has enhanced risk by allowing building on flood and seismic zones, paving over natural defences, widespread deforestation and a lack of building codes. Where we do recognise danger we have tended to deal with it ineffectively by focusing on recovery over prevention (the latter being much less costly in the long run) and failing to coordinate efforts between the public, private and community sectors in an effective way.

In recent years, projections of impending disaster have led to a future-proofing drive and to increasingly prioritise building resilience capacity to allow a system – whether a nation, state, city, community or firm – to increase its ability to withstand and recover from the shocks and stresses of disasters. Such a focus on disaster resilience is usually framed by national polices that set the tone and expected content for local resilience building, and the development of disaster resilience plans. Disaster resilience is further viewed as a collective responsibility, calling for the involvement of everyone – partners at state and local scales together with businesses, community and voluntary organisations and individuals – and not just the government.

If we are all responsible, then how we label disasters is of key importance. If they continue to be referred to as 'natural' occurrences, it becomes too easy for governments, emergency institutions and the private sector to absolve themselves of blame. To work together effectively, everyone needs to recognise that the root causes of failure and vulnerability production often lie in poor or unethical decision-making.

Future rebuilding efforts need to concentrate not just on replacing what was there before, but on replacing it with something better. We must move out of a cycle of disaster and repair that has become all too common as importance is placed on getting back to normal as quickly as possible. As Jeff Hebert, vice president for adaptation and resilience at the Water Institute of the Gulf, a Louisiana-based research group, noted in the *New York Times*: 'The fundamental problem is that the entire system is reactive . . . It would be transformational if we took the money that we spend on disasters and instead spent it on the front end on really good adaptation.'[58]

Learning from past mistakes is also imperative and we should ensure that disasters are not used as an opportunity to make money or exploit the poor. Building back better means reconstruction efforts should concentrate on those most in need and not on sites ripe for development. Reconstruction, often seen as a gold rush, is more importantly an opportunity to design in resilience to city plans so that risks are reduced. This might actually mean not building in certain areas, such as wetlands, whose overdevelopment has increased the risk of flooding in many areas. Returning such land to nature can, in many locations, act as a valuable buffer against risk.

Effective programming of disaster resilience, like all resilience actions, requires local input, coordination and an understanding of context to succeed. The needs of local communities should be well understood and adequate resources should be set aside for programmes that focus on reducing community vulnerability and improving neighbourhood preparedness. Taking a resilience perspective to disasters also means focusing on pre-disaster actions – often the poor relation of former disaster management approaches – as a means to improve post-disaster response, relief and recovery. To this end, insurance should be made more affordable and should seek to encourage risk mitigation behaviours, but it can only be an effective disaster resilience mechanism if priced right.

Resilience prompts us to think afresh and about new practices and approaches that will reduce risk and aid disaster recovery. This is more about thinking forwards and working with the inherent complexity of disaster rather than looking to the past to inform the future. Such 'backcasting', although useful as a learning resource, is likely to stymie innovative thinking that can catalyse transformation in custom and practice and lead to better ways of working to improve disaster resilience. Disaster resilience needs to work in the context of a *new normal* that implies a reboot of conventional worldviews, and an acceptance of an uncertain and volatile future. For example, after the devastating Californian wildfires of 2017, emergency services began preparing for what they talked about as the new normal in terms of the impacts of higher summer temperatures induced by climate change. The subsequent ferocity of the wildfire season of 2018 reaffirmed that they were working and acting in a new normality, despite US presidential views that it wasn't climate change but poor forest management that was primarily to blame.

We collectively need to embed foresight into our efforts to enhance disaster preparedness plans and futureproof our communities. We should be building long-term resilience and the capacities to adapt, not just focusing on short-term coping mechanisms. Many of our existing approaches are driven top-down and are short-sighted and reactive. These need to be replaced by more holistic efforts that are thought through in advance and engage with all sections of society. In many disaster zones the local population are the effective first responders. As such, organisational capacity building should involve boosting preparedness at the household level as well as focusing upon coordination between national and local levels and between responders at the city scale. The *process* of building disaster resilience is not a one-day seminar; it is an imperative to build adaptive capacity into everyday lives, strategies and plans, and governance mechanism in locations that are vulnerable. Resilience in such areas means that when disaster strikes everyone is ready for it whatever its form or severity. This is the essence of resilience for all, by all.

9

ADAPT OR DIE: FUTUREPROOFING THE TWENTY-FIRST CENTURY

The future depends on what we do in the present.

Mahatma Gandhi

Lots of companies don't succeed over time. What do they do fundamentally wrong? They usually miss the future.

Larry Page, Google founder

> And so the First Pulse and the Second Pulse, each a complete psychodrama decade, a meltdown in history; a breakdown in society, a refugee nightmare, an eco-catastrophe, the planet gone completely nuts. The Anthropocide, the Hydrocatastrophe, the Georevolution. Also great new options for investment, oh, dear, the necessity of police state crown control as expressed in draconian new laws and ad hoc practices.[1]

This is how the scene is set in Kim Stanley Robinson's future realism novel *New York 2140* which graphically depicts an urgent vision of imminent times. In this detailed story, New York has been hit by a climate change-related environmental catastrophe that has seen water rise 50 feet (15 metres), submerging much of the city so it resembles Venice. Streets have become canals with boat taxis, and an archipelago of skyscraper islands have emerged that are interconnected by sky bridges. While climate change is the cause, rampant capitalism is the real culprit, having wreaked havoc on the planet without concern for the consequences. In future New York, big business still abounds, refusing to leave its investment in the city behind. The maximisation of profit and trading opportunities has created a fragmented city of haves and have-nots and, correspondingly, a pocketed landscape of resilience where some are secure in their high-rise dwellings and corporate enclaves while others live in the downtown 'intertidal zone' of vulnerable semi-submerged dwellings.

Taking on board scientific ideas of how sea level rise might play out in a worst-case scenario, Robinson's novel is set in the aftermath of two 'pulse' events that trigger rapid and permanent flooding. These are not slow, progressive rises but events instigated by tipping points being reached. The first pulse of future Earth is caused by escalating temperatures melting Antarctic ice, leading to water rising 3 metres in a decade. This brings about not only environment destruction but also massive economic disruption and a large-scale refugee crisis:

> The first pulse was a profound shock . . . raising sea levels by ten feet. That was already enough to disrupt coastlines everywhere, also to grossly inconvenience all the major shipping ports around the world, and shipping is trade . . . So that very disregard for the consequences of their carbon burn had unleased the ice that caused sea level rise and wrecked that global distribution system and caused a depression that was even more damaging to the people of that generation than the accompanying refugee crisis, which, using the unit popular at the time was rated as fifty katrinas. Pretty bad but the profound interruption of trade was even worse as far as business was concerned.[2]

The first pulse also leads society to innovate and devise ever more elaborate geo-engineering solutions to cool the earth's temperature, but to no avail. Society has reacted too late. The oceans are too warm and subsequently trigger further ice-melt and a much larger second pulse, which raises sea levels by a further 40 feet (12 metres) across the globe. In New York, the perimeter sea wall (akin to the twenty-first-century Dryline designed by BIG Architecture described in chapter 3) is overtopped and wrecked.

New York 2140 shines a critical light on our current attempts to deal with climate change and the aftermath of the 2008 financial crash. The sense of current events still playing out in the future, where environmental change, technology, austerity and immigration overwhelm us, makes this fictional work urgently relevant. It has captured the existential threats of the current moment and presented them graphically as a genuinely grave threat to civilisation. This novel challenges us to take full account of the complex and uncertain situation we have created for ourselves, stop being complacent and take action:

> People sometimes say no one saw it coming, but no, wrong: they did. Paleoclimatologists looked at the modern situation and saw CO2 levels screaming up from 280 to 450 parts per million in less than three hundred years, faster than had ever happened in the Earth's entire previous five billion years . . . and they said, Whoa. They said, Holy shit. People! they said. Sea level rise! . . . They put it in bumper sticker terms: massive sea level rise sure to follow our unprecedented release of CO2! They published their papers, and shouted and waved their arms, and a few canny and deeply thoughtful sci-fi writers wrote up lurid accounts of such an eventuality, and the rest of civilization went on torching the planet like a Burning Man pyromasterpiece. Really.[3]

A key question raised in the book is: will we just continue to hurtle headlong into the future, and seek to protect ourselves now and just about cope, rather than looking for long-term transformation? *New York 2140* illustrates one example of how the intricate coupling of environmentally destructive behaviour, exploitative global finance, political intransigence and an overriding belief in the power of technology to provide silver bullet solutions might play out.[4] It illuminates a failure to realise how our short-term actions play out and reveal themselves over a longer time frame, providing a dire warning to us all if generational changes are not put in place now.

This theme of existential threat is repeated in the present by the most recent Intergovernmental Panel on Climate Change report written by the world's leading climate scientists, and released in October 2018.[5] Amid political moves by some of the largest polluting countries, including the US, Australia and Brazil, to remove themselves from global climate change pacts, this report warned that there are only twelve years to save the planet from the worst excesses of global warming.[6] As one of the report's authors pleaded, 'It's a line in the sand and what it says to our species is that this is the moment and we must act now . . . This is the largest clarion bell from the science community and I hope it mobilises people and dents the mood of complacency.'[7]

The plea is once again for urgent 'deep and rapid' changes and the collective political will to reduce greenhouse gas emissions. Rising temperatures will raise a multitude of risks, destroying ecosystems, producing food shortages and propagating even more extreme weather events, and lead, as in *New York 2140*, to coastal cities facing more flooding. This is *not* a natural disaster nor an act of God. It is caused by us and must be addressed by us rapidly. In the 'scenario' section of the IPCC report is speculation on what the future might bring if the world hits the 2 degrees Celsius of warming tipping point and spirals out of control. The city of Miami is used to depict the impact of a major storm in 2040 or 2050, where it is noted that 'a hurricane with intense rainfall and associated with high storm surges destroys a large part of Miami'. As we noted in chapter 3, this type of future scenario is something Miamians are well aware of.

The IPCC report also highlights the social impact of a hothouse world and argues that advancing adaptive resilience solutions should be a collective endeavour, irrespective of wealth: 'Social justice and equity are core aspects of climate-resilient development pathways . . . as they address challenges and inevitable trade-offs, widen opportunities and ensure options, visions and values are deliberated, between and within countries and communities, without making the poor and disadvantaged worse off.'[8] Here we see in stark terms the need to build resilience for all, by all. This is not just a challenge from the existential threat of a changing climate but cuts right across the myriad ways in which society should seek to deal with risk, crisis and uncertainty as we seek to futureproof in a progressive way. We have loaded the dice. Now we need to respond.

*

In the twenty-first century resilience is employed everywhere in the Western world as the futureproofing strategy of choice. In the light of 9/11, we needed a new vocabulary to articulate how we manage and govern risk given that 'we live, think and act in concepts that are historically obsolete but which nonetheless continue to govern our thinking and acting'.[9]

Although implementation methods differ depending on what is being made resilient, politicians constantly proclaim the need to enhance it, city planners and engineers are constantly being urged to adopt it, while individuals and communities are told they need to have more of it. Professional associations have rapidly incorporated resilience ideas into their existing frameworks of action for sustainability, risk management or emergency planning, in many cases extending their scale and ambition. Resilience has been further incorporated into the modus operandi of numerous policy communities and is almost ubiquitous in media portrayals and political sound bites of the latest crisis or disaster.

The many and varied depictions of resilience describe it variously in terms of bouncing back, bouncing back better or bouncing forward. We have shown how in relation to infrastructure networks, business or the economy, resilience is often framed by assessing the resistance of a system and its ability to stabilise and return to 'normal' (or business as usual) as quickly as possible. We have also provided many examples of where 'bouncing back better' is the intended outcome of planning ahead, capacity building, preparatory activities and stress-testing. This is about us gearing up to expected disruptions before they hit. In other instances of bouncing back better, we have illuminated how resilience action refers to the properties and ability of interconnected and complex ecological, technical, social and economic systems to adapt, change and learn in the midst of disruption and failure. This type of approach allows the storm to be ridden out and for bouncing back to be an improved and more positive outcome.

The final framing of resilience that we have showcased is as a bounce-forward strategy that engages with long-term planning, increasingly complex systems-thinking and works with a range of future possibilities or adaptive pathways. Approaches adopted by the IPCC and a range of localities concerned with the impact of climate change on critical infrastructure provide tangible examples of where such longitudinal thinking is being progressed. Resilience here is not a one-off action or travel towards a final destination, but a continuous journey; one that helps us to define the problems at hand while also developing solutions that mitigate emergent issues through adaptation, innovation and collaboration.

What we think of as resilience and its overall aims are therefore not fixed. As we have shown, it is a travelling concept that has risen to prominence in debates about how we seek to understand a range of 'wicked' problems in uncertain times. As the current century has progressed, resilience has become an all-encompassing approach that can be applied in a variety of national and international contexts. It can encompass a number of risk arenas such as climate change, disaster management, critical infrastructure protection, national security, economics and finance, and be put into operation across a broad range of public- and private-sector organisations.

While, in a practical sense, there is no consensus on how resilience should be applied, there does seem to be an emerging unanimity about what resilience is and what it means. Increasingly a well-understood notion of resilience abounds, prompted by the need to change the way in which we think about living with constant risk, uncertainty and fear of the future. The proliferation of resilience-speak, and its practices, is closely tied to the idea that we now live in a time of perpetual crisis and persistent uncertainty inherent in what is popularly termed the Anthropocene. At a broad level we 'get' the multitude of government pronouncements that resilience is all about coping better with adversity and being able to adapt, both now and in the future, by being prepared for the unexpected. It is this promotion of resilience – as being of positive benefit to individuals, communities, businesses, emergency responders and society as a whole – that has allowed its practices to become interwoven into contemporary life in the twenty-first century.

CONTROLLING UNCERTAINTY

In the current millennium the push for resilience is a response to existential or material vulnerability, insecurity and, ultimately, change; with the scope and importance of enhancing such properties, growing as global society seeks ways of controlling uncertainty. Overarching these numerous deployments of resilience is a fundamental futureproofing quest towards new modes of engagement with new forms of risk and risk management. Inherent in human progress has been a desire to control an uncertain future by crunching numbers and preparing plans that seek to bring the future closer to the present and in so doing, provide stability for citizens or the market. Predictability and forecasting has sought control and order so that decision-makers have had more confidence and certainty over choices they have made for the future. This is about maximising what is known and minimising what is unknown.

Whereas in the recent past, ideas of risk dominated discussions on how society could hope to control the future through probability, ideas of adaptability and adaptive capacity alongside the simultaneous rise of resilience have presented different forms of possible action. Resilience throws traditional ideas into turmoil and turns the hallmarks of the modern world – certainty, forecasting and equilibrium – on their head.[10] It forces us to work with uncertainty and to devise a range of alternative visions of the future for governing complexity in an ever-changeable world.

RESILIENCE FOR WHOM BY WHOM?

However, the advance of resilience as the policy of choice for managing future uncertainty has not been neutral and is not uncontested, placing its multiple practices under the spotlight. A key question that is often posed in such critique is whether resilience is a regressive or progressive agenda. This forces us to consider who implements resilience, for what purposes and for whose benefit? Increasingly, with talk of resilience offering radical and transformative change, there are coinciding calls to reflect on issues of social justice which ask, how does the rolling out of resilience ensure even-handedness and impartiality? How are existing systems of governance ensuring that formerly marginalised, or alternative, voices are incorporated in decision-making and the construction of alternative futures? As we have shown in previous chapters, diversity of opinion and a range of outcome options, more often than not, lead to better thought-through decisions and, in the long term, enhanced adaptive capacity, or agility, to change course when required.

A further question prompted by the uneven social impacts of resilience is, what are the consequences or knock-on implications of undertaking resilience in one location on other nearby places? Work by urban resilience expert Lorenzo Chelleri and colleagues has highlighted evidence from multiple case studies worldwide which illustrate what he terms resilience trade-offs.[11] These occur when an effort to build resilience through increasing adaptive capacity and/or reducing risk exposure leads to a reduction in adaptive capacity or an increase in other risks exposure. This introduces the relatively recent understanding that resilience is not always a positive or desirable feature. It also invites us to have a more open-ended approach to the relationship between resilience and vulnerability and make explicit that resilience is a feature that needs to be managed, rather than simply enhanced, built or engineered in.[12] For example, we illuminated how policies that seek to mitigate flooding can often enhance segregation of communities along wealth (and often racial) lines as the poorer residents are displaced as they can't afford insurance or the vast sums required to make their homes climate-resilient. Resilience here should not be seen as just a technical intervention or a checklist of necessary objectives that must be met. Instead, it should be viewed as a *process* that mediates a set of social and political relationships, grounded in an ethic of care for the most vulnerable.

POWER AND POLITICS

Concerns to ensure that resilience is socially equitable have further focused on the alleged tarnishing of resilience ideas by neoliberalism and its associated features of free market competition, deregulation and privatisation. While most starkly exposed by the deeply unethical practices of disaster capitalism, much wider economic and political shifts of the last decades have served to influence the rolling out of resilience policies in ways that some see as disciplining or controlling.

Politically, resilience has allowed us, and more particularly governments, to reframe risk, crisis and uncertainty, not as chaotic or uncontrolled, but as an opportunity to tackle risk and provide assurance in ways the state had previously found impossible to do. The emergence of resilience policies indicates a shift in government focus, reflecting a desire (or necessity, due to fiscal austerity) to step back from its conventional responsibilities to ensure the protection of the population during crisis or disruption. At the same time, this has led to a delegation of responsibility for resilience activities to certain professions, private companies, communities and individuals.

This retreat – the so called 'hollowing out' of the state – and the subsequent expansion of the private sector and civil society into its vacuum, does in theory create opportunities for new innovative institutional forms to emerge that are better able to deal with risk and vulnerability. In practice though, such retreat often makes governments less able to keep their populations safe and respond to disruption in a coordinated and controlled way. As we saw in Auckland, where fragmented electricity networks made responses to failure more difficult to action, or in Genoa where routine maintenance of bridge infrastructure was outsourced to private suppliers, neoliberal logic has in many ways facilitated, rather than alleviated, conditions of disruption.

A further shift in emphasis towards resilience being implemented by local networks also has broader implications for civic participation and the delegation of responsibility. The resilience turn emphasises the ways in which we are all now expected to be involved in enhancing the resilience of our community, our business or ourselves. Civic and individual self-reliance has become increasingly central to risk management, hazard adaptation and preparedness and, by extension, to the realisation of resilience.

Nevertheless, it is here that most critical comment on the practice of resilience can be made as individuals are *instructed* to adapt and be resilient in the face of uncertainty. While encouraging individuals, or enterprises, to autonomously act in the face of a crisis, resilience, if directed from government, tends to prescribe *how* citizens should behave and adapt. As we have shown, the reporting of suspicious behaviour to an anti-terror hotline is framed as a moral obligation to enhance community resilience. Similarly, you are deemed irresponsible if you do not adequately protect your property from rising waters or take out appropriate insurance against flooding, regardless of your ability to afford these actions. Likewise, in the financial sector, self-imposed market discipline was seen as one way of avoiding a large-scale regulatory overhaul. As such, the focus in resilience on self-regulation often comes cloaked in wider political motives that encourage particular modes of 'normal' or 'acceptable' behaviour. For some this is a dependency, or even 'a permanent condition of enslavement', rather than the independence to make our own decisions and a general empowerment of communities that the promise of resilience should bring.[13]

RESILIENCE AS THE NEW NORMAL

What we have also seen through our collective responses to exceptional risk are formally temporary short-term defensive solutions becoming normal, permanent and unchallenged under the rubric of resilience. Such approaches have been expressed largely through a variety of foresight documents, forward-looking risk management strategies, future threat assessments and associated simulated practice exercises. Resilience, in effect, has embedded the need to be constantly prepared for an array of risks, threats and disruptions into many aspects of our lives.

Take a typical day. You might wake up to a radio report talking about ongoing preparations being made to cope with the expected impact of a hurricane that is just about to make landfall in Florida.[14] You might then travel to work on public transport and be confronted by large posters at your local train station saying, 'See it, say it, sorted', encouraging you to report suspicious activity or unattended baggage to the police. If you do not see the poster, you will likely be bombarded with similar requests over the public address system, both on the platform and on the train. You might work in a business district and, having departed the train station, walk through lines of hostile vehicle mitigation bollards to exit the station forecourt and encounter further lines of these steel sentries as you approach the high-rise office building where you work. At work you are informed that today you will be involved in testing your company's cyber-attack contingency plan and spend all day role-playing how you and your colleagues would collectively act and seek to minimise disruption if this scenario came to pass. You might then go back to the train station and find your usual train has been cancelled due to points failure that will take hours to fix and which disrupts the entire regional rail network. You eventually return home and turn on the TV and watch a constant stream of images of destroyed houses and flooded cities in Florida with the news reporters telling stories of how resilient sections of the local population are or how (in)effective hurricane-proof building codes have been in this instance. The need for resilience in an array of possible disruptions is everywhere we look. It has moved from being something we need in extraordinary conditions to something we are expected to have all the time. The exception has become the norm.

We have also seen how many resilience policies are now focused on anticipating impending disaster or disruption in ways that go much further than just seeking to be proactive to possible threats. Here such policies can produce an anxious public, where 'what if' scenarios have been replaced with 'when this, then that' scenarios, where the inevitability of further disruption is assumed and planned for. Attempts to model earthquake risk in California using new computer simulations are one example of how predictive risk can both help in preparation for the 'big one', but also be turned into fearful prophecy. For some critics, such planning for the worst has become a key element of resilience development that can allow fear to be manipulated by governments through the distribution of guidance to citizens about how they can increase their resilience. In essence, the political discourse of resilience has emerged to reassure the public that they are safe, yet advise everyone to be prepared for the next attack, flood, blackout, cold snap or flu outbreak.

The emergence of such pre-emptive governance strategies asks critical questions of how political power has been organised, mobilised and retained through labelling such actions as resilient. The argument made by those who see such anticipatory modes of governing as controlling is that there is a limited range of stakeholders commonly invited into the decision-making processes, thus reducing the capacity of collective political action to transform the way in which those in control act. Resilience in this view can be seen as a way of accommodating changing requirements into discussions while promoting a stable state rather than actively pursuing the potential for transformation. This helps explain why the attempt to deal with emerging risk through resilience is often a slow and ad hoc process that 'gets stuck', rather than an approach that is transformative and committed to ripping up the current play book and starting again.

PROGRESSIVE RESILIENCE

Despite much of the criticism of resilience and resilience policy – that it makes us more precautionary and fearful, that it is a reactive and controlling tool of government, that it passes on ever-greater levels of responsibility to professions, the private sector, communities and individuals – we should try and focus on how the implementation of its 'principles' might become a progressive agenda and promote change and transformation.

While not wishing to downplay some of the problems there have been implementing resilience in an even-handed way, what we can say about resilience is that it has become intertwined in twenty-first-century life. For many, resilience offers a potential antidote to the vast challenges of coping with, and managing, future uncertainty, as well as providing a potential framework by which to respond. It can be viewed as a new conceptual approach to understanding and addressing complex problems, which may offer the possibility of transformative and adaptive change in international policy-making and government and institutional practices. It has the potential to jettison a long-held reverence to linear causal models and blueprint strategies, and embrace complexity and the unknown through increasingly collaborative and integrated solutions. As the examples used throughout this book attest, resilience-thinking and associated processes of enhancing adaptability, flexibility and agility in forward-looking plans are now providing a useful and progressive lens through which to view the future.

As has further been shown, the renegotiation of a number of international development agendas of recent years has drawn in, and embedded, resilience ideas into agreements aimed at advancing effective global policy. The 2015–2030 international framework for disaster risk reduction signed in Sendai in March 2015 highlighted the urgency to ensure resilience to disasters is embedded within development plans, policies and procedures at all scales to complement, not hinder, sustainable development. Likewise, the pact signed at the United Nations climate change conference in Paris in December 2015, as with the periodic IPCC reports, put the ideas of resilience and adaptive pathway approaches front and centre in future strategies. Perhaps most notably, though, the UN released their much-anticipated Sustainable Development Goals (SDGs) in September 2015, replacing the former Millennium Goals and setting targets in relation to future international development up until 2030. Within the SDGs, the discourse of resilience promoted the ability to respond proactively to a range of shocks and stresses and to highlight how a range of stakeholders might collectively operationalise a joined-up response. Significant emphasis was also placed on building capacities so as to reduce the vulnerability of communities, infrastructures, institutions and cities from natural hazards, economic shock, climate change and an array of other risks.[15]

Overall, these three international strategies highlighted the importance and utility of ideas and practices of resilience in tackling the integrated and complex issues of reducing the risk of disasters, advancing sustainable development and mitigating and adapting to climate change. These core agendas and their framing in resilience-thinking will ensure that resilience will be a vital area of policy-making for years to come.[16]

These international dialogues also exemplify how, at all scales from the global to the local, resilience is being seen not as a barrier to change but as a lens through which to take action, offering a possibility that resilience processes might have transformative capacities. As we have shown, a range of evolutionary approaches to thinking about, and enacting, resilience has emerged with a focus upon adaptability and flexibility to cope with an increasingly complex and volatile world. Future uncertainty has opened up a window of opportunity and stimulated innovation that has sought to break away from a 'normal' that is seen as inappropriate and undesirable. Notably, we have highlighted how the potential of adaptive transformation is being embedded in organisations of all types, from top to bottom, to enhance the ability to survive and thrive in foreseen future adversity. Here resilience is framed as both a challenge to overcome *and* an opportunity to swim in new streams and cast away obdurate ways of working and outdated customs and practices. We have also pointed to the possibilities of 'smart resilience' in appropriating digital technologies to stimulate new forms of communication and self-organisation during emergencies, as seen in Haiti in 2010, as well as for overall resilience planning and disaster recovery. Yet the promise of technological silver bullets needs to be handled carefully. Resilience reminds us to stay mindful of the limits of prediction and control. Technology can assist in better understanding complexity, but it also promotes the idea that the world is more predictable than it is. Technological fixes also prompt questions about the extent to which our world is becoming bound by automated and artificial intelligence-driven decision-making and the extent to which our interwoven digitally reliant networks and infrastructures can enhance, rather than reduce, vulnerability. While adding more devices and services to our vast digital networks is an opportunity to do things more effectively and efficiently, it is also a risk. An attack targeting such a complex system, or an accident disabling parts of it, could lead to a rapid and destructive chain reaction or cascade failure.

BECOMING FUTUREPROOF

It has always been impossible to know or predict the future, but societies have always attempted to do so. Procedures have been developed and discourses mobilised to allow us to anticipate the future and come up with narratives to discuss its likely cause and effect, whether by divine intervention, scientific innovation or the rise of human-induced mega-risk that would cause society to collapse. Such approaches have always sought to view the world through different lenses and to allow social progress to advance. Similarly, in the twenty-first century, resilience has the potential to stimulate change in the way we think about future global challenges.

To cope and prosper in conditions of persistent uncertainty requires a number of principles to be enacted in an integrated and holistic fashion if we are to effectively futureproof ourselves. Envisioning and planning for such a future through the lens of resilience must differ from conventional approaches. It must be specific to setting and circumstances, and be particular to risk assessment. It must focus on anticipating future risk while at the same time developing new approaches to deal with future stress and shocks. It must also involve a focus on both tangible results in the short and medium term as well as an appreciation that the process of how we advance longer-term resilience is all-important.

Resilience should be proactive, forward-looking and must embrace complexity. All too often conventional approaches cast the net backwards when looking at known risk and making statistically informed judgements about the future occurrence of disruption. Traditional ways of managing risk do not cope well with unknown disruptions that do not follow expected 'normal' patterns. Resilience-thinking must help us break out of the cycle of being reactive to probable crises and disruption. It must instead anticipate, plan and prepare for unpredictable future risks. We must begin to fully appreciate that the world has previously been presented to us through economic and statistical models that simplify complexity and lead us to misjudge the risk that interwoven and interconnected systems have built up. The cascading of failure through multiple systems – be that in a space shuttle in Florida, a road bridge in Genoa, the global economy, networks of utility infrastructure in Auckland or as a result of a massive cyber-attack in Estonia – showcases the need to work with rather than against complexity if we are to design solutions that are fit for purpose. Thinking in a resilient way means the future is not an extrapolation of the past. It means we have to plan for coming uncertainty, but do so in a way that is transparently organised, fair and equitable.

Resilience should bridge near-term and longer-term issues and needs. Traditional approaches in risk management and their application across fields such as emergency planning, climate change mitigation, infrastructure planning and economic forecasting have tended to focus on the more predictable short term. This has often been driven by the need to mitigate existential threats as quickly as possible and return to stability. By contrast new scenario-planning techniques, informed, but not driven, by experiences of prior disruption and trend analysis, could help decision-makers charged with enhancing resilience understand and deal better with future uncertainties in the medium and longer term. Whether this is the military thinking through war games, or Shell advancing detailed future strategies, developing a range of plausible options for how the future will pan out not only broadens stakeholder engagement but means a single Plan A, or preferred option, is replaced by a number of possible pathways. As we have showcased through examples in New York, London and general approaches promoted by the IPCC, advancing such adaptive pathway approaches puts the focus on the long-term process of resilience while addressing nearer-term needs.

Resilience is all about encouraging the *building of buffers against future uncertainty*. While many former approaches to thinking about the risk of disruption to an organisation, the fracturing of a critical infrastructure or strategies of climate mitigation have often been highly optimised (from an engineering perspective) or efficient (from an economic perspective), contemporary ideas of resilience are all about having the capacity to absorb shock and stress while continuing to operate as required. Resilience encourages the designing-in of redundancy to systems and approaches from the outset. As noted above, this might come through having a range of adaptation pathways. In technical systems with a high degree of brittleness, it might also come through the assurance of spare capacity, or slack, that is developed in order to accommodate and adapt to a range of disruptive challenges or changing circumstances.

Resilience should seek to avoid robust-yet-fragile systems where strength or toughness of components is privileged over redundancy elements. This may, for example, come through ensuring technical components can be compensated by other design elements if they become overstressed, or that a system can quickly reorganise existing practices, protocols or supply chains to avert the worst impacts of a disruption. FEMA cannot afford to be overwhelmed and short-staffed as it was during the hurricane season in 2017, and nuclear power plants cannot afford to have poorly maintained and inefficient backup systems as they did at Chernobyl and Fukushima. Deploying redundancy will require, however, a change in mindset. Having such compensatory systems is more expensive or suboptimal in the short term, and the longer-term potential benefits of having room for manoeuvre when disruption hits will need to be supported.

Resilience-thinking seeks to move beyond conventional approaches to organising the management of risk and promote *integrated and diverse* procedures rather than siloed governance styles. Such readjusted decision-making is more appropriate for dealing with complex and interconnected risk that often propagates often across different scales of operation. Resilience should be promoted not just within a singular or closed system but also across multiple networks, taking a 'system of systems' perspective. Arrangements that support resilience should encourage a wider diversity of stakeholders to have an active voice in decision-making and be rooted in the different expectations of a wide range of partners. Local knowledge – often ignored in government-driven resilience processes – should be incorporated as a priority.

As showcased by the 'Rebuild by Design' competition in New York in the aftermath of Hurricane Sandy, resilience is also about a very different kind of design – not one necessarily with a physical form, but a 'drive or desire to synthesise diverse forms of knowledge and develop collaborative cross-boundary solutions to complex problems'.[17] We have signposted numerous examples, for example at NASA and in Japan during the 2011 triple disaster, where existing procedures were not flexible enough to change, or could not take on board non-standard information. We have also seen how having a lack of diverse viewpoints in the room when decisions are being made can lead to groupthink pervading with alternative viewpoints quashed. The tendency here is to reinforce substandard and non-desired practices, for example the 'resilience creep' seen in the ubiquitous use of security bollards as a resilient design solution to counter-terrorism, where innovative alternatives are largely sidelined in discussion. Through an embrace of the principles of resilience, the governance of risk can be more integrated, holistic and build the capacity to respond to a range of future risks simultaneously.

Resilience is the outcome of and *process of learning* from undertaking many challenging and change-inducing activities in an organisation *before* disruption hits. While risk management processes have been around for a long time and in many cases have become difficult to shift, resilience necessitates change through learning and innovation. In particular, learning is key to enhancing the adaptive capacity and resourcefulness of *everyone* to respond to a multitude of disruptive challenges and in raising awareness of options that are available. The continuous journey of resilience is cyclical rather than linear; one that incorporates and acts on multiple forms of feedback. This can involve the bringing together of lessons from previous disruptions and feeding them back into refinements of risk and resilience plans. Learning is also about experimenting with new and innovative ideas and approaches. As we have exemplified through adaptive delta management in the Netherlands, we need to move out of a fail-safe environment and move towards a safe-to-fail environment. Such an approach encourages trial and error learning as a way to improve the agility of an organisation to deal with disruption and to generate the capacities required for resilience improvement.

While much of the foregoing discussion has been about how society transitions from protective-based risk management towards adaptive-based resilience, there is a still a key role for *protection and fortification* in an overall futureproofing strategy. Resilience here becomes seen in terms of mitigation and *resistance*, where such engineered-in or built-in resilience can be placed under a bounce-back model that seeks to restore normal conditions as soon as possible. It promotes ideas of *robustness* and toughness but can provide vital assurance against risk in the short term. In the name of enhancing resilience, we have seen many of our urban landscapes hardened and pepper-potted with security features to restrict terrorism, and we have seen ever-higher sea walls rebuilt on coastlines to protect against future tsunami or storm surges. We have seen numerous building codes introduced to limit the impact of hurricanes and earthquakes and we have advanced a range of measures – from simple pumps to innovative urban design features – to store or remove floodwaters.

Such short-term security is important in growing an awareness of resilience. This is underpinned by the political prioritisation of safety and security against an array of threats that can weaken the fabric of everyday life. In many countries since 9/11, resilience has been viewed as the protective logic that will make any system tougher and better able to resist disruption. Resilience policy as it emerged in the new millennium was driven by security concerns but, at the same time, security policy or any policy idea that can be loosely associated with security adopted the softer and more palatable language of resilience. Here, such 'hard' views of security and resilience should be seen as a stepping stone towards a softer path for security, including social considerations, while ensuring protection is maintained in a proportionate way.

In contrast to solutions that seek to toughen components of infrastructure or social systems, or which seek equilibrium stability or a status quo position, resilience approaches should be based on *adaptability, flexibility and agility*. Adaption should not be the poor cousin of mitigation. While conventional approaches to the problems of disruption have been based on linear trend analysis, resilience promotes the need to adapt rapidly to an uncertain future where unknown risks abound. Adapting in the face of risk, crisis and disruption has been shown to have a number of catalysts. Most notably, adaptation is stimulated from failure, or what can be termed maladaptation. We adapt by learning from experiences of infrastructure that has broken when put under pressure, sea walls that were not tall enough to avoid overtopping waves, or a planned procedure that has not worked well under disorderly conditions.

The ability to adapt can also come from enhancement of adaptive capacity – how a system, organisation, community or individual can adapt to changing circumstances while still fulfilling its core mission – that is arguably the key component of resilience-thinking. Advancing adaptive characteristics through capacity-building programmes, rolling out longer-term adaptive pathways plans and encouraging flexible, or elastic, thinking through resilience exercises and stress tests, has been shown time and time again to promote the agility to cope with and thrive in future disruptive conditions. Whether it is car markets, soft-drink manufacturers or electronics firms coping with supply chain disruption, the financial industry insisting upon annual stress-tests, the UK government and the European Union planning for a variety of Brexit scenarios, or a city resilience partnership planning for wildfires during a scorching summer, the ability to adapt is a prized advantage. We cannot afford for the future to be locked in if it turns out differently from our best guesses. The tendency when a system crashes is to reboot it, but in today's uncertain world we need to reset it.

When we are thinking through resilience practice, *context is everything*. There are no prescriptive one-size-fits-all models for advancing resilience. The world before resilience was one where the modern world developed general models that were applied elsewhere. However, today we are living in a world of less certainty and more volatility. This necessitates that resilience is customised to suit the needs of each location or system, based on risks profile, resources available, political culture, institutional set-up and data capacities. What might work in New York will not work in London or Lisbon. What has been accepted as flood control practice in the Netherlands will not exactly map onto the urban fabric in New Orleans. In reality, tensions between international policies that are encouraging local resilience measures to be implemented and the centralising tendencies of national governments still often result in countrywide strategies, 'blueprints' and 'models' being developed for local policy delivery. These often come with a requirement to meet centrally derived performance measures and visions.

This, in part, explains why in some areas resilience policy is often pulled off the shelf and mapped uncritically onto a particular organisational landscape without due care. Building the same flood protections or counter-terrorist security features across different locations in the same country as part of an overriding national strategy promotes a standardised approach which is perhaps more prone to failure and less acceptable to the majority of the population. Moving away from one-size-fits-all models and utilising local cultural history and context requires more sophisticated resilience processes and approaches that can reconcile different national and local objectives when the transfer of ideas occurs. Such ways of working are seeking to replace fixed models of change with menus of alternatives, which are selected according to local circumstances, and not centrally prescribed visions.

In order that resilience can be appropriately tailored to context, a degree of *pragmatism* is required. Acting pragmatically based on 'what matters is what works' is seen as crucial in implementing resilience. Resilience is both a concept that allows us to understand complexity and unpredictability, but also an objective of policy underpinned by pragmatic philosophy. Pragmatically futureproofing through strategies of resilience will involve closer consultation with a wider array of stakeholders to develop quality-based routes to excellence as well as giving greater managerial discretion and flexibility to those in charge. Attempts to manage the change towards resilience-working through the transformation of existing management and governance networks is not easy. As we have shown, this is often impeded by locally embedded institutional practices and political allegiances, which affect how national policy guidance is interpreted and actioned on the ground.

A pragmatic operator can acknowledge such shortcomings and work with, rather than against, the grain of custom and practice and seek new solutions. This might mean balancing out, and even trading-off, different requirements. It might mean, for example, sacrificing developable land and giving it over to marshland that will provide a buffer against flooding. It might mean increasing the price of electricity to fund extra backup capacity or redundancy in the gird. It might also mean thinking through how resilience is made affordable for an organisation rather than a sunk cost whose benefit is not seen until disruption hits.

In such cases making the business case for resilience measures in a down-to-earth way has, in some instances, encouraged and rewarded innovative measures that produce 'synergies' and 'co-benefits' that achieve a number of policy goals simultaneously. The integration of rainwater storage measures into vehicle garages, parkland and recreation areas in a number of European cities provides examples of such co-benefits in action. Likewise, the incorporation of much-needed parkland areas with a system of floodwalls, levees and dams in plans for climate-resilience in New York illuminates how pragmatism plays out in getting resilience plans implemented.

While conventional risk management has tended to largely ignore cultural aspects, instead focusing on technical and bureaucratic issues, promoting a *culture of resilience* that incorporates the possibility of many of the above-mentioned principles being enacted is key to advancing resilience as a long-term strategy of futureproofing. Building such a culture occurs across many scales of action: individually, in a community, in a business or as a nation or global community. Culture in this sense cannot be enforced or dictated. It is not something you acquire because you are told to act in a particular way, or because resilience is being prescribed in policy guidance. Advancing a culture of resilience means that resilience principles become the norm and are embedded within how you, communities or organisations think and act.

Here, resilience will often become realised not through state institutions but through localised networked responses, with governance dispersed more widely across key stakeholders and sectors. It becomes part of the collective psyche, as we saw with the Vietnamese community in New Orleans both before and after Hurricane Katrina hit. This does not mean that we should be perpetually anxious about future disruption but rather we can be assured that we are prepared to respond and adapt as required and as best we can. This means an ongoing cycle of preparing, practising, learning and preparing again. Building a culture of resilience should also be appropriate and proportionate to the likely risk, crisis and disruption faced. Building a culture of resilience should therefore utilise a range of plausible scenarios to inform change and not just be focused myopically on preparing for the worst.

ADAPT OR DIE

While the rhetoric of resilience has abounded in the twenty-first century through multiple meanings, with its merits highlighted in numerous discussions, the reality on the ground is that there is still an implementation gap. In delivering resilient solutions to complex problems, the varied ways in which resilience has been deployed has limited the transmission of consistent resilience ideas. Instead, common responses have tended to be incremental, ad hoc and reactive and with a focus on maintaining stability rather than fundamentally changing established modes of action. Simply returning to a balanced position or 'steady state' is not enough.

Resilience should be focusing on preparedness and adaptive capacity in order to manage uncertainty and facilitate transformation. It is about *bouncing forward* and embracing change. It is about shifting the inherently conservative nature of policy-making towards more progressive and flexible solutions.

Advancing what we might call 'adaptive resilience' as a key property of successful systems is vital as we plan to minimise the impact of shocks and stresses in complex and interlinked systems. This means we need to improve our governance capacity to engage in collaborative decision-making, with different networks of formal and informal institutions. Such a requirement shifts the basis of resilience away from just a focus on outcomes that have their roots in engineering and ecological models and towards an emphasis on how a process of more inclusive and deliberative governing arrangements might be fostered.

Despite the ever-expanding use of resilience, it would be fair to say that resilience efforts are currently in a transitionary phase between approaches that focus on equilibrium and evolutionary-type strategies that look to futureproof by mainstreaming forward-looking techniques and adaptability into everyday life. We have shown that the seeds of this transition have been sown and are constantly being watered by the endless stream of disruptions that society faces. However, the speed of transition is being slowed by the enduring popularity of approaches that focus on the return to stability or 'normal', and which do not disturb the status quo. Likewise, the tendency to equate resilience with emergencies and preparation for sudden shocks, or black swan events, is at present limiting the influence of more forward-thinking and adaptive strategies, particularly for 'slow burn' events that emerge over a longer time frame. This is as much a product of the backward-looking nature of forecasting undertaken by the risk industry and models of insurance cover for guarding against risk (replacing what is lost or returning to a state of normality) as it is of stimulating change. Moving out of an obsession with repairing damage in high-risk locations, or simply reconstructing infrastructure in the aftermath of extreme events, is vital. The odds are that all that will happen is that future vulnerability will be increased. As a recent commentary in the *New York Times* recently noted, 'If rebuilding in the same place once dared lightning to strike twice, it now tempts a more certain fate.'[18]

Yet, we can take the behaviour of the insurance industry as a proxy for how we might view future risk. Greater uncertainty is forcing a recalculation of risk and the placing of a value on future unpredictability. The catastrophe models used by insurers are constantly being rethought and their algorithms reprogrammed to uncover their exposure and vulnerability. This is invariably leading to altered risk probabilities that may make some areas of cover in certain locations uninsurable altogether, or at least so risky that the cost would be prohibitively expensive. The insurance voids we are already seeing in certain exposed locations for flooding, wildfires, hurricanes and for terrorist bombings are becoming more widespread as big storms and disasters are pushing many insurance companies to the point of collapse, and leaving investors wary of investing in catastrophe bonds. Rather than being reactive, insurance coverage or national reconstruction grants should refocus on the front end of the problems, and encourage and incentivise appropriate adaptation work for the long term.

FUTUREPROOFING AS METAMORPHISM

In the late 1980s and early 1990s, *Risk Society* implored us to consider how ideas of risk were reshaping the world, often in a negative way. Adapting in a risk society, argued Ulrich Beck, would need what he termed reflexivity, which would require us all to constantly monitor our behaviour and experiences, and make adjustments in the light of new information. This was about raising our awareness of cause and effect, learning from the past to inform the future, and acting proactively on feedback. *Risk Society* urged possible transformation in a modern world where change was often fleeting, temporary and did not stick. Nearly 30 years on, global society is still struggling to deal with mega-risk and requires a more rapid and deep approach to change and transformation. In *The Metamorphosis of the World*, published posthumously in 2015, Beck further argued that the series of fundamental shocks global society had experienced in recent decades had shattered our previous experiences of the world and provided moments of fresh thinking, where 'what was unthinkable yesterday is real and possible today'.[19] This, he reasoned, required not change or transformation, but metamorphosis – 'a much more radical transformation in which the old certainties of modern society are falling away and something quite new is emerging'. What is required is a complete reorientation of our worldview of the kind that the IPCC have been calling for as we lurch into climate Armageddon with our heads buried in the sand. Such metamorphosis can be a positive force and implores us to 'explore new beginnings, to focus on what is emerging from the old and seek to grasp future structures and norms in the turmoil of the present'.

Although Beck never mentions resilience, his thoughts are consistent with those who advocate resilience as a radical transformative agenda of futureproofing – where fear of future disruption is propelling us towards not only attempting to secure the future in the short term, but also building new and sustainable collaborations and relationships, and considering working and acting in ways we have never imagined before. This future is not controllable but in constant flux, and requires adaptability of approach in order to survive and thrive. Resilience, like Beck's *Metamorphosis*, also asks fundamental questions of the present. It illuminates how neither the market nor the state seems to provide coherent responses to the challenges we face. It showcases how partisan politics and a lack of coherent multilateralism at the international level often leads to inaction, the promotion of business-as-usual approaches and self-reinforcing 'gridlock' where nothing really changes.[20] Moreover, it can highlight how the vast majority of our existing approaches (some of which might be badged as resilience) do not fully embrace, or work with, complexity.

In many ways, while we have a multitude of resilience policies and resilience-thinking in many diverse areas, the fundamental essence of resilience in action is hard to find as orthodox approaches still dominate. Progressive types of resilience have seldom been fully embraced and hence have been an easy target of understandable criticism. *What has been done in the name of resilience is often nothing of the sort*. However, where resilience has – and will – increasingly prove useful in futureproofing efforts is as an explanatory framework for assisting us all in understanding and being better able to respond collaboratively and transformatively to twenty-first century risk that is characterised by high levels of interdependency, volatility, uncertainty and complexity. This is the evolution resilience requires to be a bounce-forward process of choice, not a bounce-back option of necessity.

In a famous quote attributed to Charles Darwin it was argued that it is not the strongest that survives but the most adaptable. This has given way to the shorthand version which simply urges us to 'adapt or die'. But standing, as we do, at the crossroads of history, and on the cusp of an age of permanent adaptation, we should not forget that another saying attributed to Darwin also gives us a hint about how to adapt: 'In the long history of humankind (and animal kind too) it is those who have learned to collaborate and improvise most effectively that have prevailed.'[21] And here we have it. Resilience is (or should be) a collective action problem that reframes the world around us, which draws on past experiences to inform the long future. It is a test of our capabilities to adapt and prosper in an uncertain world. It is the capacity of self-reliant individuals and communities to address complex and 'wicked' problems and secure our future. Resilience holds the potential to futureproof our world as an antidote to 'new normal' levels of uncertainty and volatility, and redesign life in the twenty-first century.

ENDNOTES

INTRODUCTION

1. White House, *Opportunities for Building Community Climate Resilience across the Nation*, Council on Climate Preparedness and Resilience, 2016, October.
2. Jon Coaffee and Peter Lee, *Urban Resilience: Planning for Risk Crisis and Uncertainty*, London: Palgrave, 2016.
3. Nassim Nicholas Taleb, *The Black Swan: The Impact of the Highly Improbable*, New York: Random House, 2017.
4. At the time of writing in late 2018, even more devastating wildfires are destroying vast tracts of land in California and have left at least 100 people dead.
5. Iain White and Graham Haughton, 'Risky Times: Hazard Management and the Tyranny of the Present', *International Journal of Disaster Risk Reduction*, vol. 22, 2017, pp. 412–19.
6. Ulrich Beck, 'The Anthropological Shock: Chernobyl and the Contours of the Risk Society', *Berkeley Journal of Sociology*, vol. 32, 1987, pp. 153–65.
7. Ulrich Beck, *Risk Society: Towards a New Modernity*, London: Sage Publications, 1992.
8. Paul Crutzen and Eugene Stoermer, 'The Anthropocene', *Global Change Newsletter*, vol. 41, May 2000.
9. Colin Waters et al., 'The Anthropocene is Functionally and Stratigraphically Distinct from the Holocene', *Science*, vol. 351, issue 6269, January 2016.
10. Roy Scranton, *Learning to Die in the Anthropocene*, San Francisco: City Light, 2015, p. 22.
11. Frank Biermann, 'The Anthropocene: A Governance Perspective', *The Anthropocene Review*, vol. 1:1, 2014, pp. 57–61.
12. Dan Gardner, *Risk: The Science and Politics of Fear*, London: Virgin Books, 2009, p. 11.
13. Yuval Noah Harari, *Homo Deus: A Brief History of Tomorrow*, London: Random House, 2016.
14. Following the first industrial revolution which was steam powered, the second electrical and the third the birth of the computer age.
15. Klaus Schwab, *The Fourth Industrial Revolution*, London: Portfolio Penguin, 2016.
16. Ibid.
17. Stephen Flynn, *The Edge of Disaster: Rebuilding a Resilient Nation*, New York: Random House, 2007.
18. David Chandler, *Resilience: The Governance of Complexity*, London: Routledge, 2014.
19. David Chandler and Jon Coaffee (eds), *The Routledge Handbook of International Resilience*, London: Routledge, 2016.
20. Isabelle Stengers, *In Catastrophic Times: Resisting the Coming Barbarism*, Paris: Meson Press, 2015.

21. Simon Dalby, 'Biopolitics and Climate Security in the Anthropocene', *Geoforum*, vol. 49, 2013, p. 189.
22. Here an array of contemporary practices and policy areas are showcased to identify the opportunities and challenges of embedding such principles into real-life situations. Detailed examples are drawn from resilience-thinking being used in tackling climate change, national security, critical infrastructure protection, economic volatility and organisational change, rapid urbanisation and disaster recovery.

1 FATE, CHOICE AND THE BIRTH OF RISK

1. Ulrich Beck, *World at Risk*, Cambridge: Polity, 2007, p. 4.
2. Svetlana Alexievich, *Chernobyl Prayer: A Chronicle of the Future*, trans. Anna Gunin and Arch Tait, London: Penguin Modern Classics, 2016.
3. Pre-modern societies can be characterised by a combination of economic, political and cultural circumstances. Notably, many people's sense of self and purpose was often expressed via a faith in some form of deity. The modern era is generally thought to have begun around AD 1500.
4. Then the Lord rained brimstone and fire on Sodom and Gomorrah, from the Lord out of the heavens (Genesis 19:24). Turning the cities of Sodom and Gomorrah into ashes condemned them to destruction, making them an example to those who afterward would live ungodly (2 Peter 2:6).
5. Peter Bernstein, *Against the Gods: The Remarkable Story of Risk*, New York: Wiley, 1998, p. 1.
6. Ibid., p. 1.
7. Peter Bernstein, *Runaway World: How Globalisation is Reshaping our Lives*, London: Profile Books, 1999, pp. 22–3.
8. The Renaissance is seen as a period of European history that provided the cultural bridge between the Middle Ages and the early modern era.
9. Gerrit Jasper Schenk, 'Disastro, Catastrophe, and Divine Judgment', in Jennifer Spinks and Charles Zika (eds), *Disasters, Death and the Emotions in the Shadow of the Apocalypse, 1400–1700*, London: Palgrave Macmillan, 2016, pp. 45–67.
10. Indeed, the origins of the term disaster come from two Latin words *dis-* and *astrum*, roughly translating as 'bad star', and were seen to relate to the unfavourable alignment of planets or stars.
11. Alexandra Walsham, 'Deciphering Divine Wrath and Displaying Godly Sorrow', in Spinks and Zika, *Disasters, Death and the Emotions*, pp. 21, 43.
12. Jon Coaffee, David Murakami Wood and Peter Rogers, *The Everyday Resilience of the City: How Cities Respond to Terrorism and Disaster*, Basingstoke: Palgrave Macmillan, 2008.
13. Augustine of Hippo, *De civitate Dei*, London: Penguin, 2003, pp. 413–26.
14. The relationship of cities to natural events is a complex one. That events become hazardous or disastrous is undoubtedly as much a consequence of the patterns and intensities of human activity as it is the destructive power of Mother Nature.
15. Robert Yeats, *Living with Earthquakes in California: A Survivor's Guide*, Corvallis, OR: Oregon State University Press, 2001, p. 193.
16. William McNeill, *Plagues and Peoples*, London: Bantam, 1998.
17. Louise Marshall, 'God's Executioners: Angels, Devils and the Plague in Giovanni Secambi's Illustrated Chronicle', in Spinks and Zika, *Disasters, Death and the Emotions*, pp. 177–99.
18. Spinks and Zika, *Disasters, Death and the Emotions*, p. 3.
19. Stories of razing or destroying cities after battles or sieges were often exaggerated and sometimes referred only to the destruction of walls or towers, so care is needed with many accounts.
20. See for example Richard Miles, *Carthage Must Be Destroyed: The Rise and Fall of an Ancient Civilization*, London: Penguin, 2012.

21. Spinks and Zika, *Disasters, Death and the Emotions*, p. 4.
22. Russell Dynes, 'The Lisbon Earthquake in 1755: The First Modern Disaster', University of Delaware Disaster Research Center, Preliminary Paper #333, 2003.
23. An inquisition was established in the city to counter what was considered the ungodly materialism of the wealthy city leading to the persecution of the Lisbon Jews, who were its bankers, financiers and moneylenders.
24. Russell Dynes, 'The Dialogue between Voltaire and Rousseau on the Lisbon Earthquake: The Emergence of a Social Science View', University of Delaware Disaster Research Center Preliminary Paper #293, 1999, p. 2.
25. François-Marie Arouet, better known as Voltaire, was a French historian who became famous for his attacks on religion, support for freedom of speech and for advocating the separation of church and state. Jean-Jacques Rousseau by contrast was an Austrian philosopher whose main concern was with the development of modern political and educational thought.
26. Such ideas were later to be embedded within Rousseau's classic 1762 work *On the Social Contract* that inspired political reforms or revolutions in Europe.
27. José Marques, 'The Paths of Providence: Voltaire and Rousseau on the Lisbon Earthquake', *Cadernos de História e Filosofia da Ciência*, Campinas: CLE-Unicamp, Série 3, 15, no. 1, 2005, pp. 33–57.
28. Immanuel Kant (1724–1804) is considered the most influential thinker of the Enlightenment era. Kant also made an important contribution to science and is considered one of the most important figures in the development of modern science and its liberation from theology.
29. He concluded that the source of the earthquake lay in cracks and caverns in the Atlantic Ocean. These impressive scientific reports are considered the start of modern seismological research.
30. This debate still rages in the contemporary period and will be further explored in chapter 8.
31. Cited in Bernstein, *Against the Gods*, pp. 20–21.
32. Descartes was convinced that as long as 'I' am a thinking being, 'I' cannot doubt my own existence, for there must be an 'I' who is doing the thinking, not God; René Descartes, *Meditations on First Philosophy* (subtitled 'In which the existence of God and the immortality of the soul are demonstrated'), first published in 1641.
33. Spinks and Zika, *Disasters, Death and the Emotions*, p. 8.
34. Written as a short essay sometime between 1613 and 1623.
35. Pascal is best known for Pascal's Triangle, a convenient tabular presentation of binomial co-efficients, where each number is the sum of the two numbers directly above it. Pascal used the Triangle to help solve problems in probability theory.
36. The probability of something occurring could be computed by totalling the number of equally likely ways it could occur, and dividing this by the total number of possible outcomes in a given situation. This allowed the use of fractions and ratios in the calculation of the likelihood of events, and the operation of multiplication and addition on these fractional probabilities.
37. Bernstein, *Against the Gods*, p. 72.
38. The origins of the word 'insurance' can be traced back to the fifteenth century, from the Anglo-Norman word 'enseurer' ('make sure'). The word 'insurance' has been commonly used with its current meaning since the sixteenth century.
39. At this time there was no organised fire brigade and attempts to extinguish the fire were futile. In the wake of the fire, London had to be almost totally reconstructed. The cost of the fire was estimated to be £10 million, at a time when London's annual income was only £12,000. Although the verified death toll was only six people it is unknown how many people died in the Great Fire of London because many more died through indirect causes.
40. www.abi.org.uk/products-and-issues/topics-and-issues/great-fire-of-london/ (accessed 1 March 2018).

41. Its full name was 'The Insurance Office for Houses, on the Backside of the Royal Exchange'. The scheme entered into around 10,000 policies, until it was dissolved around 1710.
42. Athens and other Greek cities expanded as a result of their ports, and without the Ancient Romans 'insuring' trading ships, the major port cities of the Roman Empire would never have received enough goods to expand as they did. Marine loans were essentially speculative, with merchants funding various voyages with loans to shipmasters who could not afford the journey in return for a proportion of the profit made from selling the cargo.
43. James Franklin, *The Science of Conjecture: Evidence and Probability before Pascal*, Baltimore: Johns Hopkins University Press, 2001, pp. 273–8.
44. Given the demand for its services, a dense infrastructure of insurance-related industries quickly colonised central London, helping it establish itself as the world's principal financial centre and leading to the expansion of the British Empire.
45. In growing his business, Lloyd launched *Lloyd's List* in 1696 and accumulated information and intelligence on conditions abroad and at sea in order to better determine premiums.
46. In many areas of insurance, such tables are still used when assessing risk and calculating insurance rates.
47. The work of Jacob Bernoulli and others underpins most attempts at risk management and insurance that relies upon 'normal distribution'. Conventionally this is often expressed on a bell curve and tells you how all your data is clustered around the mean. In essence, insurance exploits the statistical properties of a large number of independent risks to offer more accurate premiums.
48. Pierre Laplace, *A Philosophical Essay on Probabilities 1814*, London: Chapman & Hall, 1902.
49. The phrase 'God is Dead' or the 'Death of God' first appeared in Nietzsche's 1882 collection 'The Gay Science' (*Die fröhliche Wissenschaft*), but is most famously associated with his classic work *Thus Spoke Zarathustra*, published between 1883 and 1891.
50. Max Weber, *The Protestant Ethic and the Spirit of Capitalism*, New York: Scribner, 1958 (first published in 1905).
51. This came to represent the effective rationalisation of risk in modern society and encompasses three key elements that can be related to probability and risk assessment: efficiency, predictability (especially predicting the future and forecasting) and calculability (with a focus on numerical data, statistics and scoring).
52. See for example the work of Henri Poincaré, which has been instrumental in distinguishing chaos from randomness.
53. Bernstein, *Against the Gods*, p. 216.
54. Frank Knight, *Risk, Uncertainty and Profit*, Los Angeles: Hardpress Publishing, 2015 (first published in 1921).
55. Here likelihood is the probability of occurrence of an impact, and consequence is the impact if an event occurs.
56. Gabe Mythen, *Ulrich Beck: A Critical Introduction to the Risk Society*, London: Pluto Press, 2004, p. 1.
57. Anthony Giddens, *The Consequences of Modernity*, Cambridge: Polity, 1990, p. 139.
58. Deborah Lupton, *Risk*, London: Routledge, 1999, p. 13.
59. Ulrich Beck, *Ecological Politics in an Age of Risk*, Cambridge: Polity, 1995, p. 139.
60. Here Beck champions the idea of reflexivity that has emerged as a key concept in the social sciences in relation to thinking about risk and uncertainty as a way to constantly monitor experiences, and make adjustments in the light of new information.
61. Ibid., p. 31.
62. Cited in Martin Giles, 'On shaky ground – insurers are being asked to deal with unprecedented risks, creating pressure on governments to foot more of the bill. That would be a mistake', *The Economist*, 3 December 1994, p. 10.
63. Andrew Dlugolecki, 'Climate Change and the Insurance Industry', *The Geneva Papers on Risk and Insurance: Issues and Practice*, vol. 25:4, 2000, pp. 582–601.

64. David Lowenthal, 'The Death of the Future', in Sandra Wallman (ed.), *Contemporary Futures: Perspectives from Social Anthropology*, London: Routledge, 1992, pp. 23–35.

2 THE RESILIENCE TURN AND THE PERMANENT STATE OF ADAPTATION

1. Brian Walker and David Salt, *Resilience Thinking: Sustaining Ecosystems and People in a Changing World*, Washington DC, Island Press, 2006, p. xiv.
2. http://uk.reuters.com/article/us-britain-floods-idUKKBN0UB16I20151229 (accessed 29 December 2015).
3. Lee Bosher, 'Built-in Resilience through Disaster Risk Reduction: Operational Issues', *Building Research and Information*, vol. 42:2, 2014, pp. 240–54.
4. UN-HABITAT, *Cities and Climate Change: Global Report on Human Settlements*, London: Earthscan, 2011.
5. David Chandler and Jon Coaffee, *The Routledge Handbook of International Resilience*, London: Routledge, 2016.
6. Igor Linkov, Benjamin Trump and Jeffrey Keisler, 'Don't Conflate Risk and Resilience', correspondence to *Nature*, vol. 555, March 2018, p. 30.
7. The postmodern condition is the economic or cultural state of society which is said to exist after modernity and which rejects rational and linear approaches to the study of society or to social progress.
8. David Chandler, *Resilience: The Governance of Complexity*, London: Routledge, 2014.
9. Chandler and Coaffee, *The Routledge Handbook*.
10. Many have pointed out that what Rumsfeld forgot to add was the crucial fourth term: the 'unknown knowns'. These refer to the things we don't know that we know, for example all the unconscious beliefs and prejudices that determine how we see the world and use the power we have (or don't have) to intervene in it.
11. The United Nations Conference on Environment and Development, also known as the Earth Summit, held in Rio de Janeiro in June 1992, was especially influential in promoting ideas of sustainability.
12. www.nytimes.com/2012/11/03/opinion/forget-sustainability-its-about-resilience.html?_r=1 (accessed 4 November 2012).
13. Chandler and Coaffee, *The Routledge Handbook*.
14. Kevin Grove, *Resilience*, London: Routledge, 2018.
15. The Resilience Alliance is a research network comprised of scientists and practitioners from many disciplines who collaborate to explore the dynamics of social-ecological systems.
16. C. S. Holling, 'Engineering Resilience versus Ecological Resilience', in P. C. Schulze (ed.), *Engineering within Ecological Constraints*, Washington DC: National Academy Press, 1996, pp. 31–43.
17. This is despite supporters of ecological resilience suggesting an updated approach – Panarchy – premised upon a hierarchy of adaptive cycles, named after the Greek god Pan, the epitome of unpredictable change; Lance Gunderson and C. S. Holling (eds), *Panarchy: Understanding Transformations in Human and Natural Systems*, Washington DC: Island Press, 2002.
18. Katrina Brown, 'Global Environmental Change I: A Social Turn for Resilience?', *Progress in Human Geography*, vol. 37, 2013, pp. 1–11.
19. Judith Rodin, *The Resilience Dividend: Managing Disruption, Avoiding Disaster, and Growing Stronger in an Unpredictable World*, London: Profile Books, 2015.
20. Kathleen Tierney, *The Social Roots of Risk: Producing Disasters, Promoting Resilience*, Stanford, CA: Stanford University Press, 2014.
21. Tim Harford, *Adapt: Why Success Always Starts with Failure*, London: Abacus, 2012.
22. But while evolution in Darwinian terms was seen as a natural process, it was devoid of the foresight that the modern world has acquired through mathematics, statistics and probability that has allowed human progress through attempts to control future risk.

23. Intergovernmental Panel on Climate Change, *Third Assessment Report: Climate Change*, 2001, www.ipcc.ch/ipccreports/tar/wg2/index.php?idp=689 (accessed 1 December 2012).
24. Royal Society, *Resilience to Extreme Weather*, London: Royal Society, 2015.
25. See for example, Jean Carlson and John Doyle, 'Highly Optimized Tolerance: Robustness and Design in Complex Systems', *Physics Review Letters*, vol. 84:11, 2000, pp. 2529–32.
26. Andrew Zolli and Ann Marie Healy, *Resilience: Why Things Bounce Back*, London: Headline, 2013, p. 28.
27. Ibid.
28. Grove Karl Gilbert, 'Earthquake Prediction', presidential address to the American Association of Geographers, read at Baltimore, MD, 1 January 1909. Reproduced in *Science*, vol. XXIX:734, Friday 22 January, pp. 121–37.
29. 'Earthquake Outlook for the San Francisco Bay Region 2014–2043', *US Geological Survey*, 2016.
30. The Hayward Fault is still capable of generating destructive earthquakes just as it did in 1868. This fault is about 74 miles long on the east side of the San Francisco Bay area, running through Oakland, Fremont and San Jose. The Hayward Fault is parallel to the San Andreas Fault which lies offshore and whose rupturing caused the 1906 quake.
31. See for example Edward Lorenz, 'Deterministic Non-periodic Flow', *Journal of the Atmospheric Sciences*, vol. 20:2, 1963, pp. 130–41.
32. Forecasting regularly occurring events like the weather is more accurate, at least in the short term, than predicting less frequently occurring events as there is less historic data available from which to calculate probabilities.
33. Normally only a small number of scenarios (usually four) are produced to avoid confusion and inaction in strategic policy-makers who can struggle when confronted with too much choice and too much uncertainty.
34. In the last decade, scenario methods have also become widely used by a number of governments in Europe to plan policy-making and have alternatively been termed foresight or strategic foresight. In essence, this is a way of identifying and assessing opportunities and threats that may arise out of different possible policy scenarios and which can be used to improve decision-making and strategy setting.
35. Groupthink is a recognised psychological response that occurs within groups in which the desire for conformity in the group results in an irrational decision-making outcome. Here group members try to minimise conflict and reach a consensus decision without properly considering alternative or dissenting viewpoints and by isolating themselves from outside influences.
36. Such an approach has also been termed resilience pathways or dynamic adaptive policy pathways.
37. Marjolijn Haasnoot et al., 'Exploring Pathways for Sustainable Water Management in River Deltas in a Changing Environment', *Climatic Change*, vol. 115, 2012, pp. 795–819.
38. A weak aspect of the method, however, is that it relies on highly detailed information and the capacity of stakeholders to manage long-term pathways. As such, adaptation approaches have tended to be advanced in situations where there is a strong evidence base and where lots of data is available.
39. Work focusing on experiential learning and adaptation is central to notions of adaptive management, which formed the cornerstone of classic ecological resilience ideas.

3 ANTICIPATING CLIMATE ARMAGEDDON

1. Naomi Klein, *This Changes Everything*, London: Penguin Random House, 2015.
2. Ashley Dawson, *Extreme Cities: The Peril and the Promise of Urban Life in the Age of Climate Change*, London: Verso, 2017.

3. Shimon Wdowinski et al., 'Increasing Flooding Hazard in Coastal Communities Due to Rising Sea Level: Case Study of Miami Beach, Florida', *Ocean & Coastal Management*, vol. 26, 2016, pp. 1–8.
4. www.ucsusa.org/global-warming/global-warming-impacts/sea-level-rise-chronic-floods-and-us-coastal-real-estate-implications#.W6o9LS2ZO8X (accessed 1 October 2018).
5. www.miaminewtimes.com/news/five-the-scariest-climate-change-studies-impacting-miami-florida-9309343 (accessed 2 May 2017).
6. Dawson, *Extreme Cities*.
7. Jeff Goodell, *The Water Will Come: Rising Seas, Sinking Cities, and the Remaking of the Civilized World*, London: Little, Brown and Company, 2017.
8. Here they are being afforded the very rare opportunity to learn about issues from other cities that are grappling with similar sea level rise concerns.
9. The Greater Miami area is no stranger to leading international efforts in proactive planning. In the wake of the devastation caused by Hurricane Andrew in 1992, hurricane-resistant building codes were developed which have become best practice across the country and internationally. These passed the test of Hurricane Irma in 2017. A similar ethic of prevention – and of resilience – is needed to cope with the challenges of sea level rise.
10. http://amp.miamiherald.com/opinion/op-ed/article218581445.html (accessed 17 September 2018).
11. www.theguardian.com/environment/2018/may/18/climate-change-an-existential-security-risk-to-australia-senate-inquiry-says?CMP=Share_iOSApp_Other (accessed 17 May 2018).
12. For their work the IPCC was awarded the Nobel peace prize alongside US politician Al Gore Jr.
13. www.theguardian.com/environment/2007/dec/12/bali.climatechange1 (accessed 12 December 2007).
14. Klein, *This Changes Everything*, p. 2. Here she was referring to dirtier and more polluting forms of fossil fuel extraction, notably fracking and tar-sands exploitation.
15. Klein, *This Changes Everything*. As Naomi Klein asserts, 'Governments and scientists began talking seriously about radical cuts to greenhouse gas emissions in 1988 – the exact year that marked the dawning of what came to be called globalization' (p. 18).
16. The second assessment report was published in 1995 and the third in 2001.
17. Klein, *This Changes Everything*, p. 11.
18. Royal Society, *Resilience to Extreme Weather*, London: Royal Society, 2015.
19. Hartmut Fünfgeld and Darryn McEvoy, 'Resilience as a Useful Concept for Climate Change Adaptation?', *Planning Theory and Practice*, vol. 13:2, 2012, pp. 324–8.
20. UN-Habitat, *Cities and Climate Change: Global Report on Human Settlements*, London: Earthscan, 2011.
21. Notable international publications and work programmes include: the UN-Habitat *Cities and Climate Change Initiative* (from 2008); the World Bank primer on *Climate Resilient Cities* (2009); and more generic approaches to urban resilience which have a significant climate change adaptation component such as the UNISDR's *Making Cities Resilient Campaign* (2010), the UN-Habitat (2011) *Global Report on Human Settlements – Cities and Climate Change: Policy Directions*, and international urban capacity-building programmes such as the *Compact of Mayors* (from 2014) – an agreement by city networks to support each other in enhancing resilience to climate change.
22. Harriet Bulkeley and Rafael Tuts, 'Understanding Urban Vulnerability, Adaptation and Resilience in the Context of Climate Change', *Local Environment*, vol. 18:6, 2013, pp. 646–62.
23. Mark Pelling, *Adaptation to Climate Change: From Resilience to Transformation*, London: Routledge, 2011.
24. Brisbane City Council, *Brisbane's Total Water Cycle Management Plan*, 2013.
25. Ibid.

26. The Sponge City initiative was launched in 2015 with sixteen model sponge cities, before being extended to thirty, including Shanghai, see www.theguardian.com/world/2017/dec/28/chinas-sponge-cities-are-turning-streets-green-to-combat-flooding (accessed 5 March 2019).
27. www.un.org/apps/news/story.asp?NewsID=52710#.VnKiA2fnmUl (accessed 2 December 2015).
28. United Nations Framework Convention on Climate Change, 2015.
29. The US is known to be the world's second largest emitter of carbon after China. Together the countries produced 45 per cent of the world's carbon dioxide emissions in 2014.
30. One hundred and ninety-five countries agreed to the Paris accord; only Syria and Nicaragua didn't sign it.
31. United Nations Framework Convention on Climate Change, 2015.
32. To achieve this, the Paris Agreement stipulates that all countries shall review their contributions to reducing greenhouse gas emissions every five years.
33. https://obamawhitehouse.archives.gov/the-press-office/2015/11/30/remarks-president-obama-first-session-cop21 (accessed 1 January 2016).
34. The executive order signed by President Obama confirming the US's adoption of the agreement wasn't submitted to Congress, meaning the US's commitment could be cancelled.
35. *The Baked Apple? Metropolitan New York in the Greenhouse*, New York Academy of Sciences, 1996; *Hot Nights in the City: Global Warming, Sea-Level Rise and the New York Metropolitan Region*, Environmental Defense Fund, 1999; *Climate Change and a Global City: Potential Consequences of Climate Variability and Change*, US National Assessment & Columbia Earth Institute, 2001.
36. Of the 127 initiatives in PlaNYC, 97 per cent were launched within one year of its release and almost two-thirds of its 2009 milestones were achieved or mostly achieved. The plan was updated in 2011.
37. This multistep planning process was seen as an essential approach given the levels of uncertainty, and includes evaluation of plans and strategies and monitoring of results.
38. Cited in Melissa Wagner et al., 'Adaptive Capacity in Light of Hurricane Sandy: The Need for Policy Engagement', *Applied Geography*, vol. 50, 2014, pp. 15–23.
39. www.theguardian.com/cities/2015/mar/09/bjarke-ingels-new-york-dryline-park-flood-hurricane-sandy (accessed 9 March 2015).
40. New York State 2100 Commission, *Recommendations to Improve the Strength and Resilience of the Empire State's Infrastructure*, 2013.
41. Urban Green Building Council, *Building Resiliency Task Force*, June 2013.
42. Henk Ovink and Jelte Boeijenga, *Too Big: Rebuild by Design: A Transformational Approach to Climate Change*, Netherlands: nai010, 2018.
43. Ibid.
44. Ibid.
45. Some research is arguing that the overriding idea of resilience is obscuring some of the uneven distribution of actual resilience initiatives in New York.
46. www1.nyc.gov/office-of-the-mayor/news/459-18/2019-to-onenyc-plan-strong-just-city-launches-today (accessed 5 September 2018).
47. www1.nyc.gov/office-of-the-mayor/news/271-17/mayor-new-resiliency-guidelines-prepare-city-s-infrastructure-buildings-for (accessed 28 April 2017).
48. Klein, *This Changes Everything.*
49. Ovink and Boeijenga, *Too Big.*

4 RESPONSIVE CRITICAL INFRASTRUCTURE LIFELINES

1. National Infrastructure Advisory Council (NIAC), *Critical Infrastructure Resilience Final Report and Recommendations*, NIAC, 2009.

2. Less than two years previously, 9/11 had proved a classic case of cascading failure on New York's interdependent infrastructures where building collapse triggered water-main breaks that flooded the subway and the vault containing all of the main telecommunication cables that kept the city linked into the global economy.
3. Thomas Fisher, *Designing to Avoid Disaster: The Nature of Fracture-critical Design*, London: Routledge, 2012.
4. https://placesjournal.org/article/fracture-critical (accessed 20 October 2012).
5. Auroop Ratan Ganguly, Udit Bhatia and Stephen E. Flynn, *Critical Infrastructures Resilience: Policy and Engineering Principles*, London: Routledge, 2018.
6. National Association of Counties, *Improving Lifelines: Protecting Critical Infrastructure for Resilient Counties*, 2014.
7. Gianluca Pescaroli and David Alexander, 'A Definition of Cascading Disasters and Cascading Effects: Going Beyond the "Toppling Dominos" Metaphor', *Planet@Risk* Glob Forum Davos, vol. 3:1, 2015, pp. 58–67.
8. A further result of this trend has been the expansion of infrastructures considered to be critical and which has seen a shift from the line-based systems of public utilities to more complex social infrastructures which safeguard the well-being of citizens and private enterprises performing socially significant roles.
9. Siemens, *Toolkit for Resilient Cities*, 2013.
10. Brad Evans and Julian Reid, *Resilient Life: The Art of Living Dangerously*, Cambridge: Polity, 2014, p. 18.
11. Richard Little, 'Holistic Strategy for Urban Security', *Journal of Infrastructure Systems*, vol. 10:2, 2004, p. 52.
12. Michel Bruneau et al., 'A Framework to Quantitatively Assess and Enhance the Seismic Resilience of Communities', *Earthquake Spectra*, vol. 19:4, 2003, pp. 733–52.
13. Ronald Fisher and Michael Norman, 'Developing Measurement Indices to Enhance Protection and Resilience of Critical Infrastructure and Key Resources', *Journal of Business Continuity & Emergency Planning*, vol. 4:3, 2010, pp.191–206.
14. Ganguly et al., *Critical Infrastructures Resilience*.
15. Lewis Perelman, 'Shifting Security Paradigms: Toward Resilience', *Critical Thinking: Moving from Infrastructure Protection to Infrastructure Resilience*, George Mason University, 2007, p. 24.
16. Amory Lovins, 'Energy Strategy: The Path Not Taken?', *Foreign Affairs*, vol. 55:1, 1976, p. 88.
17. Igor Linkov and José Manuel Palma-Oliveira (eds), *Resilience and Risk: Methods and Application in Environment, Cyber and Social Domains*, Dordrecht, The Netherlands: Springer, 2017.
18. Christine Pommerening, 'Resilience in Organizations and Systems: Background and Trajectories of an Emerging Paradigm', *Critical Thinking: Moving from Infrastructure Protection to Infrastructure Resilience*, George Mason University, 2007, p. 10.
19. Barack Obama, Presidential Policy Directive 21: *Critical Infrastructure Security and Resilience*, Washington DC, 2013.
20. Australian Government, *Critical Infrastructure Resilience Strategy*, 2010.
21. Such attacks are increasingly seen as a new and emerging military strategy. This has been increasingly termed hybrid warfare which blends conventional warfare, irregular warfare and cyber warfare.
22. A botnet is a number of Internet-connected devices, each of which is running one or more bots. Botnets can be used to perform distributed denial of service (DDoS) attacks, steal data, send spam and allow the attacker to access the device and its connection.
23. https://e-estonia.com/how-estonia-became-a-global-heavyweight-in-cyber-security (accessed 1 October 2018).
24. www.nytimes.com/2017/07/06/technology/nuclear-plant-hack-report.html (accessed 6 July 2017).
25. www.symantec.com/blogs/threat-intelligence/dragonfly-energy-sector-cyber-attacks (accessed 20 October 2017).

26. www.reuters.com/article/us-usa-cyber/u-s-homeland-security-unveils-new-cyber-security-strategy-amid-threats-idUSKCN1IG2L9 (accessed 15 May 2018).
27. Lance Gunderson and C. S. Holling (eds), *Panarchy: Understanding Transformations in Human and Natural Systems*, Washington DC: Island Press, 2002.
28. A traditional 'science first' approach that starts with projections and predicted impacts and only then focuses on adaptation options to reduce these impacts.
29. Environment Agency, *TE2100 Plan: Managing Flood Risk through London and the Thames Estuary*, 2012.
30. Tim Reeder and Nicola Ranger, 'How Do You Adapt in an Uncertain World? Lessons from the Thames Estuary 2100 Project', *World Resources Report*, Washington DC, 2011.
31. Ibid.
32. Ibid.
33. Ibid.
34. Delta Alliance, *Towards a Comprehensive Framework for Adaptive Delta Management*, 2014, p. 2.
35. Han Meyer, Dale Morris and David Waggonner, *Dutch Dialogues – New Orleans – The Netherlands – Common Challenges in Urban Deltas*, Amsterdam: SUN, 2009.
36. As the World Economic Forum noted in their 2014 report into *Risk and Responsibility in the Hyperconnected World*, 'The collective ability to manage cyber risk in this shared digital environment is fundamental. It forms the crux of cyber resilience.'

5 SECURITY, RESILIENCE AND PREPAREDNESS

1. Lord Toby Harris, 'London's Preparedness to Respond to a Major Terrorist Incident', london.gov.uk, 2016.
2. www.theguardian.com/australia-news/2016/aug/18/melbourne-wins-worlds-most-liveable-city-award-sixth-year-in-a-row (accessed 18 August 2016).
3. Australia's Strategy for Protecting Crowded Places from Terrorism, 2017.
4. 'Premier announces anti-terror bollards for Melbourne's CBD', *The Age*, 10 June 2017.
5. Sandra Walklate and Gabe Mythen, *Contradictions of Terrorism: Security, Risk and Resilience*, London: Routledge, 2014, p. 144.
6. Dan Gardner, *Risk: The Science and Politics of Fear*, London: Virgin Books, 2009, p. 296.
7. Walklate and Mythen, *Contradictions of Terrorism.*
8. www.bbc.co.uk/news/world-europe-44502949 (accessed 15 June 2018).
9. www.dailystar.co.uk/news/latest-news/586889/paris-wall-france-eiffel-tower-barrier-security-terror-threat (accessed 9 February 2018).
10. Ulrich Beck, *World Risk Society*, Cambridge: Polity, 1999, p. 153.
11. Mary Douglas, *Purity and Danger: An Analysis of the Concepts of Pollution and Taboo*, London: Routledge, 1966.
12. A vehicle bomb left in a parking area below the iconic World Trade Center in February 1993 exploded, killing six and injuring over 1,000 people,
13. Patricia-Lee Brown, 'Designs in a Land of Bombs and Guns', *New York Times*, 28 May 1995, p. 10.
14. The Alfred P. Murrah Federal Building in Oklahoma City was devastated by a truck bomb in April 1995, killing 168 and injuring over 800.
15. Executive Order 12977 – 19 October 1995.
16. Eve Hinman and David Hammond, *Lessons from the Oklahoma City Bombing: Defensive Design Techniques*, Reston, VA: American Society of Civil Engineers, 1997.
17. Martha Baer, Katrina Heron, Oliver Morton and Evan Ratliff, *Safe: The Race to Protect Ourselves in a Newly Dangerous World*, New York: HarperCollins, 2005, p. 2.
18. The proactive defence of buildings and structures from explosions *per se* at this time was not new and hence military experts who had developed expertise in 'blast resistant

design' for missile silos or Cold War bunkers were drafted in to assist in the protection of civic buildings.

19. Martin Pawley, *Terminal Architecture*, London: Reaktion, 1998.
20. Most notably the Provisional Irish Republican Army (IRA) and Real IRA.
21. The counter-response came from the IRA in February 1991 when, during a 'Gulf War' cabinet meeting, the IRA fired a number of mortar bombs at the prime minister's residence.
22. In November 1992 a bomb was found under One Canada Square in the London Docklands, and in February 1996 the IRA succeeded in bombing the London Docklands, at South Quay Station.
23. Cited in Jon Coaffee, *Terrorism, Risk and the City*, Aldershot: Ashgate, 2003.
24. Ibid.
25. This removal of insurance coverage is further detailed in chapter 6.
26. *An Phoblacht*, April 1993 edition.
27. Locally, the ring of steel was referred to as the 'ring of plastic' as the temporary access restrictions were based primarily on the funnelling of traffic through rows of plastic traffic cones.
28. Within London, the ring of steel was promoted in terms of traffic management and environmental improvements with attempts to remove any references to the ongoing terrorist threat.
29. This technology was developed during the first Gulf War. These digital cameras were capable of processing the information and giving feedback to the operator within four seconds.
30. Walter Laqueur, 'Post-modern Terrorism', *Foreign Affairs*, vol. 75:5, 1996, pp. 24–36.
31. Stephen Flynn, *The Edge of Disaster: Rebuilding a Resilient Nation*, New York: Random House, 2007, p. 154.
32. See Nancy Chang, *The Silencing of Political Dissent: How the USA Patriot Act Undermines the Constitution*, New York: Seven Springs, 2002.
33. Australian Government, *Counter-Terrorism White Paper: Securing Australia, Protecting Our Community*, 2010.
34. One key difference between the American and UK models that emerged after 9/11 is that 'UK Resilience' is a wide net cast to encompass a range of civil, natural and anthropogenic risks, hazards and threats from the beginning, whereas in the USA widespread criticism was levied at the Office of Homeland Security for its focus on foreign threats at the expense of indigenous natural hazards. Another example of differential focus occurred in Australia in the early 2000s where the focal point of security was on immigration, border control and foreign relations.
35. For example, in the UK the overarching *Strategy for Countering International Terrorism* (CONTEST) is a long-term strategy for developing resilience for counter-terrorism. This strategy was developed from 2003 but only made public in 2006. Updated versions were released in 2009, 2011 and 2018. This 'resilience' strategy is divided into four strands: PREVENT, PURSUE, PROTECT and PREPARE, which collectively seek to reduce the threat of, vulnerability to and ultimately risk of terrorist attack.
36. On the morning of 11 March 2004 ten bombs exploded on four trains in and around Madrid central train station, leaving 191 dead and more than 1,800 injured. On 7 July 2005, often referred to as 7/7, a series of coordinated terrorist attacks using homemade bombs took place on London's transport network, killing 52 and injuring over 700. On 26 November 2008, a series of twelve coordinated shooting and bombing attacks lasting four days took place across Mumbai, killing 164 people and injuring over 300. On 22 July 2011, two sequential lone-wolf terror attacks took place in Norway. First, a car bomb exploded in the centre of Oslo killing eight and injuring over 200, followed by a shooting spree on the nearby island of Utoya, killing 68 and injuring over 100.
37. Kevin Grosskopf, 'Evaluating the Societal Response to Antiterrorism Measures', *Journal of Homeland Security and Emergency Management*, vol. 3:2, 2006, p. 2.

38. Lisa Benton-Short, 'Bollards, Bunkers, and Barriers: Securing the National Mall in Washington DC', *Environment and Planning D: Society and Space*, vol. 25:3, 2007, p. 426.
39. Jon Coaffee, 'Rings of Steel, Rings of Concrete and Rings of Confidence: Designing Out Terrorism in Central London pre and post 9/11', *International Journal of Urban and Regional Research*, vol. 28:1, 2004, pp. 201–11.
40. Jon Coaffee, Paul O'Hare and Marian Hawkesworth, 'The Visibility of (In)Security: The Aesthetics of Planning Urban Defences against Terrorism', *Security Dialogue*, vol. 40:4/5, 2009, pp. 489–511.
41. Home Office, *Working Together to Protect Crowded Places*, London: Home Office, 2009, p. 11; Jon Coaffee et al., 'The Visibility of (In)Security'
42. Trevor Boddy, 'Architecture Emblematic: Hardened Sites and Softened Symbols', in Michael Sorkin (ed.), *Indefensible Space*, Abingdon: Routledge, 2007, pp. 277–304.
43. https://cityroom.blogs.nytimes.com/2013/01/13/times-square-bow-tie-is-to-get-a-belt-of-steel-and-granite (accessed 13 January 2018).
44. The threat was seen to come from a number of sources: drunken drivers, drivers who lost control of their vehicles for other reasons, terrorists who planned to drive into crowds (al Qaeda propaganda had called for such attacks), and would-be bombers who could leave car bombs in the Square (as they did in 2010).
45. https://snohetta.com/news/362-snohettacelebrates-opening-of-times-square-redesign (accessed 19 April 2017).
46. Ibid.
47. www1.nyc.gov/office-of-the-mayor/news/003-18/mayor-de-blasio-extensive-planinstall-security-bollards-protect-new-yorkers (accessed 2 January 2018).
48. Australia's Strategy for Protecting Crowded Places from Terrorism, 2017.
49. See *Safe Places – A Comprehensive Guide for Owners, Operators and Designers*, 2012.
50. www.standard.co.uk/news/london/campaigners-plan-safety-gardens-around-london-to-replace-barriers-after-terror-attacks-a3561631.html (accessed 13 June 2017).
51. Although Italy has not suffered any major terror attacks on its territory, there have been repeated warnings that the country is on terrorist hit lists.
52. www.dezeen.com/2017/08/24/stefano-boeri-treebarriers-prevent-vehicle-terror-attacks-news (accessed 24 August 2017).
53. UK Cabinet Office, *Strategic National Framework on Community Resilience*, London: Cabinet Office, 2011.
54. Ibid., p. 4.
55. Ibid., p. 3.
56. Joshua Reeves, *Citizen Spies: The Long Rise of America's Surveillance Society*, New York: NYU Press, 2017.
57. See for example 'Help Us Spot the Terrorists Urge Police', *Manchester Evening News*, 5 March 2007, p. 1.
58. Security Service (MI5), 'Police Launch New Counter-terrorism Campaign', *MI5 News Update*, 25 February 2008 (message from the Security Service/MI5 mailing list).
59. The Communities Defeat Terrorism campaign was part of a much broader approach that was launched in March 2017 called Action Counters Terrorism (ACT) that called on 'communities to act on their instincts to help prevent atrocities taking place': '*don't worry, don't delay, just act*'.
60. Pat O' Malley, 'Resilient Subjects: Uncertainty, Warfare and Liberalism', *Economy and Society*, vol. 39:4, 2010, p. 448.
61. Michael Kackman, *Citizen Spy: Television, Espionage, and Cold War Culture*, Minneapolis: University of Minnesota Press, 2005.
62. Jon Coaffee, David Murakami Wood and Peter Rogers, *The Everyday Resilience of the City: How Cities Respond to Terrorism and Disaster*, Basingstoke: Palgrave Macmillan, 2008.
63. UK Home Office, *Revised Prevent Duty Guidance for England and Wales*, London: HM Government, 2015.

64. Charlotte Heath-Kelly, 'The Geography of Pre-criminal Space: Epidemiological Imaginations of Radicalisation Risk in the UK Prevent Strategy, 2007–2017', *Critical Studies on Terrorism*, vol. 10:2, 2017, pp. 297–319.
65. Clive Norris and Michael McCahill, 'CCTV: Beyond Penal Modernism?', *British Journal of Criminology*, vol. 46:1, 2006, pp. 97–118.
66. Marc Andrejevic, 'The Work of Watching One Another: Lateral Surveillance, Risk, and Governance', *Surveillance and Society*, vol. 2:4, 2005, pp. 479–97.
67. 9/11 further catalysed these developments and shepherded in many new coercive and automated analytical applications. Most recently, attention has turned to the enormous data-harvesting operations of UK and US intelligence agencies, sanctioned by 9/11-related legislation such as the Patriot Act.
68. Jon Coaffee and Pete Fussey, 'Driving Resilience Through Security: The Practices and Impacts Of Security-driven Resilience', *Security Dialogue*, vol. 46:1, 2015, pp. 86–105.

6 STRESS-TESTING ECONOMIC RESILIENCE

1. www.washingtonpost.com/news/wonk/wp/2017/06/15/its-time-to-stop-blaming-poor-people-for-the-financial-crisis/?noredirect=on&utm_term=.46d4f459662e (accessed 15 June 2017).
2. Michael Lewis, *The Big Short: Inside the Doomsday Machine*, New York: W.W. Norton, 2010.
3. www.nytimes.com/2010/03/15/books/15book.html (accessed 16 March 2010).
4. Adam Tooze, *Crashed: How a Decade of Financial Crises Changed the World*, London: Allen Lane, 2018.
5. Ibid.
6. James Brassett and Christopher Holmes, 'Building Resilient Finance? Uncertainty, Complexity, and Resistance', *British Journal of Politics and International Relations*, vol. 18:2, 2016, pp. 370–88.
7. Thomas Piketty, *Capital in the Twenty-first Century*, Cambridge, MA: Harvard University Press, 2014.
8. Lino Briguglio, Gordon Cordina, Stephanie Bugeja and Nadia Farrugia, *Conceptualizing and Measuring Economic Resilience*, Department of Economics, University of Malta, 2006.
9. Ibid.
10. Adam Rose, 'Defining and Measuring Economic Resilience to Disasters', *Disaster Prevention and Management*, vol. 13:4, 2003, pp. 307–14.
11. Howard Chernick (ed.), *Resilient City: The Economic Impact of 9/11*, New York: Russell Sage Foundation, 2005.
12. *Liberty Street Economics*, 'Lower Manhattan since 9/11: A Study in Resilience', 19 October 2016.
13. At this time, fears of climate change impacts dented the insurance market, resulting in the insolvency of eleven separate insurers. It also catalysed interest in the use of catastrophe 'cat' models among insurers and reinsurers.
14. Two features of the market compounded this situation at this time. First, insurance premiums were dropping because of increased corporate competition. Second, many 'old' risks were being claimed against, such as asbestos-related illnesses, genetic engineering and many different types of pollution. Insurance companies therefore began to closely examine the risks they were prepared to underwrite.
15. As early as October 1991, the Association of British Insurers was in discussions with the government to review the existing cover against terrorism, as during the first Gulf War it was far from clear who would be financially responsible for associated acts of terrorism in the UK.
16. 9/11 also stimulated the development of catastrophic modelling for man-made hazards, complementing its advance in the field of natural hazards.

17. Chernick, *Resilient City*, p. 155.
18. Cited in Peter van Aartijk Jr, 'Can Terrorism Insurance Pool Calm Insurers Fears?', *Independent Agent*, December 2001.
19. Subsequently the insurance industry put forward a suggested model called Homeland Security Mutual Reinsurance Company based on Pool Re as part of the Insurance Stabilization and Availability Act of 2001 which was formally proposed on 10 October. Five days later the Bush Administration published their own 'terrorism insurance plan', which proposed that the insurers picked up a great amount of the risk up to a certain level ($100 million). A further scheme was mooted on 1 November 2001, the Terrorism Risk Protection Act, which would be triggered only in the event of a $100 million loss. The federal government would, it was proposed, then pick up 90 per cent of the loss, leaving the insurance companies to pick up the remaining 10 per cent.
20. Econophysics is an interdisciplinary field of research that seeks to apply theories and methods from physics, to solve economic problems that engage with uncertainty and non-linearity (some also refer to it as statistical finance).
21. Such models are developed by harnessing loss and hazard observations, building upon existing data, testing existing models and incorporating these lessons into future catastrophe modelling advances.
22. Catastrophe bonds (also known as cat bonds) were created and first used in the mid-1990s in the aftermath of Hurricane Andrew in the US, emerging from a need by insurance companies to reduce some of the risks they would face if a major catastrophe occurred. As they might incur damages that they could not cover by charging premiums they created cat bonds that are issued through an investment bank and then sold to investors.
23. James Brassett and Christopher Holmes, 'Building Resilient Finance?'.
24. The Big Bang was pre-dated by changes in US legislation, notably the Depository Institutions Deregulation and Monetary Control Act, signed into law by President Jimmy Carter in 1980. The act hoped to increase deregulation and to improve the control of monetary policy by the Federal Reserve.
25. The wider Financial Crisis Inquiry Commission's final report released in 2011 further identified 'widespread failures in financial regulation', 'dramatic failures of corporate governance and risk management' and 'lack of transparency' as key causes of the financial collapse.
26. Cited in Brassett and Holmes, 'Building Resilient Finance?'.
27. Grahame Thompson, 'Financial Globalisation and the "Crisis": A Critical Assessment and "What is to be Done?"', *New Political Economy*, vol. 15:1, 2010, pp.127–45.
28. Christopher Holmes, 'Ignorance, Denial, Internalisation, and Transcendence: A Post-structural Perspective on Polanyi's Double Movement', *Review of International Studies*, vol. 39:2, 2012, pp. 273–90.
29. Innovation brought about by fintech should go hand in hand with effective and transparent governance structures and risk management practices that can build a platform by which fintech developments and enabling technologies might be identified, managed and monitored and their impact on financial resilience assessed.
30. 'The Bank of England's Approach to Operational Resilience', speech by Charlotte Gerken given at Operational Risk Europe 2017 Conference, London.
31. As recent high-profile disruptive events have shown, the speed and effectiveness of communications with the people most affected, including customers, is an important part of any firm's – or the financial sector's – overall response to an operational disruption.
32. Blockchain technology is a digital, distributed transaction ledger with identical copies maintained on each of the network's members' computers. When transactions occur they are grouped in blocks, and recorded sequentially in a chain of blocks. The digital linkages between the blocks in the chain are protected by cryptography.
33. Impact tolerance is expressed by reference to specific outcomes and metrics such as the maximum tolerable duration of disruption. In assessing impact tolerance there is an assumption that a particular risk has crystallised and will impact soon.

34. www.ecb.europa.eu/press/key/date/2017/html/sp170313.en.html (accessed 2 February 2018).
35. www.theguardian.com/business/2017/nov/26/bank-stress-tests-resilience-to-30bn-losses-bank-of-england-britain-lenders-rbs (accessed 26 November 2017).
36. www.telegraph.co.uk/business/2018/06/13/bank-england-demands-lenders-prepare-better-failures-tsb-visa (accessed 13 June 2018).
37. The Dodd–Frank Wall Street Reform and Consumer Protection Act was financial reform legislation passed by the Obama administration in 2010 as a response to the 2008 crisis and named after sponsors US Senator Christopher Dodd and US Representative Barney Frank. Its aim was to decrease various risks in the US financial system. As recently as May 2018 President Trump has pledged to repeal Dodd-Frank.
38. https://financefeeds.com/bank-england-push-enhanced-operational-resilience-cyber-incidents-banks (accessed 13 June 2018).
39. https://www.theguardian.com/business/live/2018/nov/28/markets-us-china-trade-war-trump-xi-bank-of-england-stress-tests-business-live (accessed 28 November 2018).
40. https://uk.reuters.com/article/uk-eu-banks-tests/eu-to-put-banks-through-brexit-mill-in-toughest-stress-test-yet-idUKKBN1FK2KA (accessed 31 January 2018).
41. www.cnbc.com/2018/09/11/stress-testing-the-trade-war-possible-bear-market-in-stocks-looms-for-us.html (accessed 11 September 2018).
42. Resilience programmes were also put in place to map the impact of the financial crisis and austerity policies on local and regional economies.
43. This refers to the 1980s economic polices associated with US President Ronald Reagan and UK Prime Minister Margaret Thatcher commonly associated with free market economics and reduced levels of government intervention and regulation.
44. Kate Raworth, *Doughnut Economics: Seven Ways to Think like a 21st Century Economist*, London: Random House, 2017.
45. Chris Clarke, 'Learning to Fail: Resilience and the Empty Promise of Financial Literacy Education', *Consumption Markets & Culture*, vol. 18:3, 2015, pp. 257–76.
46. Raworth, *Doughnut Economics*, p. 160.
47. www.theguardian.com/commentisfree/2018/jul/29/city-of-london-desperate-gamble-china-vulnerable-economy (accessed 29 July 2018).

7 THE SEARCH FOR ORGANISATIONAL AGILITY

1. Frank Landy and Jeffery Conte, *Work in the 21st Century: An Introduction to Industrial and Organizational Psychology*, London: John Wiley & Sons, 2010.
2. www.compete.org/reports/all/2802-transform-the-resilient-economy-integrating-competitiveness-and-security (accessed 12 October 2017).
3. Yossi Sheffi, *The Resilient Enterprise: Overcoming Vulnerability for Competitive Advantage*, Cambridge, MA: MIT Press, 2005.
4. Ibid.
5. Yossi Sheffi, *The Power of Resilience: How the Best Companies Manage the Unexpected*, Cambridge, MA: MIT Press, 2017.
6. Masahiko Haraguchi and Upmanu Lall, 'Flood Risks and Impacts: A Case Study of Thailand's Floods in 2011 and Research Questions for Supply Chain Decision-making', *International Journal of Disaster Risk Reduction*, 2014, pp. 256–72.
7. In 2017, Intel was ranked No. 6 by Gartner in its annual global Supply Chain Top 25 list.
8. Intel Business brief, When Disaster Strikes, Intel Keeps Supply Chains Moving, June 2018.
9. Ibid.
10. www.huffingtonpost.com/muhtar-kent/the-cocacola-company-and-_b_2564580.html?guccounter=1 (accessed 29 March 2013).

11. Ibid.
12. Ibid.
13. https://coca-colahellenic.com/en/about-us/business-resilience-and-risk-management/business-resilience (accessed 1 June 2017).
14. Coca-Cola HBC won 'The Risk Management Award – In House & Insurable Risk Managers' at the 2016 British Insurance Awards.
15. The failure to the O-rings and how this propagated through the rest of the space shuttle was a significant stimulus to the emergence of the field of resilient engineering.
16. Arjen Boin and Michel van Eeten, 'The Resilient Organization', *Public Management Review*, vol. 15:3, 2013, p. 439.
17. This highlights the difficulties of ensuring resilience in austerity as the maintenance of strategic reserves and redundant capacity becomes unrealistic.
18. Christopher Hood, 'A Public Management for All Seasons?', *Public Administration*, vol. 69, 1991, p. 14.
19. David Woods and John Wreathall, *Managing Risk Proactively: The Emergence of Resilience Engineering*, Columbus, OH: Ohio State University Press, 2003.
20. Fast rising rates of urbanisation mean that by 2050 it is expected that 75 per cent of an expanded global population will be urban.
21. Simon Marvin, Andrés Luque-Ayala and Colin McFarlane (eds), *Smart Urbanism: Utopian Vision or False Dawn?* London: Routledge, 2016.
22. Jon Coaffee, 'Rescaling and Responsibilising the Politics of Urban Resilience: From National Security to Local Place-Making', *Politics*, vol. 33:4, 2013, pp. 240–52.
23. www.morethangreen.es/en/smarter-cities-by-ibm (accessed 2 December 2017).
24. Shannon Mattern, 'Mission Control: A History of the Urban Dashboard', *Places Journal*, March 2015.
25. Stephen Few, 'Dashboard Confusion', *Intelligent Enterprise*, 20 March 2004.
26. Rio invested in strategic-level technologies to co-ordinate and control its various security and disaster management processes in the build-up to the 2016 Olympic Games.
27. www-03.ibm.com/press/us/en/pressrelease/33303.wss, 2010 (accessed 1 June 2011).
28. www.thalesgroup.com/en/worldwide/security/press-release/mexico-city-telmex-and-thales-selected-double-capacity-worlds-most (accessed 4 November 2014).
29. Commando, Control, Comunicaciones, Cómputo, Inteligencia, Integración, Información e Investigación is patterned after Thales's C4ISTAR defence systems (Command, Control, Communications, Computers, Intelligence, Surveillance, Target Acquisition and Reconnaissance), which enable remote commanders to monitor data and coordinate personnel in the field.
30. Five years after the *Ciudad Segura* project was launched, there has been a significant reduction in crime, more arrests and lower police response times.
31. Hillary Mushkin, 'Reconnaissance: Inside the Panopticon: A Low-tech Visit to Mexico City's High-tech Urban Surveillance Center', *Places Journal*, February 2016.
32. Marvin et al., *Smart Urbanism*, p. 7.
33. Mattern, 'Mission Control'.
34. Rob Kitchin and Martin Dodge, 'The (In)Security of Smart Cities: Vulnerabilities, Risks, Mitigation, and Prevention', *Journal of Urban Technology*, published online, 12 December 2017.
35. www.100resilientcities.org/pages/about-us#/-_/ (accessed 18 December 2013). In April 2019 it was announced that the 100 Resilient Cities programme would be discontinued by the Rockefeller Foundation.
36. www.greenbiz.com/blog/2014/08/12/michael-berkowitz-community-secret-ingredient-urban-resilience (accessed 12 August 2014).
37. Jon Coaffee, Marie-Christine Therrien, Lorenzo Chelleri, Daniel Henstra, Daniel P. Aldrich, Carrie L. Mitchell, Sasha Tsenkova and Éric Rigaud, 'Urban Resilience Implementation: A Policy Challenge and Research Agenda for the 21st Century', *Journal of Contingencies and Crisis Management*, vol. 26, 2018, pp. 403–10.

38. Robert Olshansky and Laurie Johnson, *Clear as Mud: Planning for the Rebuilding of New Orleans*, Chicago and Washington DC: American Planning Association, Planners Press, 2010.
39. This inundated 27,000 square miles of land around the Mississippi River despite a misplaced confidence among the engineering fraternity that the levee system in place would not be breached. This led to advanced flood defences being constructed, under the Flood Control Act of 1928 when creating the world's longest system of levees and floodways. Socially, the Great Flood also displaced many thousands of low-income, largely African American residents, and was a significant factor in accelerating the Great Migration of African Americans to northern US cities.
40. Olshansky and Johnson, *Clear as Mud*, p. 11.
41. A range of high-level workshops (including one in March 2005 at the National Academies of Science), scenario exercises (including one centred on New Orleans run in 2004 – called Hurricane Pam) and simulated modelling had made clear that New Orleans would be severely affected if a significant hurricane hit – its levees protection system would likely fail, the entire city would be flooded for many weeks or months and a large proportion of the population would have to be evacuated to other US regions.
42. Olshansky and Johnson, *Clear as Mud*, p. 20.
43. The Urban Water Plan received the American Planning Association's 2015 National Planning Excellence Award for Environmental Planning.
44. City of New Orleans, *Resilient New Orleans*, 1 September 2015.
45. www.iso.org/news/Ref2189.htm (accessed 31 May 2017).
46. www.iso.org/obp/ui#iso:std:iso:22316:ed-1:v1:en (accessed 1 February 2018).
47. Similarly, the world first standard on organisational resilience published in Britain in 2014 (BS 65000) argued, 'Organisational resilience is the ability of an organisation to anticipate, prepare for, respond and adapt to incremental change and sudden disruptions in order to survive and prosper.'
48. Ibid.
49. David Denyer, *Organizational Resilience: A Summary of Academic Evidence, Business Insights and New Thinking*, BSI and Cranfield School of Management, 2017.
50. www.iso.org/obp/ui#iso:std:iso:22316:ed-1:v1:en (accessed 1 February 2018).
51. https://disaster-recovery.cioreview.com/cxoinsight/thriving-in-the-face-of-disasters-nid-26887-cid-106.html (accessed 1 October 2018).

8 DISASTER RESILIENCE: WHERE IT ALL COMES TOGETHER

1. For example, in October 2016 Hurricane Matthew led to catastrophic flooding killing nearly 600 people and leaving 35,000 homeless.
2. Antony Loewenstein, *Disaster Capitalism: Making a Killing out of Catastrophe*, London: Verso, 2015.
3. Lee Bosher and Ksenia Chmutina, *Disaster Risk Reduction for the Built Environment*, Oxford: Wiley/Blackwell, 2017.
4. Neil Smith, 'There's No Such Thing as a Natural Disaster', The Social Science Research Council, 1 June 2006.
5. Ibid.
6. Ksenia Chmutina, Jason von Meding, J-C Gaillard and Lee Bosher, 'Why Natural Disasters Aren't All That Natural', openDemocracy, 14 September 2017.
7. Phil O'Keefe, Ken Westgate and Ben Wisner, 'Taking the Naturalness Out of Natural Disasters', *Nature*, vol. 260, 1976, pp. 566–7.
8. Chmutina et al., 'Why Natural Disasters'.
9. Jon Coaffee, *Terrorism, Risk and the City*, Aldershot: Ashgate, 2003; Mike Davis, 'The Flames of New York', *New Left Review*, 12, November–December 2001.

10. Naomi Klein, *The Shock Doctrine: The Rise of Disaster Capitalism*, Toronto: A.A. Knopf Canada, 2007.
11. Jon Coaffee, David Murakami Wood and Peter Rogers, *The Everyday Resilience of the City: How Cities Respond to Terrorism and Disaster*, Basingstoke: Palgrave Macmillan, 2008.
12. David Lyon, *Surveillance after September 11*, Cambridge: Polity, 2003.
13. This included border control, the running of prisons and many aspects of intelligence gathering.
14. Klein, *Shock Doctrine*.
15. Such companies provided heavily armed private security who patrolled the streets to stop 'looters' whose only crime was to go in search of much-needed supplies.
16. www.theguardian.com/us-news/2017/jul/06/naomi-klein-how-power-profits-from-disaster (accessed 6 July 2017).
17. Smith, *There's No Such Thing as a Natural Disaster*.
18. Siambabala Bernard Manyena, 'The Concept of Resilience Revisited', *Disasters*, vol. 30:4, 2006, pp. 434–50.
19. In January 2005, 168 governments adopted a ten-year plan to make the world safer from hazards at the World Conference on Disaster Reduction, held in Kobe, Hyogo, Japan.
20. UNISDR, Hyogo Framework for Action 2005–2015: *Building the Resilience of Nations and Communities to Disasters*, World Conference on Disaster Reduction, 18–22 January 2005, Kobe, Hyogo, Japan. A/CONF.206/6. UNISDR.
21. These include disaster risk reduction, climate change adaptation, social protection, working in fragile contexts and humanitarian preparedness and response.
22. Department for International Development (DFID), *Saving Lives, Preventing Suffering and Building Resilience: The UK Government's Humanitarian Policy*, London: DFID, 2011.
23. This replaced the Homeland Security Presidential Directive on National Preparedness issued in 2003.
24. The National Academies of Sciences, Engineering and Medicine provide nonpartisan, objective guidance for decision-makers on pressing issues. When faced with a complex question, they bring together experts from across disciplines to look at the evidence with fresh eyes and openness to insights from other fields. The aim is a shared understanding of what the evidence reveals and the best path forward; National Academies, *Disaster Resilience: A National Imperative*, Washington DC: National Academies Press, 2012.
25. Working with eight federal agencies and a community resilience group, the National Research Council appointed a committee of experts to examine ways to increase disaster resilience in the United States and to develop a plan of action for the nation.
26. Subsequent research published in early 2018 by the US National Institute of Building Sciences places this figure even higher at $6 saved for every $1 spent.
27. Available evidence also supported the impression that the Vietnamese communities were more resilient than others in New Orleans with psychologists finding a much higher rate of return for Vietnamese-Americans than that for blacks and whites, and much less post-traumatic stress.
28. United Nations, *Sendai Framework for Disaster Risk Reduction 2015–2030*, Geneva: UN, 2015, p. 10.
29. Ibid.
30. Ibid.
31. One example of rumour spreading came in the aftermath of Hurricane Sandy in 2012, where members of the public widely used Photoshop to manipulate images and photographs. As a result, false news stories about which places in New York were flooded were circulated and spread from social media to television.
32. Daniel Aldrich, *Building Resilience: Social Capital in Post-Disaster Recovery*, Chicago: University of Chicago Press, 2012.

33. The total cost for each disaster is calculated from insured and uninsured losses, including physical damages to buildings and infrastructure, and other related costs such as business disruption and crop damage. $306 billion is a conservative estimate with actual costs likely rise to over $400 billion as the actual financial destruction from disasters becomes clearer in the longer term.
34. According to data released by the National Centers for Environmental Information (NCEI), which tracks the nation's major weather and climate events.
35. https://edition.cnn.com/2018/09/14/us/hurricane-florence-flood-insurance-uninsured/index.html (accessed 15 September 2018).
36. Because of development pressures, it is almost impossible to expand flood zones, meaning they don't accurately reflect the risk on the ground.
37. United States Government Accountability Office, *Report to Congressional Addressees, 2017 Hurricanes and Wildfires: Initial Observations on the Federal Response and Key Recovery Challenges*, September 2018.
38. For example, it was noted how FEMA and each state-based responder had conducted a range of simulated emergency exercises in recent years that helped develop relationships and led to quicker decision-making during the disasters of 2017.
39. The Cajun Navy were first formed to assist the rescue operation after Hurricane Katrina and are credited with rescuing thousands of citizens during subsequent disasters in the southern states.
40. www.csmonitor.com/USA/Society/2017/0828/In-all-hands-on-deck-response-to-Harvey-lessons-learned-from-earlier-storms (accessed 28 August 2017).
41. In this case, immediate warnings were issued as emergency responders did not want to repeat the mistakes of 2005, when dithering over an order to evacuate more than 2 million people led to the city's disastrous evacuation as Hurricane Rita bore down leaving over 100 people dead.
42. www.chron.com/news/houston-weather/hurricaneharvey/article/East-Texas-county-tells-residents-GET-OUT-OR-12162456.php (accessed 30 August 2017).
43. More than 17,000 sustained major damage and around 32,000 sustained minor damage.
44. Sixty-eight were attributed to direct effects, including flooding, and 35 to indirect effects in the hurricane's aftermath.
45. www.vox.com/energy-and-environment/2017/12/28/16795490/natural-disasters-2017-hurricanes-wildfires-heat-climate-change-cost-deaths (accessed 26 March 2018).
46. https://news.nationalgeographic.com/2017/08/heavy-rain-harvey-houston (accessed 1 September 2017).
47. A 500-year flood is one that has a one in 500 (0.2 per cent) chance of occurring in any given year.
48. www.dezeen.com/2017/09/01/urban-design-caused-hurricane-harvey-disaster-houston-flooding-ilan-kelman-opinion (accessed 1 September 2017).
49. https://apps.texastribune.org/harvey-reservoirs (accessed 12 October 2017).
50. This complies with federal law, which requires property owners to purchase flood insurance to qualify for a federally backed mortgage.
51. In the wake of Hurricane Harvey there was much discussion about changing the law to require full disclosure of flood risk. Such disclosure came up against significant resistance from the real estate industry who feared house prices would crash.
52. www.nytimes.com/2017/08/30/us/houston-flooding-growth-regulation.html?_r=0 (accessed 30 August 2017).
53. www.houstonchronicle.com/opinion/outlook/article/Fleming-Houston-deserves-a-truly-democratic-12199101.php (accessed 14 September 2017).
54. Ibid.
55. www.chron.com/news/transportation/article/Houston-wins-9-4M-for-flood-warning-on-roads-12736772.php (accessed 8 March 2018).
56. Over 100 other cities around the globe are part of this network, including many in the US such as Boston, New York, Pittsburgh, St Louis, San Francisco and Minneapolis.

57. www.100resilientcities.org/city-houston-selected-join-100-resilient-cities-global-network (accessed 29 August 2018).
58. www.nytimes.com/2018/10/08/us/fema-disaster-recovery-climate-change.html (accessed 8 October 2018).

9 ADAPT OR DIE: FUTUREPROOFING THE TWENTY-FIRST CENTURY

1. Kim Stanley Robinson, *New York 2140*, London: Orbit Books, 2017, p. 34.
2. Ibid., p. 139.
3. Ibid., p. 140.
4. When his book was published, Robinson in a number of media interviews noted a number of current projects in coastal cities that resemble his vision 100+ years hence, notably floating islands in Singapore that are being contemplated due to fears of sea level rise.
5. Intergovernmental Panel on Climate Change, *Global Warming of 1.5°C:* an IPCC special report on the impacts of global warming of 1.5°C above pre-industrial levels and related global greenhouse gas emission pathways, in the context of strengthening the global response to the threat of climate change, sustainable development, and efforts to eradicate poverty: Summary for Policymakers, IPCC, 8 October 2018.
6. The call here is to keep warming to a maximum of 1.5 degrees Celsius. Beyond this figure, even half a degree will significantly worsen the risks of drought, floods, extreme heat and poverty across the globe. This benchmark is lower than the one set by the global Paris Agreement, which aimed to prevent the planet from warming by 3 degrees.
7. www.theguardian.com/environment/2018/oct/08/global-warming-must-not-exceed-15c-warns-landmark-un-report?CMP=Share_iOSApp_Other (accessed 8 October 2018).
8. IPCC, *Global Warming of 1.5°C*, section D.6.1.
9. Ulrich Beck, 'The Silence of Words: On Terror and War', *Security Dialogue*, vol. 34:3, 2003, p. 256.
10. Libby Porter and Simin Davoudi, 'The Politics of Resilience for Planning: A Cautionary Note', *Planning Theory & Practice*, vol. 13:2, 2012, pp. 329–33.
11. Lorenzo Chelleri, James Waters, Marta Olazabal and Guido Minucci, 'Resilience Trade-offs: Addressing Multiple Scales and Temporal Aspects of Urban Resilience', *Environment and Urbanization*, vol. 27:1, 2015, pp. 181–98.
12. Jon Coaffee, Marie-Christine Therrien, Lorenzo Chelleri, Daniel Henstra, Daniel P. Aldrich, Carrie L. Mitchell, Sasha Tsenkova and Éric Rigaud, 'Urban Resilience Implementation: A Policy Challenge and Research Agenda for the 21st Century', *Journal of Contingencies and Crisis Management*, vol. 26, 2018, pp. 403–10.
13. David Chandler and Julian Reid, *The Neoliberal Subject: Resilience, Adaptation and Vulnerability*, London: Rowman and Littlefield, 2016.
14. This vignette was written as Hurricane Michael was just about to slam into Florida in October 2018.
15. For example, Target 1.5 focuses on community resilience: 'By 2030 build the resilience of the poor and those in vulnerable situations, and reduce their exposure and vulnerability to climate-related extreme events and other economic, social and environmental shocks and disasters.' The SDGs also promise to promote climate change adaptation: 'Strengthen resilience and adaptive capacity to climate-related hazards' (target 13.1); improve critical infrastructure resilience – 'Develop quality, reliable, sustainable and resilient infrastructure' (target 9.1); and 'Build sustainable and resilient buildings utilizing local materials' (target 11c).
16. Jon Coaffee and Peter Lee, *Urban Resilience: Planning for Risk Crisis and Uncertainty*, London: Palgrave, 2016.
17. Kevin Grove, *Resilience*, London: Routledge, 2018.

18. www.nytimes.com/2018/10/08/us/fema-disaster-recovery-climate-change.html (accessed 8 October 2018).
19. Ulrich Beck, *The Metamorphosis of the World*, Cambridge: Polity, 2015.
20. Thomas Hale and David Held, *Beyond Gridlock*, Cambridge: Polity, 2017.
21. Some have attributed this quotation to Darwin's *On the Origin of the Species* (1859) and some to *Descent of Man* (1871) although some dispute it as a Darwin saying at all.

SELECT BIBLIOGRAPHY

Aldrich, Daniel, *Building Resilience: Social Capital in Post-disaster Recovery*, Chicago: University of Chicago Press, 2012

Alexievich, Svetlana, *Chernobyl Prayer: A Chronicle of the Future*, trans. Anna Gunin and Arch Tait, London: Penguin Modern Classics, 2016

Augustine of Hippo, *De civitate Dei*, London: Penguin, 2003

Baer, Martha, Katrina Heron, Oliver Morton and Evan Ratliff, *Safe: The Race to Protect Ourselves in a Newly Dangerous World*, New York: HarperCollins, 2005

Beck, Ulrich, *The Metamorphosis of the World*, Cambridge: Polity, 2015

——, *Risk Society: Towards a New Modernity*, London: Sage Publications, 1992

——, *World at Risk*, Cambridge: Polity, 2007

——, *World Risk Society*, Cambridge: Polity, 1999

Bernstein, Peter, *Against the Gods: The Remarkable Story of Risk*, New York: Wiley, 1998

Bosher, Lee, and Ksenia Chmutina, *Disaster Risk Reduction for the Built Environment*, Oxford: Wiley/Blackwell, 2017

Chandler, David, *Resilience: The Governance of Complexity*, London: Routledge, 2014

Chandler, David, and Jon Coaffee (eds), *The Routledge Handbook of International Resilience*, London: Routledge, 2016

Chandler, David, and Julian Reid, *The Neoliberal Subject: Resilience, Adaptation and Vulnerability*, London: Rowman and Littlefield, 2016

Chang, Nancy, *The Silencing of Political Dissent: How the USA Patriot Act Undermines the Constitution*, New York: Seven Springs, 2002

Chernick, Howard (ed.), *Resilient City: The Economic Impact of 9/11*, New York: Russell Sage Foundation, 2005

Coaffee, Jon, *Terrorism, Risk and the City*, Aldershot: Ashgate, 2003

Coaffee, Jon, and Peter Lee, *Urban Resilience: Planning for Risk Crisis and Uncertainty*, London: Palgrave, 2016

Coaffee, Jon, David Murakami Wood and Peter Rogers, *The Everyday Resilience of the City: How Cities Respond to Terrorism and Disaster*, Basingstoke: Palgrave Macmillan, 2008

Dawson, Ashley, *Extreme Cities: The Peril and the Promise of Urban Life in the Age of Climate Change*, London: Verso, 2017

Douglas, Mary, *Purity and Danger: An Analysis of the Concepts of Pollution and Taboo*, London: Routledge, 1966

Evans, Brad, and Julian Reid, *Resilient Life: The Art of Living Dangerously*, Cambridge: Polity, 2014

Fisher, Thomas, *Designing to Avoid Disaster: The Nature of Fracture-critical Design*, London: Routledge, 2012

Flynn, Stephen, *The Edge of Disaster: Rebuilding a Resilient Nation*, New York: Random House, 2007

Franklin, James, *The Science of Conjecture: Evidence and Probability before Pascal*, Baltimore: Johns Hopkins University Press, 2001
Ganguly, Auroop Ratan, Udit Bhatia and Stephen E. Flynn, *Critical Infrastructures Resilience: Policy and Engineering Principles*, London: Routledge, 2018
Gardner, Dan, *Risk: The Science and Politics of Fear*, London: Virgin Books, 2009
Giddens, Anthony, *The Consequences of Modernity*, Cambridge: Polity, 1990
——, *Runaway World: How Globalisation Is Reshaping Our Lives*, London: Profile Books, 1999
Goodell, Jeff, *The Water Will Come: Rising Seas, Sinking Cities, and the Remaking of the Civilized World*, London: Little, Brown and Company, 2017
Grove, Kevin, *Resilience*, London: Routledge, 2018
Gunderson, Lance, and C. S. Holling (eds), *Panarchy: Understanding Transformations in Human and Natural Systems*, Washington DC: Island Press, 2002
Hale, Thomas, and David Held, *Beyond Gridlock*, Cambridge: Polity, 2017
Harari, Yuval Noah, *Homo Deus: A Brief History of Tomorrow*, London: Random House, 2016
Harford, Tim, *Adapt: Why Success Always Starts with Failure*, London: Abacus, 2012
Hinman, Eve, and David Hammond, *Lessons from the Oklahoma City Bombing: Defensive Design Techniques*, Reston, VA: American Society of Civil Engineers, 1997
Kackman, Michael, *Citizen Spy: Television, Espionage, and Cold War Culture*, Minneapolis: University of Minnesota Press, 2005
Klein, Naomi, *The Shock Doctrine: The Rise of Disaster Capitalism*, Toronto: A.A. Knopf Canada, 2007
——, *This Changes Everything*, London: Penguin Random House, 2015
Knight, Frank, *Risk, Uncertainty and Profit*, Los Angeles: Hardpress Publishing, 2015 (first published 1921)
Landy, Frank, and Jeffery Conte, *Work in the 21st Century: An Introduction to Industrial and Organizational Psychology*, London: John Wiley & Sons, 2010
Laplace, Pierre, *A Philosophical Essay on Probabilities 1814*, London: Chapman & Hall, 1902
Lewis, Michael, *The Big Short: Inside the Doomsday Machine*, New York: W.W. Norton, 2010
Linkov, Igor, and José Manuel Palma-Oliveira (eds), *Resilience and Risk: Methods and Application in Environment, Cyber and Social Domains*, Dordrecht, The Netherlands: Springer, 2017
Loewenstein, Antony, *Disaster Capitalism: Making a Killing out of Catastrophe*, London: Verso, 2015
Lupton, Deborah, *Risk*, London: Routledge, 1999
Marvin, Simon, Andrés Luque-Ayala and Colin McFarlane (eds), *Smart Urbanism: Utopian Vision or False Dawn?* London: Routledge, 2016
Meyer, Han, Dale Morris and David Waggonner, *Dutch Dialogues - New Orleans - The Netherlands - Common Challenges in Urban Deltas*, Amsterdam: SUN, 2009
Miles, Richard, *Carthage Must Be Destroyed: The Rise and Fall of an Ancient Civilization*, London: Penguin, 2012
Mythen, Gabe, *Ulrich Beck: A Critical Introduction to the Risk Society*, London: Pluto Press, 2004
Olshansky, Robert, and Laurie Johnson, *Clear as Mud: Planning for the Rebuilding of New Orleans*, Chicago and Washington DC: American Planning Association, Planners Press, 2010
Ovink, Henk, and Jelte Boeijenga, *Too Big: Rebuild by Design: A Transformational Approach to Climate Change*, Rotterdam, Netherlands: nai010 publishers, 2018
Pawley, Martin, *Terminal Architecture*, London: Reaktion, 1998
Piketty, Thomas, *Capital in the Twenty-first Century*, Cambridge, MA: Harvard University Press, 2014
Raworth, Kate, *Doughnut Economics: Seven Ways to Think like a 21st Century Economist*, London: Random House, 2017

Reeves, Joshua, *Citizen Spies: The Long Rise of America's Surveillance Society*, New York: NYU Press, 2017
Robinson, Kim Stanley, *New York 2140*, London: Orbit Books, 2017
Rodin, Judith, *The Resilience Dividend: Managing Disruption, Avoiding Disaster, and Growing Stronger in an Unpredictable World*, London: Profile Books, 2015
Schwab, Klaus, *The Fourth Industrial Revolution*, London: Portfolio Penguin, 2016
Scranton, Roy, *Learning to Die in the Anthropocene*, San Francisco: City Light, 2015
Sheffi, Yossi, *The Power of Resilience: How the Best Companies Manage the Unexpected*, Cambridge, MA: MIT Press, 2017
——, *The Resilient Enterprise: Overcoming Vulnerability for Competitive Advantage*, Cambridge, MA: MIT Press, 2005
Sorkin, Michael (ed.), *Indefensible Space*, Abingdon: Routledge, 2007
Spinks, Jennifer, and Charles Zika (eds), *Disasters, Death and the Emotions in the Shadow of the Apocalypse, 1400–1700*, London: Palgrave Macmillan, 2016
Stengers, Isabelle, *In Catastrophic Times: Resisting the Coming Barbarism*, Paris: Meson Press, 2015
Taleb, Nassim Nicholas, *The Black Swan: The Impact of the Highly Improbable*, New York: Random House, 2017
Tierney, Kathleen, *The Social Roots of Risk: Producing Disasters, Promoting Resilience*, Stanford, CA: Stanford University Press, 2014
Walker, Brian, and David Salt, *Resilience Thinking: Sustaining Ecosystems and People in a Changing World*, Washington DC: Island Press, 2006
Walklate, Sandra, and Gabe Mythen, *Contradictions of Terrorism: Security, Risk and Resilience*, London: Routledge, 2014
Weber, Max, *The Protestant Ethic and the Spirit of Capitalism*, New York: Scribner, 1958 (first published 1905)
Woods, David, and John Wreathall, *Managing Risk Proactively: The Emergence of Resilience Engineering*, Columbus, OH: Ohio State University Press, 2003
Zolli, Andrew, and Ann Marie Healy, *Resilience: Why Things Bounce Back*, London: Headline, 2013

INDEX